William Henry Lowe

The Hebrew Student's Commentary on Zechariah

Hebrew and LXX with excursus on syllable-dividing, metheg, initial dagesh, and

siman rapheh

William Henry Lowe

The Hebrew Student's Commentary on Zechariah
Hebrew and LXX with excursus on syllable-dividing, metheg, initial dagesh, and siman rapheh

ISBN/EAN: 9783337419448

Printed in Europe, USA, Canada, Australia, Japan

Cover: Foto ©Lupo / pixelio.de

More available books at **www.hansebooks.com**

THE
HEBREW STUDENT'S COMMENTARY

ON

ZECHARIAH

HEBREW AND LXX.

WITH

EXCURSUS ON SYLLABLE-DIVIDING, METHEG,
INITIAL DAGESH, AND SIMAN RAPHEH.

By W. H. LOWE, M.A.
HEBREW LECTURER AT CHRIST'S COLLEGE.

London:
MACMILLAN AND CO.
1882

[*The Right of Translation and Reproduction is reserved.*]

Cambridge:
PRINTED BY C. J. CLAY, M.A. & SON,
AT THE UNIVERSITY PRESS.

PREFACE.

SINCE the founding of the Theological Tripos Examiners have frequently complained, that the Candidates for it do not, as a rule, take pains to acquire an accurate knowledge of even the Elements of the Sacred Tongue. This has been, doubtless, in great measure the fault of the *Curriculum*, to the requirements of which they have been obliged to conform their studies. It need, however, be a matter of surprise to none, that the Regulations for a Tripos Examination in the chief subjects of a field of learning so wide as that of Theology, should not at the first have been perfect: for כל התחלות קשות, *i.e.* Il n'y a que le premier pas qui coûte. We have every reason to hope that from the inauguration of the New Regulations for that Tripos will date a new era in the Hebrew scholarship of the University, and that the Theological Tripos will thenceforth send forth into the world scholars as sound in their knowledge of the Elements of Hebrew as did the 'Voluntary Examination' which it superseded. This Student's Commentary has been written with a view to aiding this New Scheme of Theological Studies. The plan of it is as follows:

Words and sentences are treated from a purely grammatical point of view, and in so doing no difficulties have been wittingly avoided, but, rather, some have at times been intentionally raised, when by so doing an opportunity has been afforded of explaining some of the *minutiæ* of Hebrew Syntax. Unpointed Hebrew, and Transliteration, have been freely used from considerations of economy. But, if the student will point for himself the unpointed Hebrew words, and afterwards correct his own vowel-points from a pointed Text, this apparent incompleteness in the Notes will thus be transformed into a distinct advantage. The Hebrew Text quoted in reference to matters of punctuation is that of Baer, in the Books Genesis, Isaiah, Job, Proverbs, Psalms, and The Minor Prophets; in the case of the other Books various editions have at times been consulted.

The 'Remarks' (on the interpretation of the prophecies) are looked upon as of secondary importance, and are consequently printed in smaller type. Enough has, we hope, been given in them, to enable the Student (who is supposed to be studying the Book chiefly with a view to learning the language) to read the prophecies with an intelligent notion of their contents. But, if he should wish to see such questions discussed at much greater length, he may refer to Wright's *Bampton* Lectures.

The Excursus treat of matters, which may perhaps be of some interest to riper Scholars than those, for whom the bulk of the book is intended.

I am much indebted to Rev. A. T. Chapman, Fellow and formerly Tutor of Emmanuel College, for reading the proof-sheets, and for several valuable suggestions, which he has made to me in the course of so doing.

W. H. L.

CAMBRIDGE,
   May, 1882.

INTRODUCTION.

PROLEGOMENA TO CHAPTERS I.—VIII.

Personal to the Prophet.

OF the personal history of the Prophet Zechariah hardly anything is recorded. He styles himself "Zechariah, son of Berechiah, son of Iddo, the prophet," which certainly implies that he was the grandson of Iddo. But in Ezra v. 1, vi. 14 he is spoken of as "son of Iddo." This, however, presents no difficulty, for similarly *Jehu* is mentioned as *son of Jehoshaphat son of Nimshi* (2 Kings ix. 14), while (ver. 20) he is called merely *son of Nimshi*. The father of Zechariah, and the father of Jehu, seem to have been (to use an illustration from modern times) somewhat in the position of *Abraham Mendelssohn*[1], they could both boast of being the father and the son of a man of reputation. Knobel's supposition, then, that "son of Berechiah" (Zech. i. 1, 7) is an interpolation from Is. viii. 2, where Zechariah son of *Jeberechiah* is mentioned, is unnecessary. In Ezra v. 1, 2 "Zechariah son of Iddo" is mentioned as prophesying in conjunction with "Haggai the prophet," and being instrumental in bringing about the resumption of the work of rebuilding the Temple. We know nothing further for certain about him, except that he prophesied up to the month of Cislev in the 4th year of Darius. Something may, however, be deduced from circumstantial evidence.

Among the Priests and Levites who came up with Zerubbabel is mentioned "Iddo" (Neh. xii. 4), as one of heads of the priestly families

---

[1] Son of the philosopher *Moses Mendelssohn*, from whose Biblical Commentary we quote the opinions of Arnswald, and father of *Felix Mendelssohn Bartholdy* the musician.

(*rāshē haccōh'nīm*) in the days of Joshua (see p. 32) the High Priest. Again in the days of Joiakim, the son of Joshua (the High Priest), a Zechariah son of Iddo is mentioned (ver. 10, 12, 16) as one of the heads of families (*rāshē hā'ābhōth*), and that evidently among the Priests. From these facts it is deduced by many (and not unreasonably), that Zechariah (like Jeremiah and Ezekiel) was a priest as well as a prophet: and that (supposing the Iddo of Neh. xii. 4, 16 to be the same person that is mentioned in Zech. i. 1), while Zechariah began his ministry during the High-priesthood of Joshua, he was head of his family in the days of Joiakim the son of Joshua. Thus Zechariah's father, probably, died early and never became the head of his family, and Zechariah was a young man at the time of the return from the Captivity.

The times of the Prophet, and occasion of his Mission.

In the first year of his reign in Babylon B.C. 538 (*Rawlinson*) Cyrus the Great made a decree for the return of the Jewish exiles to Jerusalem, and for the rebuilding of the House of the LORD God of Israel, which was in Jerusalem (Ezr. i. 3). The sum total of the "Congregation" (*qāhāl*) which came up on this occasion was 42,360 (*fathers of families*, probably, i.e. about 200,000 free men, women and children), besides male and female slaves to the number of 7,337 (Ezr. ii. 64, 65, Neh. vii. 66, 67). These came up under Zerubbabel (or *Sheshbaççar* comp. Ezr. iii. 8, v. 16, Zech. iv. 8), the Head of the Captivity (*Rēsh Gālūthā*) son of Shealtiel (Ezr. iii. 2, 8, v. 2 &c., Hagg. i. 1, 12 &c., Matt. i. 12, Luke iii. 27), and Joshua the son of Josedech the High Priest. Zerubbabel is called (1 Chron. iii. 19) son of Pedaiah (son of Jeconiah, son of Jehoiakim), Shealtiel having probably died without male issue, and his brother Pedaiah having (in accordance with Deut. xxv. 5—10) taken his deceased brother's wife. Zerubbabel was thus legal heir of Jehoiachim, king of Judah. Feeble indeed was the people's response to the Persian king's invitation to return to their own country, and remarkably so with those who ought to have been most eager to avail themselves of it, viz. the priesthood. Of them but 4 out of the 24 orders, and of the Levites only 74 (*households*, probably) returned. After the returned exiles had arrived at their respective cities, as the seventh month was approaching they were assembled, as one man, to Jerusalem, and rebuilt the altar of burnt offerings, and from the 1st day of Tishri (see page 10) reestablished the daily sacrifices. They kept also in that month the Feast of Tabernacles[1] (Ezra iii. 1—6) "according to the scripture" (viz. from the 15th to the 22nd[2] of the 7th month, Lev. xxiii. 33—42). Then in the second month (*Iyyár*) of the second year of their return (whether this was the second or third year of Darius cannot be decided) energetic measures began to be taken for the building of the Temple, and the foundation thereof was shortly laid amid the blasts of trumpets, the clashing of cymbals, and songs and praises to the LORD "for His mercy (endureth) for ever upon Israel," while some shouted for joy, and the ancient men, who had seen the Former House, wept, when the foundation of this House was laid before their eyes (Ezr. iii. 8—13). But the building was not destined to be completed at this time. When the Samaritans heard that the community, which had returned from the Captivity, were beginning to rebuild the Temple, they came to Zerubbabel, and to the chiefs of the people, and desired to take part in the work. On their cooperation being declined they set themselves to hinder the Jews in their work, and bribed some of the favourites at the Court of Persia so effectually, that they frustrated the purpose of the people of Judah during the rest of "the reign of Cyrus, even up to the reign of Darius" (Ezra iv. 1—5);—i.e. from about B.C. 536 to B.C. 529 when Cyrus died, and during the reign of Cambyses, son of Cyrus (B.C. 529—522), and the 10 months (or less) of the reign of the pseudo-Smerdis (or Bardes) B.C. 522—1, and during one year of the reign of Darius, who succeeded Bardes in 521—in all about 15 years[3]. In the second year of Darius, God raised up Haggai the prophet, and Zechariah the son of Iddo (Ezr. v. 1, 2) to prophesy to the Jews which were in Judah and Jerusalem, so that Zerubbabel and Joshua the High Priest and the rest of the people "came and worked at the House of the Lord of Hosts in the 24th day of the 6th month of the second year of Darius," (Hag.

---

[1] The fact that this was the first Festival, which they kept on their return, may be an additional reason for the prominence given to it in Zech. xiv. 16, 18. There does not appear to be any sufficient ground for doubting the genuineness of Ezr. iii. 4—6ª.

[2] The 22nd called *Sh'míní 'açéreth* is looked on as a separate Festival, *régel biph'ne 'açmo* (T. B. *Succah* 47ᵇ–48ª).

[3] For further particulars with regard to the events of this interval see the book of Ezra.

i. 15). Although it is true that the enemies of Judah and Benjamin were a chief cause of this long neglect of the work of rebuilding, still such neglect seems to have been in great measure caused by remissness on the part of Zerubbabel and Joshua, and the heads of the people. For Haggai on the 1st of the 6th month (i. 1—11) administered to them a scathing rebuke, when he said to them "Is it time for you, *you indeed*, to dwell in your houses all ceiled, while this House lieth waste?" He calls on them too to "consider their ways," to call to mind, *why* it was that they "sowed much, and brought in little," it is (says he) because "My House is waste, and ye run every one to his own house." In the 7th month the word of the LORD came again to Haggai, and he foretells the "shaking of the heavens and the earth and the sea," encourages the people by the promise that "the choicest things of the nations should come" to glorify God's House (ii. 7, 8), and assures them that "the glory of that House will in later times be greater than at the first" (ver. 9). At this juncture it was, that the first recorded revelation came to Zechariah, in the 8th month, and he is commanded to exhort the people to repentance, and to warn them against neglecting the words of the prophets as their fathers had done before them, if they would not experience their chastisements (i. 1—6).

Contents of Chap. i.—viii.

After the (1) introductory verses (Chap. i. 1—6), Chapters i. 7—viii. 23 fall into two divisions, divided from each other, and from the introduction, by the mention of the exact date of each revelation. They comprise (2) Chap. i. 7—vi. 15, and (3) Chap. vii. and viii.

(2) Chap. i. 7—vi. 15 consists of a series of seven visions, with two appendices —chaps. ii. 6—13—vi. 9—15.

First Vision (chap. i. 7—17).—*The horsemen between the myrtles.* This vision was intended to convey to the prophet the truth that, though as yet there may be little sign of God's "overthrowing the kingdoms" (Haggai ii. 22), yet He, with His all-watchful eye, was scanning the horizon, and preparing to fulfil His word.

Second Vision (chap. i. 18—21).—*The four horns and four workmen* indicate that God would continue to remove the hostility of the Persians, even as He had already broken the power of the Assyrians, Egyptians, and Babylonians.

Third Vision (chap. ii. 1—5).—*The man with the measuring line.* The enlargement and perfect security of the people of God. An appendix (chap. ii. 6—13), prophetic of the ingathering of the nations in the days of BRANCH, the Messiah.

Fourth Vision (chap. iii.)—*Joshua, the high priest, arraigned before the angel of* the Lord. The forgiveness of the sins of the priesthood and people, whose representative he was.

Fifth Vision (chap. iv.).—*The candlestick with the two olive-trees.* The diffusion of God's grace by means of His two channels—the priesthood and civil power. It contains a promise (ver. 9) that Zerubbabel's hands should finish the building of the Temple.

Sixth Vision (chap. v. 1—11).—*The flying roll, and the woman in the ephah,* denoting the curse on sinners, and the banishment of sin.

Seventh Vision (chap. vi. 1—8).—*The four chariots.* God's judgments on the nations. An appendix (chap. vi. 9—15) describing the crowning of Joshua, which foreshadows the twofold office of BRANCH, as king and priest. A probable *lacuna* in the text.

(3) Chaps. vii., viii.—The inquiry concerning the fasts. The prophet's rebuke of the people for their formalism. The answer to their inquiry, in the form of a promise that their fasts should be turned into feasts.

PROLEGOMENA TO CHAPTERS IX.—XIV.

Integrity, Date and Authorship.

The first to call in question the genuineness of these chapters was Mede (the great English writer on Prophecy, who died 1638). He was led to do so in defence of the correctness of the Text of the New Testament. Observing that in Matt. xxvii. 9 a passage, which is evidently a quotation from Zech. xi. 12, 13, is ascribed to Jeremiah, he felt bound to support this authoritative statement of the Evangelist (as he considered it), and in endeavouring so to do he came to the conclusion that there is much in these Chapters which argues their pre-exilian origin. Since his time the question has been repeatedly discussed, with such inconsistent results, that while Hitzig places chaps. ix.—xiv. as early as B.C. 772, in the reign of Uzziah, Eichhorn refers them to "after the battle of Issus, B.C. 333," and Böttcher "after B.C. 330" (see Pusey's "*Table of Dates* &c."). We now proceed to review the arguments which have been brought forward by the impugners of the genuineness of these chapters, bearing in mind Pusey's weighty remark "It is obvious that there must be some mistake either in the tests applied, or in their application, which admits of a variation of at least 450 years."

I. A difference has been alleged between chaps. i.—viii., and chaps. ix.—xiv., (1) with regard to Style, (2) with regard to Historical Standpoint.

(1) With regard to style it has been urged:

(α) *That the style of chaps. i.—viii. is utterly different to that of chaps. ix.—xiv.* This (speaking generally) we are free to admit. But we cannot admit it as a valid argument against the Unity of Authorship. For, upon the argument of mere *style* it might be maintained that the same author could not have written Zech. i. 1—6, vii. and viii., and i. 7—vi. 15; the first-mentioned passages consist chiefly of rebuke, and in them there is no mention of *Çemach*, while in the other passage there is nothing but a series of visions, with passages of encouragement and promise interspersed (ii. 10—17, iii. 7—10, vi. 9—15). As for the heading of chap. vii. 1, which ascribes it to Zechariah, it might be put out of the argument for one side or the other, since such critics are in the habit of rejecting such verses as spurious, when they are subversive of their preconceived conclusions. Again, we may adduce cases in which the argument from style has no weight with these critics: e.g. the style of Hos. i.—iii. is utterly different to that of iv.—xiv. and that of Ezek. iv. v. to that of vi. vii. or of xxvii. xxviii. and yet the general integrity of these books is universally admitted.

(β) *That in i. 7—vi. 15 there is nothing but visions, while in ix.—xiv. there are none.* But, there can surely be no reason why a prophet should not relate visions when he sees them, while there is every reason why he should not relate them when he does not see them; neither can there be any reason in the nature of things why a prophet, who *once* in his life saw a series of visions *in one night*, should be expected to have all revelations made to him in that particular manner. Zech. i. 1—6, vii. viii. contains no visions, and yet the genuineness of those passages is not doubted. Similarly, Amos vii.—ix. consists wholly of visions, while in i.—vi. there are none; Isaiah, too, and Ezekiel related such visions as they saw, but when they saw none they delivered their message in a different manner. If the thoughtful reader will compare this objection with that which we have said *might* be brought against the unity of authorship of chap. i. 1—6, vii., viii., and chap. i. 7—vi. 15, he will probably come to the conclusion, that one is of as little weight as the other.

(γ) *That the angel interpreter, and Satan, and the Seven Eyes disappear from chaps. ix.—xiv.* This is quite natural. They were part of the visions, and when the visions disappear, they disappear also. It might as reasonably be argued that the Prophet was bound in the latter portion of his prophecies to refer continually to Horses, Chariots, Candlesticks, Horns &c., because, forsooth, he had seen such in his visions!

(δ) *That* (*a*) *Exact dates are given in the former chapters, but none in the latter.* So, too, are dates prefixed to Is. vi. 1, Ezek. i. 1—3, viii. 1, xl. 1, &c.—*That* (*b*) *in chaps. i.—viii. introductory formulas constantly occur, which are wanting in the latter chapters.* Similarly Hosea uses introductory formulas in the first five chapters, but none in the last nine. And yet (as we have said) no doubt is entertained of the integrity of that book.

Finally the argument from style must always be a doubtful one. Pusey has given an instance of the precarious nature of such arguments in the following. The *Laws of Plato* an acute German critic imagined to have proved from their style to be not the work of Plato. And yet Jowett (*Transl. Plato Dialog.* iv. p. 1) has shown their genuineness by 20 citations in Aristotle (who must have been intimate with Plato for some 17 years), by allusions of Isocrates (writing a year after Plato's death), by references of the comic poet Alexis (a younger contemporary), besides the unanimous voice of later antiquity. Further, critics of similar tendencies do not agree on points of style: e.g. Rosenmüller speaks of the first eight chapters as being "prosaic, feeble, poor," and of the remaining six as "poetic, weighty, concise, glowing," (comp. Maurer and Hitzig). Böttcher on the other hand says "In comparison with the *lifeless language* of these chapters (ix.—xiv.), as to which we cannot at all understand how any can have removed them into so early pre-exile times, the Psalms attributed to the time of the Maccabees are amazingly fresh." When critics so disagree as to the respective merits of the styles of the two sections, it seems hardly worth while to consider the argument. We will merely remark, that neither sweeping statement is correct. In the first chapters when Zechariah is describing his visions, he uses the natural language of narrative, viz. prose. When (ii. 10—17, vi. 12, 13) he looks forward to the distant future, he speaks in glowing language such as will bear comparison with anything contained in the latter chapters.

(2) A difference with regard to the Historical Standpoint has been urged (α) in *particular* passages, (β) in the two sections *generally*.

(a) We have shown in the Commentary that the arguments of those who see in certain passages of chap. ix.—xiv. positive indications of the pre-exilian origin of these chapters are inconclusive. See especially "Remarks" on ix. 1—8, pp. 82—84; ix. 9—17, p. 90; x. 2, p. 91; x. 3—12, pp. 95, 96; xi. 1—3, p. 97, 8, p. 101; xi. 14, p. 104; xii. 1—9, p. 110, 111; xii. 11, p. 16; xiv. 5, p. 124; xiv. 1—21, p. 131, 132.

(β) With regard to the historical standpoint *generally*, it has been alleged *that in chap. i.—viii. the prophet is continually mentioning the rebuilding of the Temple, and the re-inhabiting of Jerusalem; while in chap. ix.—xiv. he is occupied with quite different matters. In the former he mentions his contemporaries, such as Zerubbabel and Joshua, but not so in the latter portion.* As regards the Temple and the prophet's contemporaries this is perfectly true, but it is no argument for the pre-exilian authorship of chap. ix.—xiv., nor against their contents having been delivered by Zechariah. For, if our theory as to the date of these chapters be correct, they were written at a time when the rebuilding of the Temple had been long completed, and when those abuses of the Temple-service, which occupy so much of the attention of the Prophet Malachi, had not as yet crept in. The Prophet *is* occupied in the latter chapters with matters quite different from those with which he is concerned in the former chapters, hence the frequent recurrence in the latter section of the expression "in that day" (ix. 16, xii., xiii., xiv. *passim*). But, that in the latter section there is no mention of the re-inhabiting of Jerusalem is certainly untrue, see (ix. 16, 17), x. 6, 7, xii. 6, xiv. 10.

The arguments, however, against the pre-exilian origin of these chapters are not merely of a negative kind.

II. We now proceed to adduce from (a) parallel passages, (β) notes of time, &c., what we consider to be

Internal Evidence in favour of the hypothesis of the Post-exilian Origin of Chap. ix.—xiv.

(a) The writer of chap. ix.—xiv. shows such a familiarity with the writings of the *later* prophets as seems to some reconcileable only with the supposition that he wrote at a date posterior to them: thus with the so-called *Deutero-Isaiah*[1]. Compare

Zech. ix. 12ᵃ with Is. xlii. 7, xlix. 9, lxi. 1.	Zech. xii. 1 with Is. li. 13.
Zech. ix. 12ᵇ with Is. lxi. 7.	— — 2 ,, — li. 22, 23.
— x. 10 ,, — xlix. 19, 20.	— xiii. 9 ,, — xlviii. 10.
— xi. 15, 16 — lvi. 11.	— — 16 ,, — lx. 6—9, lxvi. 23.
	— — 17 ,, — lx. 12.

Zephaniah. Compare Zech. ix. 5, 6 with Zeph. ii. 4, 5.

Jeremiah. Compare

Zech. ix. 12 with Jer. xvi. 18.	Zech. xi. 6 with Jer. xxvi. 29—33.
— xi. 3 ,, — xxv. 34—36.	— xiii. 9 — — xxx. 22.
— —— ,, — xii. 5, xlix. 19, l. 44. (The only passages in which *Geon hay Yarden* occurs).	(Comp. also with these Zech. viii. 8, and Hos. ii. 23.)
	Zech. xiv. 7 with Jer. xxx. 7, 8.
Zech. xi. 5 with Jer. ii. 3, l. 7.	— — 10 ,, — xxxi. 38—40.
	— — 20, 21 — xxxi. 40.

Obadiah. Compare

Zech. xii. 6 with Obad. ver. 18.	Zech. xiv. 9 with Obad. ver. 9.

Ezekiel. Compare

Zech. ix. 2—4 with Ezek. xxviii. 1—23.	Zech. xiii. 1, 2 with Ezek. xxxvi. 25, xxxvii. 23.
— x. 2 ,, — xxxiv. 5, 8.	
— x. 3 ,, — xxxiv. 12, 17, 20, 22, 31.	— xiii. 8, 9 ,, — v. 2, 12; xi. 20.
	— xiv. 2 (xii. 2—9) xxxviii. 14—18.
— xi. ,, — xxxiv.	— — 4 with Ezek. — 19, 20.
especially verr. 4, 5, 16 with verr. 3, 4, and ver. 9 with ver. 16.	— — 8 ,, — xlvii. 1.
	— — 13 ,, — xxxviii. 21.
— xi. 7, 14 ,, — xxxvii. 16—22	— — 14 ,, — xxxix. 10.
— xii. 10 ,, — xxxix. 29.	— — 21 ,, — xliv. 9.

Haggai. Compare
Zech. xiv. 13 with Hag. ii. 21, 22.

Similarly chap. i.—viii., which are of undeniable post-exilian authorship, show a thorough acquaintance with the *later* prophets. Compare, for example:

chap. ii. 6 (E.V.) with Isa. xlviii. 20, or with Isa. lii. 11 and Jer. li. 6, 9;
chap. ii. 9, 11 (E.V.), and chap. iv. 9, with Ezek. vi. 7, 10, xxxix. 10, &c.;
chaps. iii. 8, vi. 12, with Jer. xxiii. 5, xxxiii. 15 (Isa. iv. 2);
chap. vi. 15 with Jer. xvii. 24;

---

[1] The date of Is. xl.—lxvi. need not come under consideration here, since most critics who regard Zech. ix.—xiv. as pre-exilian, consider Is. xl.—lxvi. as contemporary with the *later* prophets.

chap. vii. 5—10 with Isa. lviii. 3—7;
chap. vii. 9 with Ezek. xviii. 8, and Jer. vii. 5—7, xxii. 3;
chap. vii. 12 with Ezek. xi. 19;   chap. viii. 4 with Isa. lxv. 20;
chap. vii. 13 with Jer. xi. 11;   chap. viii. 6 with Jer. xxxii. 17, 27;
chap. vii. 14 with Jer. xvi. 13, &c.;   chap. viii. 7 with Isa. xliii. 6;
chap. viii. 3 with Jer. xxxi. 23; chap. vii. 8 with Isa. xlviii. 1.

This argument seemed so convincing to de Wette that, after having in the first three editions of his *Einleitung* declared for two authors, he felt compelled to change his mind, and in his fourth edition admitted the post-exilian origin of Chap. ix.—xiv., and even the possibility of their having been written by Zechariah. We are not, however, prepared to regard this argument as conclusive. We own the difficulty that there is in computing the exact weight due to the argument derived from the consideration of parallel passages, and concur with Cheyne's pertinent remarks on the subject (*The Prophecies of Isaiah*, II. p. 210):

"The argument from parallel passages is sometimes much overrated. How prone we are to fancy an imitation where there is none, has been strikingly shown by Munro's parallel between the plays of Shakspeare and Seneca (*Journal of Philology*, Vol. VI. Camb. 1876, pp. 70—72), and even when an imitation on one side or the other must be supposed, how difficult it is to choose between the alternatives!...A recent revolution of opinion among patristic students may be a warning to us not to be too premature in deciding such questions. It has been the custom to argue from the occurrence of almost identical sentences in the *Octavius* of Minucius Felix and the *Apologeticum* of Tertullian, that Minucius must have written later than the beginning of the third century, on the ground that a brilliant genius like Tertullian's cannot have been such a servile imitator as the hypothesis of the priority of Minucius would imply. But Adolf Ebert (*Tertullians Verhältniss zu Minucius Felix*) seems to have definitely proved that Tertullian not only made use of Minucius, but did not even understand his author rightly."

(β) There are certain notes of time, &c. in chaps. ix.—xiv. which seem to compel us to admit their post-exilian origin.

1. No mention is made of any king of Israel or Judah, except the Messiah (ix. 9). For chap. xi. 6 evidently refers to the different nations of the world (i.e. *hā'ādām* means "mankind," and *hā'áreç* "the world"). The expression "from *their* hand" indicates that several kings are referred to; and so, if "his king" meant an Israelite king, the expression "(and each) into the hand of his king" would imply that each Israelite had a separate king. But the meaning is

"I will deliver mankind into the hand of one another and (each people) into the hand of its king."

2. The manner in which Greece is named (ix. 13) as the chief enemy of Zion (quite different from that of Joel iv. 6, Is. lxvi. 19), besides other historical references, which we have pointed out in our "Remarks," leave us no choice but to understand chap. ix.—xi. as descriptive of the Macedonian and Maccabean periods. While the prophecies of chap. xii.—xiv., which manifestly form one section, would be simply untrue if uttered in reference to any pre-exilian epoch.

3. Except in Mal. i. 1 the expression *Maṣṣá d'bhár YHVH* occurs only in chap. ix. 1 and xii. 1.

4. In xii. 11 a place in the tribe of Issachar is called by an *Assyrian* name.

The reader will perceive that the arguments adduced in II. (a) and (β) answer from the positive side of the argument those objections which in I. (a) and (β) we treated merely from the negative side.

We conclude, therefore, that chap. ix.—xiv. are, equally with chap. i.—viii., of post-exilian origin.

III. *The Integrity of Chap. ix.—xiv.*

The theory, which Bunsen has called one of the triumphs of modern criticism, that chap. ix.—xi. and chap. xii.—xiv. are the work of two different prophets: viz. chap. ix.—xi. that of a contemporary of Isaiah, perhaps Zechariah son of Jeberechiah (Is. viii. 2), and chap. xii.—xiv. possibly that of Urijah son of Shemaiah (Jer. xxvi. 20—23), falls to the ground with the establishment of the post-exilian origin of the whole section. Archbishop Newcombe, who originated this theory, concluded that chap. ix.—xi. were written much earlier than the time of Jeremiah, and before the captivity of the tribes; but was not so positive as his followers with regard to the pre-exilian authorship of chap. xii.—xiv., though he thinks the mention of idols (xiii. 2) to be in favour of that supposition. We must, therefore, discuss a little more fully what have been termed *the grounds for separating chap. xii.—xiv. from chap. ix.—xi.*

(1) *Chap. xi. has a distinct introductory formula.* But since this formula is the same as that of chap. ix. 1, and that a formula which recurs only in Mal. i. 1, this

argument tends rather in the other direction.—(2) *The former chapters speak of Israel and Judah, but the latter do not mention "Israel."* On the contrary chap. xii. 1 states that the whole of the following prophecy is concerning "Israel."—(3) *In the former Syrians, Phoenicians, Philistines, and Greeks are mentioned, but Assyrians and Egyptians described as the most powerful. These chapters belong therefore to early times.* We have already shown that the manner in which the Greeks are here described as enemies of Israel fixes the date of these chapters to the post-exilian period. Egypt and Assyria are spoken of (x. 10) as the nations who had carried off the people, and whence they were to be brought back, while in ver. 11 the stereotyped language of former prophets is evidently used in a figurative sense.—(4) *The anticipations of the two prophets are different. The first trembles for Ephraim, but for Judah he has no fear.* On the contrary, Ephraim and Judah are included equally in the promised protection. *The second prophet does not mention the northern kingdom, but is full of alarm for Judah, and sees the enemy laying siege to Jerusalem.* "Ephraim" does not denote "the northern kingdom" in chap. ix.—xi. (see Remarks). If Jerusalem was to be besieged at any time after its rebuilding (but see Remarks, p. 132), there is no reason why the same prophet who spoke before in general terms of wars, should not afterwards speak more particularly of a siege. In prophesying concerning a siege of Jerusalem it is only natural that Judah, in which tribe it partly stood, should be especially mentioned. Moreover, as we remarked above, the section is expressly addressed to all "Israel."—(5) *Difference of style:* "And it shall come to pass" *does not occur in ix.—xi.*, "in that day" *which occurs so often in xii.—xiv.* occurs only once in ix.—xi., and "n*'um YHVH*," *occurs only twice in ix.—xi.* There are also favourite expressions in xii.—xiv., such as "all peoples," "all nations round about," "family of Egypt," &c. This is true, but chap. xii.—xiv. are admitted by all to be a separate section, delivered probably on a different occasion to the former section, and pointing on the whole to a much further distant future. These facts are quite sufficient to account for such very slight differences of style.

IV. *The Integrity of the whole Book.*

With regard to the integrity of the book we must premise, that the fact that a passage occurs in a certain book is not to be regarded as a proof that it was looked upon by those who drew up the Canon as necessarily an integral portion of that book. For, the principle was to insert short compositions into longer ones lest from their lack of bulk they should be lost (אײדי דזוטר מירבם *Baba Bathra* 14ᵇ). Thus (*Vayyiqra Rabba* xv. 2) the two verses Is. viii. 19, 20 are ascribed to Beeri (father of Amos), and are said to have been placed there because they were not long enough to form a book by themselves. Again, in T. B. *Maccoth* 24ᵇ the verse Mic. iii. 12 is ascribed, without remark, to Urijah the priest, the co-witness with Zechariah son of Jeberechiah (Is. viii. 2). If therefore it should be thought that Zech. xi. 1—3, and xiii. 7—9 have no apparent connection with the context in the places in which they stand, it would be quite admissible to suppose them to be fragments, say of Ezekiel, and Jeremiah respectively, which had not been included in those books, and which were now inserted in the prophecies of Zechariah to prevent their being lost. There is no doubt, that we are aware of, expressed in Talmudim or Midrashim as to the genuineness of the last six chapters of Zechariah. On the contrary, chap. xi. 1 is distinctly ascribed to "Zechariah son of Iddo" (T. B. *Yoma* 39ª). While, on the other hand, Rabbi Akivah, in a remarkable piece of exegesis (*Maccoth ibid.*), identifies *Zechariah the son of Jeberechiah* with *the author of Zech. viii. 4*, although he is perfectly aware, that Zechariah prophesied during the time of the Second Temple. (See further *Introduction to Zechariah* in Bishop Ellicott's "Old Testament Commentary for English Readers.")

We have given reasons for assigning the whole of chap. ix.—xiv. to the post-captivity period: we have shown, too, that there is nothing in the style or contents of the two sections of this division (ix.—xi. and xii.—xiv.) to cast any serious doubt on the unity of authorship. We now proceed to adduce some arguments to prove that there is sufficient correspondence between chap. i.—viii. and ix.—xiv. to justify us, in default of any positive evidence to the contrary, in regarding the whole book as the work of one prophet.

(1) Both portions exhibit, as we have shown, an extensive acquaintance with the writings of the *later* prophets.

(2) They both exhibit also an extensive acquaintance with the *earlier* books, thus: in chap. i. 4—6, chap. vii. 12, reference is made to "the former prophets" generally;

    chap. ii. 12 (E.V. 8) recalls the thought, though not the phraseology, of Ps. xvii. 8;
    chaps. iii. 8, vi. 12, allude to Isai. iv. 2, as well as to Jer. xxiii. 5, and xxxiii. 15;
    chap. iii. 10 is from Mic. iv. 4;
    chap. vi. 13 evidently refers to Ps. cx. 4;
    chap. viii. 8 recalls Hos. ii. 21 (E. V. 19);
    chap. viii. 20—22, in substance may be compared with Mic. iv. 1, 2, Isa. ii. 2, 3.

And in the second part,
    chap. ix. 1—8 bears some resemblance to Amos i. 3, ii. 6;

chap. ix. 10 (first half) is borrowed from Mic. v. 10, and (second half) from Ps. lxxii. 8;

chap. xiii. 2 is a quotation from Hos. ii. 17, or Mic. v. 12, 13 (comp. Is. ii. 18, 20); and verse 9 from Hos. ii. 20 (E.V. 23);

comp. also chap. ix. 16 with Is. xi. 12;

chap. x. 12 with Mic. iv. 5;

chap. x. 10—12 with Is. xi. 15, xiv. 25, x. 24—27, xxx. 31, &c.;

chap. xii. 8 with Joel iv. 10;

chap. xii. 10 with Joel iii. 1, 2.

chap. xiv. 3 with Is. xxxiv. 1—4;

chap. xiv. 6, 7 with Amos v. 18, 20, Joel iv. (E.V. iii.) 15, Is. xxx. 26;

chap. xiv. 8 with Is. xi. 9, ii. 3, Mic. iv. 2;

chap. xiv. 11 with Amos ix. 13—15;

chap. xiv. 20 with Is. xxiii. 18;

chap. xiv. 21 with Is. iv. 3, xxxv. 8, Joel iv. (E.V. iii.) 17: *etc.*

But we cannot lay much stress on this argument, since prophets, belonging as they did in most cases to a school, were in all probability acquainted with the works of their predecessors.

(3) In both divisions there are similar if not identical expressions to represent the whole people such as "the house of Israel, and the house of Judah" (viii. 13), "the house of Judah, and the house of Joseph" (x. 6). See further on pp. 90, 110.

(4) Chap. xi. 11 is very similar to ii. 9, 11 [13, 15 Hebr.]. And the promise of x. 1 to that of viii. 12. In both portions Jerusalem is bid rejoice (ii. 10 Hebr. ver. 14, ix. 9), and in both the only king of Israel mentioned is the Messiah.

(5) In both portions there are promises of the bringing back of the exiles (comp. ii. 10—17, viii. 6—8 with ix. 11, 12 and x. 10—12).

(6) In both there is the habit of dwelling on the same thought or word (e.g. ii. 14, 15, vi. 10, vi. 12, 13, viii. 4, 5, viii. 23, xi. 7, xiv. 10, 11, xiv. 4, xiv. 5). In both the whole and its part are mentioned together for emphasis as v. 4, x. 4, and in xii. 11 we have "every family apart," and then in ver. 12, 13 the specification. In both parts we have the unusual number of *five* sections to a verse, e.g. vi. 13, ix. 5, 7.

(7) Both divisions are written in Hebrew free from Aramaisms. In both the expression *mē'ōbhēr ūmishshābh* occurs (vii. 14, ix. 8), an expression which occurs elsewhere only in Ezek. xxxv. 7.

(8) The highly poetic language and deep prophetic insight of chap.

ix.—xiv. we consider as an additional argument in favour of the unity of authorship of the whole book. For the man, to whom in his youth such mystic visions as those of chap. i.—vi. were vouchsafed, is just such an one to whom we should not be surprised to find, that in his later years such profound revelations as those contained in chap. ix.—xiv. were revealed, and who from his poetic and imaginative temperament would be likely to find suitable poetic language and metaphors, wherewith to clothe them when revealed to him.

The *internal* evidence being favourable to the hypothesis of the post-exilian origin of chap. ix.—xiv., as well as of chap. i.—viii., and to that of unity of authorship, rather than adverse to it, and there being no positive *external* evidence to the contrary, we conclude that it is probable that the whole of the so-called book of Zechariah (except perhaps xi. 1—3, and xiii. 7—9) is the work of Zechariah, grandson of Iddo.

V. *Probable date of Zech. ix.—xiv.*

Holding the view that by divine inspiration prophets are able to predict events, we cannot agree with those who assert that they must always have written after the events which they describe. Further, in the case before us, while chap. ix.—xiii. are a sufficiently accurate description of the chief features of the Macedonian and Maccabean periods to be interpreted as *prophetic* thereof, they are so vague in detail, and of such an imaginative and idealistic character as to render the supposition that they are *descriptive* of events which had already taken place extremely improbable. We conclude, therefore (apart from any consideration of authorship), that they were written before Alexander's victorious march through Palestine (B.C. 333). But, though a prophet could foretell events, he would not speak of matters, which could be of no interest to his contemporaries. Zechariah would not, therefore, prophesy concerning the wars of the sons of Zion with the sons of Greece before the Greeks had begun to attract attention in the East (comp. p. 132). Now the first event in connection with the Greeks, which would become notorious in the East, is the burning of Sardis by the Ionians (B.C. 499). These chapters must, then, have been composed after that date (viz. between 499—333 B.C.). Now

Zechariah was, as we have shown, in all probability a young man when he came from Babylon. Suppose he was 25 years of age in the second year of Darius (520), he would have been but 46 in the year of the burning of Sardis, or 55 in the year of the battle of Marathon (490), or 65 in the year of the battle of Salamis (480). Now, this last great victory, being a naval one, was likely to attract the most attention among the Jews. For, the fleets of the Phœnicians had been requisitioned by the Persians for the subjugation of the Ionians, and the Jews might well have feared that the Greeks, confounding them with the Phœnicians, would wreak a speedy and bitter vengeance on them. We consider therefore that about 479 B.C. (the year after the battle of Salamis) is the date to which the last six chapters of Zechariah may most reasonably be assigned.

Contents of Chap. ix.—xiv.

These chapters consist of two sections: (1) Chap. ix.—xi., (2) Chap. xii.—xiv., each of which commences with the formula *Massâ d'bhár Adōnāy*.

(1) Chap. ix., x. Doom of adjacent nations. The struggles, but eventual triumph and security, of Israel. The coming of the King (chap. ix. 9, *seqq*.).
,,   xi. [xiii. 7—9 (?)]. The storm threatens the shepherds (?). Rejection of the Good Shepherd. Doom of the foolish shepherd.
(2) Chap. xii. 1—9. Struggles of Israel with the nations.
,,   xiii. 1—4. Zeal against prophets in general.
,,   xii. 10—14. Mourning over him whom they pierced.
,,   xiii. 5, 6. General disclaiming of prophetic powers. [chap. xiii. 7—9 (?)].
,,   xiv. "The last things," as seen in the light of the old dispensation.

ZECHARIAH.

CHAPTER I.

IN the eighth month, in the second year of Darius, came the word of the LORD unto Zecha-riah, the son of Berechiah, the son of Iddo the prophet, saying,

---

"Came," lit. *was* (and so elsewhere): LXX. ἐγένετο. "Iddo the prophet," this is, in part, the meaning of the Hebr. according to the traditional accentuation; but the words "the prophet" were originally intended, doubtless, to apply to Zechariah, not to Iddo[1]. Verse 1. Translation.

שְׁתַּיִם is the fem. of שְׁנַיִם "two": it (with its constr. שְׁתֵּי) is the only word which has a בגדכפת letter *with dagesh* after a *moving* shᵉva. The *dagesh* is *forte*, representing the lost נ. The full form of the word would be either (Gesen.) שְׁנָתַיִם (which, however, is used as the dual of שָׁנָה "a year"), or rather שִׁנְתַּיִם. The Arabic has a prosthetic Alef[2], being masc. *ithnāni*, fem. *ithnatāni* (or dropping Words.

---

[1] The tradition is: "When a prophet's name is mentioned *and* that of his father, then *he* is a prophet, and the *father also*. When only the prophet's name is mentioned, then his father was not a prophet." א״ר יוחנן כל נביא שנתפרש שמו ונתפרש שם אביו, נביא ובן נביא, וכל נביא שנתפרש שמו ולא נתפרש שם אביו, הוא נביא, ואביו אינו נביא. ר׳ אלעזר בשם ר׳ יוסי בן זמרא מייתי לה מן הדא (עורא ה, א.) והתנבי...זכריה בר עדוא נבאיא, שהיה נביא בן נביא ויקרא רנה, ופרשה, ו (5). But, there is no reason on account of this to saddle Tradition with the anachronism of supposing the grandfather (or father) of Zechariah to have been "Iddo the prophet" (2 Chron. xiii. 22), who lived more than four centuries earlier, for the name was an old one in the Priesthood (see 1 Chron. vi. 6, E.V. v. 21). At any rate, according to common sense (not to mention that it is in accordance with the usual custom of other Semitic languages), the title, which comes at the end of a genealogical string like this, belongs naturally to that person of whom the writer is especially speaking.

[2] R. David Qimchi in his Grammar (*Sha'ar diqdūq hash-shēmōth, sha'ar*

the prefix and retaining the Nun) *thintāni*, which is exactly שְׁנָתַיִם, since Arab. *Th* often corresponds to Hebr. שׁ, as שׁוֹר "an ox," Arab. *Thour*.

דָּֽרְיָ֫וֶשׁ "Darius," has a *metheg* under the first letter, to indicate that the *sh'va* under the *rēsh* is moving[1]. The pointing דָּרְיָ֫וֶשׁ[2] in Tregelles' English edition of *Gesenius* (1846) is contrary to the authority of MSS., neither is the word so pointed in Gesen. *Thesaurus*. [By a remarkable coincidence the sum of the numerical values of the consonants of דריוש (4 + 200 + 10 + 6 + 300 = 520) gives the date B. C. of the second reign of Darius, when the prophecies of Haggai and those of the first six chapters of Zechariah were delivered.]

יְהוָֹה, the Jews always read this word as אֲדֹנָי "The LORD," with the vowels of which it is furnished; unless it is preceded or followed by the word אֲדֹנָי itself, when it is read as אֱלֹהִים (and pointed יֱהוִֹה). Consequently the prefixes בּ, כּ, ל, (·)מ, when placed before this word, are pointed as though actually prefixed to אֲדֹנָי, or אֱלֹהִים, as the case may be.—זְכַרְיָה is compounded of the stem זכר and יה, the latter half of the Sacred Name יְהוָֹה. The Sacred Name as a termination of Proper names occurs in various forms, e.g. יָה, יָהוּ, ־יָה־, and even simply י. Thus יְשַׁעְיָה, יְשַׁעְיָהוּ, צִדְקִיָּהוּ, and אֲבִי (2 Kings xviii. 2)

hash-sh'vā) bears witness to the fact that the orientals (בני מזרח) read the Hebrew words as *eshtaim*, *eshté*.

[1] The cuneiform contract-tablets of the time of Nebuchadnezzar all point to a moving *sh'va* under the *rēsh*, for a moving *sh'va* before a *yūd*, even if the *yūd* be pointed with quite a different vowel, should always incline towards an *i* sound (Qimchi, ibidem), and in them the syllable is always *ri*. The forms are (1) Da-ri-ya-us, (2) Da-ri-ah-us, (3) Da-ri-ya-mu-us, (4) Da-ri-ya-a-mu-us, (5) Da-ri-ah-u-su, (6) Da-ri-ya-a-uts, (7) Ta-ri-ah-mu-su (Budge). All of these exhibit in the second syllable what could, at the least, be represented in Hebrew only by a *moving sh'vā*. Nos. (2), (4),

(5), (6) and (7) point clearly to a long *ā* after the *yūd*. The Hebrew was prevented from representing properly the *u* or *ū* of the ultimate before the שׁ, by the fact that two vowels cannot fall together in Hebrew. It could only have been done by inserting an awkward א after the י, thus דָּרְיָאוֶשׁ.

[2] But, for all that, the Persic inscription of Behistan points to a short (*a*). There we read, over and over again, a-d-m D-a-r-y-w-u-sh "I Darius," in which the first letter of a-d-m is the same as the second of the name. Now *Adm* is the Sanscrit *ăhăm*, Zend *ăzem*, whence I conclude (but I am open to correction) that the first *a* of Darius was *originally* short.

for אֲבִיָּה (2 Chron. xxix. 1).—בֶּן־בֶּרֶכְיָה. The construct of בֵּן unlike that of שֵׁם (which is but six times ‍-שֶׁם) is generally joined to its consequent by a hyphen (*maqqēph*), which has the effect of making the two words into one (which seems to be the effect also of *mahpac* in הַלָּבָן Gen. xvii. 17): and then, since a long vowel cannot stand in a closed syllable unless it have the accent or *metheg* (see Excurs. I. 8), the long *ē* is changed into *ĕ* or *ĭ* as בֶּן־מֶלֶךְ, בֶּן־נוּן. The first vowel of בֶּרֶכְיָה has *methey* or rather *munach*. (See Excurs. II. A. 1 and 9 N.B.)—לֵאמֹר "saying," though sometimes it means "to say." The infinitive construct is אֱמֹר, when לְ is prefixed to it the vowel of לְ is *ē* and the א becomes quiescent; but this is not the case with the prefixes בְּ and כְּ, thus בֶּאֱמֹר (Deut. iv. 10), כֶּאֱמֹר (Josh. vi. 8). With the word אֱלֹהִים, however, the change takes place with all three suffixes, thus, לֵאלֹהִים, בֵּאלֹהִים, כֵּאלֹהִים.

בַּחֹדֶשׁ הַשְּׁמִינִי means simply "in the eighth month," without stating the day of the month. Some have maintained that the word חֹדֶשׁ (which means "new-moon" and then "month") is used here in a *constructio prægnans* to denote "the first day of the month." In 1 Sam. xx. 5 חֹדֶשׁ does mean "new moon"; comp. 2 Kings iv. 23; Is. i. 13. But, never does the word when used with the def. art. and followed by an ordinal have this meaning. It is true that the בַּחֹדֶשׁ הַשְּׁלִישִׁי of Ex. xix. 1 is by Jewish Tradition said to mean the 1st of Sivān, but the Tradition is hung on the words which come after בַּיּוֹם הַזֶּה (see Mᶜcilta, T. B. *Shabbath* 86ᵇ and Rashi), and not on any such special meaning of חֹדֶשׁ (the Pentateuchal expression for "new moons" being רָאשֵׁי חֳדָשִׁים, Numb. x. 10, &c.). Moreover Haggai (Zechariah's contemporary), when wishing to express the 1st day of the month distinctly, adds the words בְּיוֹם אֶחָד לַחֹדֶשׁ (i. 1). Comp. Gen. viii. 5, 13; Ex. xl. 2, 17; Numb. i. 1; xxix. 1; xxxiii. 38, &c. It would be possible to make the words of our text denote "the 1st day of the 8th month" only by altering the pointing to בְּחֹדֶשׁ הַשְּׁמִינִי which would mean "on the new moon of the eighth [scil. month]."—בִּשְׁנַת שְׁתַּיִם לְ-. This is the regular way of expressing a date

Constructions.

2 The LORD hath been sore displeased with your fathers.
3 Therefore say thou unto them, Thus saith the LORD of hosts; Turn ye unto me, saith the LORD of hosts, and I will turn unto you, saith the LORD of hosts.

from (or rather *with respect to*) a certain starting point: viz. בְּ is prefixed to the *constr.* of שְׁנָה, which is followed by the fem. numeral in the *absolute*, and that again by לְ: e.g. (2 Kings xxiv. 12) בִּשְׁנַת שְׁמֹנֶה לְמָלְכוֹ, lit. "In the year eight with respect to his reigning." N.B. The Hebr. construct-form simply denotes a close relation (or annexation) to the following word. "Of" is only *one* of the meanings expressed by the construct.

LXX. This version seems to make Addo identical with Barachias: πρὸς Ζαχαρίαν τὸν τοῦ Βαραχίου υἱὸν Ἀδδὼ τὸν προφήτην. But, possibly, υἱόν is a corruption of υἱοῦ caused by the collocation. In any case τὸν προφήτην must refer to Ζαχαρίαν.

Remarks. In point of time this prophecy in the 8th month, comes in between Hag. ii, 1—9, in the 7th month, and Hag. ii. 10—23, in the 9th month.

Verse 2. Constructions. קָצַף...קֶצֶף: קֶצֶף (the pausal form of קֶצֶף) is the acc. of the cognate subst. following the verb קָצַף. Even intransitive verbs can take such an acc. (the case-ending being, however, almost lost in Hebr.), e.g. (Ps. xiv. 5) פָּחֲדוּ פָחַד. The use of the absolute infinitive (which is but a subst.) before a finite verb, to intensify its meaning, is only another form of this construction. In Arabic, also, both transitive and intransitive verbs take this cognate acc. (with the case-ending retained), e.g. ḍaraba ḍaraban "he struck a blow," and intrans. nāma nouman "he slept a sleep"; the Hebr. פֶּן־אִישַׁן הַמָּוֶת "lest I sleep death" (Ps. xiii. 4) is but a slight extension of this construction (comp. for the idea כַּד דְּמַךְ "when he slept," i.e. died—Talm. Jerush.; οὐ γὰρ ἀπέθανε τὸ κοράσιον, ἀλλὰ καθεύδει, Matt. ix. 24; and the Syr. *d'mec* he slept, died).

Verse 3. Words. The student may here observe that אֲלֵהֶם is written first without a י after the לְ, and afterwards (as usually) with the י, thus אֲלֵיהֶם. It is convenient to say that אֶל and עַל take the plural pron.-suff.; but as a matter of fact the י which appears before the suffixes is part of the word itself, as the poetic forms אֱלֵי (Job iii. 22,

&c.), עָלַי (Ps. l. 5, &c.), and the Arab. forms distinctly show. נְאֻם is a subst. (of the form of גְּבוּל "boundary") from a verb, which only occurs once, and then followed by נְאֻם as the cognate accusative (Jer. xxiii. 31) וַיִּנְאֲמוּ נְאֻם "and say *God saith*." Such nouns are the same in the absol. and in the constr. state. N.B. the *u* of this word is only וּ written *defective*, and is no more a *short* vowel, than is the ִ of זְבוּלֻן.

וְאָמַרְתָּ אֵלֵי. When וְ is prefixed to the perfect tense, 2nd pers. sing. masc., or 1st sing. com., if the accent remains in its proper place (viz. on the second root-letter) the perfect retains its ordinary meaning; if, however, the verb is to have the force of a future, subjunctive, imperative, &c. the accent[1] is (as a rule) thrown on the last syllable, e.g. (Deut. iv. 30) וְשַׁבְתָּ, (Numb. xiv. 15) וְהָמַתָּה, (Gen. vi. 18) וַהֲקִמֹתִי, (Ps. lxxxix. 24) וְכַתּוֹתִי, (Gen. xvii. 6) וְהִפְרֵתִי. In such a case, if the vowel of the first letter be not supported by a *sh'va*, or *dagesh forte*, that vowel will require *metheg* (Excurs. II. A. 1): thus we have וַאֲמַרְתָּ אֲלֵהֶם "therefore say unto them." But there are certain cases in which the accent is not thrown on the last syllable: (1) When such a perfect is immediately followed (without a *distinctive* accent) by the *tone*-syllable of the succeeding word, as (Deut. xiv. 26) וְאָכַלְתָּ שָּׁם "and thou shalt eat there." This is in order to avoid the concurrence of two *tone*-syllables. (On the *dagesh* in the שׁ see Excurs. III.): (2) With a *disjunctive* as (Deut. viii. 10) וְאָכַלְתָּ וְשָׂבָעְתָּ "and thou shalt eat and be satisfied": (3) In the *Qal* only of verbs *quiescent* ל"ה and ל"א, thus (2 Kings xxi. 13) וּמָחִיתִי "and I will wipe out," (Gen. xvii. 19) וְקָרָאתָ "and thou shalt call." A Perfect thus changed, as *V'âmartâ*[2] is here, into an Imperative has usually

Constructions.

---

[1] Unless we wish to indicate the kind of accent used, we shall mark the tone-syllable (i.e. the *accentuated* syllable) by a vertical line placed over the consonant bearing the tone-vowel.

[2] In transliteration *metheg* will in future be represented by ˋ, and the tone-accent by ˊ.

4 Be ye not as your fathers, unto whom the former prophets have cried, saying, Thus saith the LORD of hosts; Turn ye now from your evil ways, and *from* your evil doings: but they did not hear, nor hearken unto me, saith the LORD.

---

some other verb preceding it. But sometimes, as here, it stands alone, comp. (2 Sam. xiv. 10) וַהֲבֵאתוֹ אֵלָי הַמְדַבֵּר "Anyone that saith [ought] unto thee bring him unto me."—*Adōnāy Çʾbā'ōth*. Since neither the NAME *YHVH*, nor its substitute *Adōnāy*, has a constr. form, some Jewish grammarians say that between THE NAME and *Çʾbā'ōth* the word אֱלֹהֵי is to be understood (though not read). Thus the expression means "THE LORD (God of) HOSTS."—וְאָשׁוּב אֲלֵיכֶם. The E. V. "and I will turn, &c." is admissible; but it would, perhaps, be better to render the words "that I may return unto you." The ordinary form to express "and I will return" is with the final ה,ָ, e.g. Mal. iii. 7 וְאָשׁוּבָה אֲלֵיכֶם. In speaking of the Hebr. Imperfect, we must always remember that Arabic, which retains distinctive terminations, and their distinctive meanings, more than any Semitic language, has four (or five) forms of the Imperfect: (1) the Indicative ending in *u*, (2) Subj. in *a*, (3) Jussive without final vowel (like the Hebr. and colloquial Arab. Imperf.), (4 and 5) the Energetic in *anna* and *an*. Now, while we maintain that the Hebr. Imperf. in *āh* is often used, merely for the sake of variation of sound, in the same sense as the ordinary Imperf., still it seems to us evident that the final *āh* sometimes represents the *a* of the Arab. Subj. and sometimes the *anna* of the Energetic. But as the case-endings (where found) have in Hebrew (for the most part) lost their distinctive meaning, so too the mood-endings.

Remarks. Though God had declared (Hag. i. 13, ii. 4) that He was "with them," Hag. ii. 14, 17 shows how much need the people still had of repentance.

Verse 4. Words. הָרִאשֹׁנִים. Baer (with Leusden) has the *methey* incorrectly under the ה (Excurs. II. A. 1). But he places it correctly in vii. 7, 12, viii. 11, &c.—וּמַעַלְלֵיכֶם with the note יָתֵר י, which means that the י between ל and ל is superfluous. In such a case the vowels given above are to be read with the consonants which the note declares are to be read. Thus here we are to read וּמַעַלְלֵיכֶם. Since there is not, elsewhere, such a word as מַעֲלִיל, while the word מַעֲלָל (in the plur. form only) is very common, it is natural that the traditional reading should be וּמַעַלְלֵיכֶם. But, there is a way in which the letters as they stand ומעליכם *might* be read, and that is וּמַעֲלִילֵיכֶם; the objection, however, to this reading is that there is no *known* plur. עֲלִילִים, the plur. of עֲלִילָה being always עֲלִילוֹת. But, there is yet another difference of reading, viz. that, while the Western Jews read וּמַעַל(י)לֵיכֶם, the Oriental Jews read וּמִמַּעַל(י)לֵיכֶם (but the *Codex Petropolitanus*, A.D. 916, inferior in age only to the Camb. MS. *Mm*. 5. 27, A.D. 856, and that only with respect to the consonants, while it has the Oriental reading in the *margin* marked as the "*correct reading*," has in its *text* the Western variant). The Oriental may be the correct reading, but the prefixed מ is quite unnecessary, as it might well be supplied from the preceding מִדַּרְכֵיכֶם, as (Hag. i. 10) מ may be supplied before יְבוּלָהּ from the מִטַּל which precedes; compare Zech. xiv. 10. But, on the whole, it appears that וּמַעַלְלֵיכֶם is a reading which cannot be improved on, the prefix מ being naturally understood after מִדַּרְכֵיכֶם, and the more easily omitted since the word already begins with a מ.

The student need hardly be reminded that since מדרכיכם is *defined* by the pron. suff. (כם) the adjective which follows it (being simply an epithet) takes the definite article. When on the contrary the article is omitted the adj. becomes a tertiary predicate, thus Hag. i. 4 should be rendered " Is it time for you, *you* [I say], to dwell in your houses coiled as they are (בבתיכם ספונים), while this House is in ruins?"

Constructions.

οἱ προφῆται ἔμπροσθεν is a very free rendering of the Hebr. It ought to have been rather οἱ ἔμπροσθεν προφῆται, or οἱ πρότεροι προφῆται.—מעללים is generally rendered correctly (as here) by ἐπιτηδεύματα (comp. i. 6, Hos. ix. 15, xi. 3, Mich. iii. 4, vii. 13).— עלילות is also similarly rendered in Zeph. iii. 4 (but in v. 7 by ἐπιφυλλίς). But in Hos. iv. 9, v. 4, vii. 2 διαβούλια is given as the equivalent of מעללים.

LXX.

ZECHARIAH I. 5, 6.

5 Your fathers, where *are* they? and the prophets, do they live for ever?
6 But my words and my statutes, which I commanded my servants the prophets, did they not take hold of your fathers? and they returned and said, Like as the LORD of hosts thought to do unto us, according to our ways, and according to our doings, so hath he dealt with us.

Verse 5. Words.
אַיֵּה־הֵם. This appears to us an instance of a slight loss of purity in the Hebr. of the Post-Captivity. Elsewhere we find אַיָּם for "where are they?" and nowhere, except in Job xv. 23 (where there is nothing at all following the word) do we find אַיֵּה except followed by a suff. or subst. The other extant Biblical forms with a suffix are: אַיֶּכָּה "where art thou?" (Gen. iii. 9), and אַיּוֹ "where is he?" (Job xx. 7, &c.), or "where is," with a noun following (2 Kings xix. 13, Mich. vii. 10). On the *ga'yā* under the ה of הַלְעוֹלָם and the י of יִחְיוּ see Excurs. II. B. 2, and A. 7. In any but very incorrect editions there is also *sillūq* placed under the *second yūd*, thus: יִחְיוּ (compare תָּהֵין at the beginning of ver. 4). *Yich'yū* is the real Imperfect "did they keep on living?" comp. (1 Sam. xxii. 12) הֲלֹא לֹזֶה יְעַנּוּ "did not they keep praising this man?"

Versions.
Both LXX. and Syr. have (according to the interpunctuation) "Your fathers, where are they and the prophets? Will they live for ever?" But there is no reason why the interpunctuation should not be rejected, and both read "Your fathers, where are they? And the prophets, will they live for ever?" The order of the Hebr. words, apart from interpunctuation, shows that this is the collocation intended.

Remarks.
Rābh[1] (who brought the Mishnah and other traditions into Babylon, and was in a manner the founder of the Talmud Bablī) interprets this verse as containing a saying of the Prophet which is objected to by the people. The prophet says "Your fathers, where are they?" The people answer "It is true enough that our fathers are dead — but are the prophets any more alive than they?" To which the Prophet replies "The prophets, indeed, are dead — but their words have come to pass" (T. B. *Synhédrim* 105 *a*). This is the only interpretation, which seems to us to give good sense, and it is certainly in accordance with the controversial, not to say colloquial, style of the Post-captivity Prophets. We are glad to see that Keil has adopted this interpretation. Another view of the matter is that Zechariah's words are equivalent to this: The light of prophecy is dying out: while ye have the light, walk as children of the light. But to us it appears, that to put the words "Do (or did) the prophets live for ever?" into the mouth of Zechariah, is to destroy utterly his argument.

[1] Contemporary with Artaban IV. king of Persia, who died A.D. 226.

"But (אַךְ) [in spite of what you say]." The word אַךְ when used as an affirmative particle denotes the result of some mental process, sometimes incorrect (as in Gen. xliv. 28, Ps. lxxiii. 13), sometimes correct (as in Ps. lxxiii. 1).—הִשִּׂיג is of course the Hif. of נָשַׂג, and must not be confounded with a verb, parts of which have the same pronunciation, viz. סוּג, Hif. הִסִּיג, תַּסֵּג Mich. vi. 14, as though from נָסֹג which actually occurs in Is. lix. 13, comp. יִסֹּג Mich. ii. 6) "to remove," Nif. יִסֹּגוּ אָחוֹר (Ps. xxxv. 4) "let them start back." Sometimes the former verb is construed with לְ (as in Lev. v. 11), or is even used absolutely as (Lev. xxv. 47) וְכִי תַשִּׂיג יַד גֵּר "and if the hand of a stranger acquire (wealth)."

<small>Verse 6. Words.</small>

After the words τὰ νόμιμά μου they introduce δέχεσθε: perhaps they dittographed the word חקי, and read הֻקַּי קְחוּ. After ἐντέλλομαι they introduce ἐν πνεύματί μου, which they borrowed from vii. 12. οἱ κατελάβοσαν may be a corruption of οὐ κατ., comp. Lam. i. 12, where they have οἱ πρὸς ὑμᾶς for אֲלֵיכֶם ; or, they may have read הֲלוֹא as hēllū, and thought that it was equivalent to the Aram. אֲלֵי = Hebr. אֵלֶּה: the former supposition is, perhaps, the more probable. For vayyāshūbhū they give καὶ ἀπεκρίθησαν, reading vayyāshībhū, and understanding it in the uncommon biblical (without an acc. of the thing answered) but later Hebr. sense of replying, comp. Syr. pannī, and Arab. radda.

<small>LXX.</small>

The Prophet quotes an historical case (from Jeremiah) in proof of what he says; עָשָׂה יְיָ אֲשֶׁר זָמָם (Lam. ii. 17). The first prophecy ends here.

<small>Remarks.</small>

The Vision of the Horseman among the Myrtles (vv. 7—17).

There are two expressions in Hebr. for the numeral *eleven*, viz., עַשְׁתֵּי עָשָׂר אַחַד עָשָׂר (masc.), אַחַת עֶשְׂרֵה (fem.); and עַשְׁתֵּי עָשָׂר (masc.), עַשְׁתֵּי עֶשְׂרֵה. In Assyrian the numeral *one* in the *masc.* is expressed by *istin* (עֶשְׁתֵּן): the Hebr. seems to have retained this old numeral in the second form of the compound numeral *eleven* (comp. ἕν-δεκα, &c.) *in the fem. as well as in the masc.* "Sebat": the names of the months as found in the books of Zech., Esth., and Neh., are most of them of Assyrio-Babylonian origin: they are in use among the Jews to this day. The following is a table of the months:

<small>Verse 7. Words.</small>

No. of Month.	Old Hebrew Name.	Assyrio-Babylonian.	Later Hebrew.	No. of days in an ordinary year.	Corresponding to our
1.	הָאָבִיב חֹדֶשׁ (Ex. xiii. 4—Deut. xvi. 1).	Ni-sa-an-nu.	נִיסָן (Neh. ii. 1, Esth. iii. 7).	30.	March—April.
2.	זִו (1 Kings vi. 1, 37).	Ai-ru.	אִיָּר (Non-biblical).	29.	April—May.
3.	No name occurs.	Si-va-nu.	סִיוָן (Esth. viii. 9).	30.	May—June.
4.	,,	Dhu-mu-zu.	תַּמּוּז (Non-biblical as the name of a month, but see Ezek. viii. 14, which seems, however, to refer to the sixth month, see ver. 1).	29.	June—July.
5.	,,	A-bu.	אָב (Non-biblical).	30.	July—August.
6.	,,	U-lu-lu.	אֱלוּל (Neh. vi. 15).	29.	August—Sept.
7.	הָאֵתָנִים יֶרַח (1 Kings viii. 2).	Tas-ri-tu.	תִּשְׁרִי (Non-biblical).	30.	Sept.—Oct.
8.	בּוּל (1 Kings vi. 38).	"The eighth month."	מַרְחֶשְׁוָן (Rt. חרשׁ cogn. in senso to בּוּל).	29.	Oct.—Nov.
9.	No name occurs.	Ki-si-li-vu.	כִּסְלֵו (Neh. i. 1, Zech. vii. 1).	30.	Nov.—Dec.
10.	,,	Ti-bi-tuv.	טֵבֵת (Esth. ii. 16).	29.	Dec.—Jan.
11.	,,	Sa-ba-tu.	שְׁבָט (Zech. i. 7).	30.	Jan.—Feb.
12.	,,	Ad-da-ru.	אֲדָר (Esth. iii. 7).	29.	Feb.—March.
13 (intercalary).		"The month after Addaru."	וְאֲדָר (Non-biblical).	30.	

It will be observed that in an ordinary year the months consist alternately of 30 and 29 days. A month containing 30 days is called מָלֵא "full," one containing 29 days is called חָסֵר "defective."

7 Upon the four and twentieth day of the eleventh month, which *is* the month Sebat, in the second year of Darius, came the word of the LORD unto Zechariah, the son of Berechiah, the son of Iddo the prophet, saying,

8 I saw by night, and behold a man riding upon a red horse, and he stood among the myrtle trees that *were* in the bottom; and behind him *were there* red horses, speckled, and white.

The name "*Iddō*" is here (as in Ezr. v. 1, vi. 14, Neh. xii. 4, 16) spelt with a final א; but in i. 1 and in Chronicles it is without the final א.

In mentioning the months, if the numeral required have an *ordinal* form, that form is used as (i. 1) בַּחֹדֶשׁ הַשְּׁמִינִי; but, if the numeral be higher than ten it has no ordinal form, and therefore there is no choice but to use the cardinal: hence we get עַשְׁתֵּי־עָשָׂר חֹדֶשׁ "the eleventh month." (On the *metheg* see Excurs. II. A. 1.) Constructions.

לַיְלָה has the accent on the penultimate because it is a *masc.* nom. (לֵיל and לַיִל) with an additional final ה. But all *fem.* nouns (subst., adj., and part.) which end in ה have the acc. on the *last* syll.[1]: thus Verse 8. Words.

נַחֲלָה is a *fem.* noun meaning inheritance, but נַחַל (Ps. cxxiv. 4) is a *masc.* noun = נַחַל "a valley." The additional ה is a remnant of the ending of the accusative case, though in many instances the force of the case is lost, and לַיְלָה is simply the nominative. The Semitic case-endings were Nom. *um*, Oblique *im*, Acc. *am*, in Arab. they are still *un*, *in*, *an*, and after the def. article simply *u*, *i*, *a*. In Hebr. traces of these cases are found, e.g. of Nom. in *o* as the final ו of חַיְתוֹ (Gen. i. 24), בְּנוֹ (Numb. xxiv. 3): the Oblique is *i*, as the final י of דִּבְרָתִי and מַלְכִּי (Ps. cx. 4), and of בְּנִי (Gen. xlix. 11), &c.: the Acc. in *ôm* used adverbially as פִּתְאֹם "suddenly," or in *âm* as חִנָּם "in vain," רֵיקָם, &c.: or in *âh* as לַיְלָה "by night" (Ps. i. 2), and in the final ה denoting "motion to" as נַחְלָה מִ "to the river of Egypt" (Numb. xxxiv. 5). The nom. and oblique case terminations have quite lost their force, it is only the accusatival ending which has (and that in

---

[1] Such fem. forms as יְשׁוּעָתָה (Ps. iii. 3) have the *additional* ה.

the majority of cases) retained its force.—The word הֲדַס (Is. xli. 19, lv. 13, Neh. viii. 15) "a myrtle," by the absorption of the *d* and the change of ה into א, becomes in Talmudic (Traditional Pronunciation) *assā*, in Aram. *āsā*, and in Arab. *ās*.—מְצֻלָה has the *sīmān rāpheh* (see Excurs. IV.) over the ל, to show that the ל is not to be doubled after the *qibbuṣ* (see on verse 13), and that it is therefore from the Root צוּל, and means "depth," "hollow"; and not from Root צלל, and meaning "shady place." The *qibbuṣ* (ֻ) is only *shūriq* (וּ) written defectively (compare note on נְאֻם in verse 3).—אֲדֻמִּים (plur. of אָדוֹם). Observe the *dagesh* in third root-letter, similarly in the next word, and in עֲרוּמִּים "naked" (Gen. ii. 25), only that there the *shūriq* is anomalously written instead of *qibbuṣ* before *dagesh forte*.—שְׂרֻקִּים. It is impossible to speak with any certainty about this word, as it does not occur elsewhere as an adj. of colour. There is, however, a Persian word *surch* "red," "dun," used of the hair of camels (שְׂרֻח, Zend *çukhra*, Sanscrit *çukhrá* "red," "bright"), which the Prophet *might* have brought from Persia, only that (if Justi be correct) the form of the word in Persian must at that time have been *thukhra*. Again, there is an Arabic word with the ר and ק transposed שְׁקַר, from which comes the adj. *ashqar* "red," used of men or horses, with which most commentators are inclined to identify our word. But, we cannot with some connect it with Talmudic שְׂרָק, סְרָק and שִׁירְקוֹן "red paint" or "rouge," because that is probably the Greek συρικόν. While, however, שְׂרָק does not occur elsewhere in Bibl.-Hebr. as an adj. of colour, it does occur, viz. in (Is. xvi. 8) שְׂרוּקֶיהָ (another instance of *dagesh forte* after *shūriq*), as "its [the vine's] branches" or "clusters." Comp. שׂרֵק (Is. v. 2, Jer. ii. 21), and שׂרֵקָה (Gen. xlix. 11), a choice kind of vine, which Abu-l-Walîd (*Hebr.-Arab. Dict.* ed. Neubauer, col. 751) calls *sherīq*, and says that it is the choicest kind grown in Syria. Also שְׂרִיקוֹת "combs" is used with reference to working "flax" (Is. xix. 9).

לַיְלָה would mean "by night," but הַלַּיְלָה (comp. הַיּוֹם "to-day")

Constructions. means properly "to-night" (Gen. xix. 5, 34, xxx. 15), and here "on this night" (the night of the 24th) is equivalent to בַּלַּיְלָה הַזֶּה (Ex. xii. 12). For, though it is true that the Jews count from the evening, so that the evening of the 24th is regarded as

9 Then said I, O my lord, what are these? And the angel that talked with me said unto me, I will shew thee what these be.

10 And the man that stood among the myrtle trees answered and said, These are they whom the LORD hath sent to walk to and fro through the earth.

the 25th, yet, when a particular day is mentioned, and then such an expression occurs as "in the evening," &c. (Ex. xii. 18), it denotes the evening of that day.—בַּמְּצֻלָה "in a certain hollow": the article is used in the (practically) *indefinite* sense, as in הַפָּלִיט "a certain fugitive" (Gen. xiv. 13), see my *Fragment of T. B. P°sachim*, p. 94, note 36.

Hallåy'lăh, τὴν νύκτα. *Bên hă°dassîm* "*sher bamm°çulăh*, ἀναμέσον τῶν ὀρέων τῶν κατασκίων. For הֲהַדַסִּים they seem to have read הֶהָרִים, a plur. of הַר "mountain," which occurs often in the constr. (e.g. Ps. l. 10), and also with suffixes (e.g. Deut. viii. 9). Some have supposed that they may have read הַהֲדוּרִים, which they translate ὄρη in Is. xlv. 2. Either solution supposes ר to have been read for ס. Others have suggested that the LXX. merely translated conjecturally, and imagined that "mountains" must be the meaning here, because of the mention of "the two mountains" in vi. 1. For the colours of the horses we have (1) "*dummîm* πυρροί; (2) *s°ruqqîm* ψαροί "starling-grey" καὶ ποικίλοι; (3) *l°bhānîm* λευκοί. In chap. vi. they are as follows: (1) as here, both in Hebr. and LXX.; (2) *sh°chōrîm* "black" LXX. μέλανες; (3) as here, both in Hebr. and LXX.; and then there is (4) בְּרֻדִּים אֲמֻצִּים LXX. ποικίλοι ψαροί. Whence it would appear that the LXX., being unable to understand *s°ruqqîm*, rendered it ψαροὶ καὶ ποικίλοι in order to give *four* colours as in chap. vi. We may note here that the colours in Rev. vi. are λευκός (*lābhān*); πυρρός (*ādōm*); μέλας (*shāchōr*); and χλωρός "pale" (the equivalent, probably, of *bārōd*). For *hăh°dassîm* Aq. and Symm. give correctly τῶν μυρσινεώνων.

Strong *Vav* with the Imperfect has the power of drawing back the accent from the ultimate to the penultimate, when no quiescent *sh°va* or *dagesh forte* intervenes between the two syllables. Consequently (since we cannot have a long vowel in a closed syllable) the last vowel must be shortened. Thus יֹאמַר becomes וַיֹּאמֶר. But in the case of a pausal accent it remains in its original place, thus: וַיֹּאמַר (ver. 10)[1]. In the 1st pers. sing. the accent is not

Verse 9. Words.

---

[1] See further in notes on ch. v. 5.

11 And they answered the angel of the LORD that stood among the myrtle trees, and said, We have walked to and fro through the earth, and, behold, all the earth sitteth still, and is at rest.

drawn back, even when not in pause: thus we have וָאֵלֵךְ פְּרָתָה (Jer. xiii. 7), but the verbs quiescent ל״ה are an exception[1], e.g. the form וָאֵרֶא (ii. 1), and וָאַעַן (iv. 4); so וָאֹפֶן, וָאַעַל, and וָאַעַשׂ.—דֹּבֵר, the pres. partic. is the only part of the Qal of this verb that is commonly used in the sense of "speaking" (but we find the past partic. דָּבֻר in Prov. xxv. 11, and the infin. with suff. דָּבְרְךָ Ps. li. 6).—אֵרְאֲךָ happens never to occur except with a disjunctive accent, therefore it is always אֶרְאֶךָּ (Gen. xii. 1, Judg. iv. 22) with *segōl* under the second א, and *dagesh forte* in the ך. The pausal form of the suffix when it is *possessive* (not *objective*) is ךָ without *dagesh*: thus צִדְקָךְ "thy righteousness" (Job viii. 6). Out of pause such a verb would take simply ךָ as אֶעֱשֶׂךָ (Gen. xii. 2).—On the *metheg* of *v'hithhalléch* see EXCURS. II. D. 4.

Haddōbhér bí (LXX. ὁ λαλῶν ἐν ἐμοί). The verb *dibbér* is found generally construed with אֶל, לְ, or עִם of the person spoken to. But, in the case of God's speaking by revelation, the preposition בְּ is often used, perhaps on account of the subjective nature of revelation (comp. Numb. xii. 6, 8, Jer. xxxi. 30, Hab. ii. 1). *Māh-hémmāh élleh*, the pronoun הֵמָּה discharges the office of the verb "are": "*I* [emphatic] will show thee what these *are*" (LXX. τί ἐστι ταῦτα). But above the emphasis is on *these*: *māh-élleh* "what (are) these?" (LXX. τί οὗτοι). Observe the same constructions in iv. 4 and 5; and comp. Ps. xxiv. 8 and 10.

Constructions.

Verse 11. Words. On the first *metheg* on *Vayya'ănu* see Excurs. II. B. 3.—*Hā'ísh hā'ōméd*, "the man who was standing," i.e. who has already been mentioned as standing, and therefore, necessarily, to be identified with the man "riding on a bay horse" of verse 8, and also, doubtless, with "The Angel of the LORD" of ver. 11.—*Yōshébheth v'shōqáteth* is, hardly, a hendiadys for "dwelling at ease" (יוֹשֶׁבֶת לָבֶטַח

---

[1] See further in notes on iv. 4.

ZECHARIAH I. 12, 13.

12 Then the angel of the LORD answered and said, O LORD of hosts, how long wilt thou not have mercy on Jerusalem and on the cities of Judah, against which thou hast had indignation these threescore and ten years?

13 And the LORD answered the angel that talked with me *with good words and comfortable words*.

Judg. xviii. 7), since יָשַׁב sometimes (as in Mich. v. 3) has that meaning when standing alone; but, rather, יָשְׁבָה means "dwelling at ease," and וְשַׁקְטָה "and that, in a state of insolent assumption of security" (comp. יָשְׁבָה וְשָׁלֵוָה vii. 7, and וְשָׁלֵוָה וְשֹׁקֶטֶת 1 Chron. vi. 40). LXX. for *Yōshĕbheth* has κατοικεῖται, as in ii. 5 (Hebr. 9) κατοικηθήσεται (correctly there) for *Tēshēbh*.

Since the NAME *YHVH* cannot take the article, and the article cannot be put before a noun in construct., it might have been difficult to say whether מַלְאַךְ יְיָ meant "*an* angel of the LORD," or "*the* Angel of the LORD." But, considering that *eth* is prefixed (which is, as a rule, the case only with defined nouns), and the participle *hā'ōmēd* occurs afterwards (with the *def. article*), and that *Mal'ac Adōnāy* occurs so frequently to denote a particular Angel, it must needs be so here. He is, of course, to be identified with "the man" of verses 8, 10. For, had he been a fresh person introduced here, the construction in the next clause must have been וְגַם הוּא עֹמֵד. Constructions.

רָחַם "he pitied" is *usually* construed (as here) with a direct object, or absolutely (as Jer. xxi. 7). But sometimes (e.g. Ps. ciii. 13) with עַל. The construction of זָעַם is exactly similar (the only passage in which it is construed with עַל is Dan. xi. 30). זֶה שִׁבְעִים שָׁנָה, this is just the construction in the English: "this seventy years," compare vii. 3, and זֶה פַעֲמַיִם "this twice" (Gen. xxvii. 36). Verse 12. Constructions.

Zā'amtāh ὑπερεῖδες, translating euphemistically. For *zĕh shibh'ĭm shānāh* τοῦτο ἑβδομηκοστὸν ἔτος. LXX.

נִחֻמִים (as in Is. lvii. 18, ed. Baer). The *sīmān rāphēh* over the מ denotes (as in מַצָּלָה ver. 8) that the letter is not doubled, and that the *qibbuç* is only a *shūriq* written short (see Excurs. IV.). So, the word is the same as that which occurs (with suffix) in Hos. xi. 8 נִחוּמָי. It is a pi'elistic *substantive* (not an ad- Verse 13. Words.

14 So the angel that communed with me said unto me, Cry thou, saying, Thus saith the LORD of hosts; I am jealous for Jerusalem and for Zion with a great jealousy. 15 And I am very sore displeased

jective) of the form of שִׁמֻּרִים "special observance" (Ex. xii. 42); on the *metheg* see Excurs. II. A. 1. Another form of substantive also from the Pi'el of the same verb, and having a meaning similar to that of תַּנְחוּמִים, is תַּנְחוּמִים. These nouns (here mentioned) are used in the plural for the sake of strengthening their meaning.

דְּבָרִים נִחֻמִים. Had *nichumím* been an adjective agreeing with *d'bhārím* there would have been no need to place a conjunctive accent on דְּבָרִים (as there is in the preceding clause); for, see the first words of the chapter בַּחֹדֶשׁ הַשְּׁמִינִי, where *hashsh'míní* agrees with *chódesh*, and yet חֹדֶשׁ is furnished with a disjunctive accent *pashtā* (which is always placed on the last letter of the word: while, if the tone-syllable be the penultimate, an additional accent of the same form is placed on the consonant which bears the vowel of that syllable). But *nichumím* is, as we have said, a substantive: we must therefore either take it as in apposition with *d'bhārím* meaning "words [viz.] comfort," or understand דְּבָרִים נִחֻמִים as standing for דְּבָרִים [דִּבְרֵי] נִחֻמִים "words [viz. words of] comfort," like אֲרוֹן הַבְּרִית (Josh. iii. 14), which may be taken as equivalent to הָאָרוֹן [אֲרוֹן] הַבְּרִית "the ark [viz. ark of] the covenant." But see note on iv. 7.—By LXX. *Nichumím* is rendered as an adj. παρακλητικούς.

Constructions and interpunctuation.

Verse 14. Words and constructions.

קִנֵּאתִי is the perfect used to denote the immediate past, the action being continued in the present: it is best translated by the English present[1]. "Thus saith the LORD" in this verse is the same use of the tense. This verb קָנָא when construed with לְ (as here, Numb. xxv. 13, &c.) denotes "to be jealous, or zealous, *for*," but with the acc. (Numb. v. 14), or בְּ (Gen. xxx. 1), "to be jealous *against*." On *qin'āh g'dōlāh* compare note on ver. 2.

Verse 15. Words.

The adj. שַׁאֲנָן is of the same form as רַעֲנָן "green" (which latter has no fem. or plur. in use). The doubling of the last letter, substituting a *pathach* followed by *dagesh forte* for *qāmāç*, before the plur. termination occurs also in such forms as the

---

[1] Driver (*Hebrew Tenses* § 10) compares, rightly, the so-called "aorist of immediate past" in Greek, as ἐδεξάμην "I welcome."

with the heathen *that are* at ease: | and they helped forward the afflic-
for I was but a little displeased, | tion.

following; מַטְעַמִּים (Gen. xxvii. 4), מַטְעַמּוֹת (Prov. xxiii. 3, 6); compare also גָּמָל plur. גְּמַלִּים, קָטָן plur. קְטַנִּים &c., and our note on *^adummīm* (verse 8). On מְעָט the Massoreth says קמץ בזקף, i.e. the *pathach* of the word is turned into *qāmāṣ*, although the disjunctive accent on the syllable (viz. *zāqēf*) is not strong enough to have such an effect in most cases.

^Ani qōçēf is the Present Tense. It seems to be used here, in preference to the Perfect (compare *qinnethi* ver. 14), because the very word קצפתי is required in the second section of the verse to be used as an actual Perfect, and it would have been extremely awkward to use the same tense of the same verb in two different ways in the same verse.—*^Ashér* means here "for," "because" (= יַעַן אֲשֶׁר or יַעַן כִּי), comp. Gen. xxx. 18, xxxiv. 13, 27, &c.—*V^ehēmmāh* "and *they*" is emphatic; but not the *^ani* above (except in so far as there is a contrast between "I" and "they") because the pronoun is, as a rule, required with the participle, when it represents the Pres. Tense; for a case in which the pronoun of the First Person is supplied with a partic. from a verb in the First Person, which comes in the next verse, see chap. ix. ver. 12.—עָזְרוּ לְרָעָה. Some would render this "helped the evil," after the analogy of such passages as לַעְזוֹר לַהֲדַדְעֶזֶר "to help Hadadezer" (2 Sam. viii. 5). But it seems better to understand לְרָעָה (as in Jer. xliv. 11) in the sense of "for evil," the prefix לְ being used as it is after *'ā͞z^erū* in 2 Chron. xx. 23, עָזְרוּ אִישׁ בְּרֵעֵהוּ לְמַשְׁחִית "they helped, each against other, for destruction," i.e. "they helped to destroy each other." In this example the verb עָזַר is construed with בְּ "against," and the substantive with לְ is merely complementary. The verb, here, we take as used absolutely, as in Is. xxx. 7, "And as for Egypt, utterly in vain, do they help." So that we should render והמה עזרו לרעה "But *they* helped for evil," meaning "And they cooperated [with me, *but*] for evil."

Constructions.

16 Therefore thus saith the LORD; I am returned to Jerusalem with mercies: my house shall be built in it, saith the LORD of hosts, and a line shall be stretched forth upon Jerusalem.

17 Cry yet, saying, Thus saith the LORD of hosts; My cities through prosperity shall yet be spread abroad; and the LORD shall yet comfort Zion, and shall yet choose Jerusalem.

LXX. הַשֻּׁאַנִּים τὰ συνεπιτιθέμενα. The נ‍ג seems to have been read as ת, so that they read הַשָּׁאתִים, partic. of שִׁית; comp. the form קָאם 3rd perf. (Hos. x. 14). For this meaning of *shīth* comp. (Ps. iii. 7) אֲשֶׁר סָבִיב שָׁתוּ עָלָי. For עׂרָן they give συνεπέθεντο. The עׂ written close together might give שׁ, and ר seems to have been read as ת, giving שָׁתוּ.

Verse 16. Words.
Observe that יְרוּשָׁלַםִ (except in Jer. xxvi. 18, Esth. ii. 6, 1 Chr. iii. 5, 2 Chr. xxv. 1, xxxii. 9) is always spelt defectively, i.e. without *yōd* in the last syllable.—On the accent of יִבָּנֶה, and the *dagesh* in בָּה, see Excurs. III. The K'thīb קוה (which form occurs only as k'thīb, and that only again in 1 Kings vii. 23, Jer. xxxi. 39) must be read קָוֶה, after the analogy of קָצֶה (Gen. xix. 4). The K'rī is קָו (or, rather, קָו, ed. Baer); comp. צַו. Either word would mean "a line."

Constructions.
Shābhtī should be rendered "I am returned," as the Present complete, rather than as the Prophetic Perfect "I will return" (which *grammatically* would be equally admissible).

Verse 17. Words.
תְּפוּצֶנָה stands for תְּפוּצֶינָה; Baer correctly edits it תְּפוּצֶנָה with the *sīmān rāphēh* over the נ, as he does also תְּהִימֶנָה (Mich. ii. 12); see Excurs. IV. In chap. xiii. 7 the same word is used of "being scattered," in a bad sense, and such is the ordinary use of the verb. But in Gen. x. 18 the Niph. (it is exactly equivalent to the Qal in this verb) is used of "being spread," not in a bad sense. And so the Qal is, undoubtedly, used here. The corresponding Arab. *fāḍa yafʿalu* means "to be abundant," in which sense פרץ is, however, the common word in Hebr. See note on ii. 10.—The מן of מִטּוֹב denotes "on account of," as in מֵרֹב "on account of the multitude of" (ii. 8).

LXX. has ἔτι διαχυθήσονται...ἐν ἀγαθοῖς.

נחם (Qal *Nāqám* unused) may, as far as grammatical form is concerned, be either the Perf. Niphal or Pi'el. But the Niph. means "to pity," and is construed with על, אל, or ל, or מן (see Dictionaries); while in the Pi'el it means "to comfort," and is construed with the direct object as in Gen. l. 21, Job ii. 11, and here (and sometimes with a complementary על or מן of the thing concerning which the comfort is given, as in Is. xxii. 4, Gen. v. 29).— בחר "to choose" is (normally) construed with ב of the thing chosen.

Constructions.

Except '*od* for ἔτι there is nothing in the Hebr. to correspond with the words καὶ εἶπε πρὸς μὲ ὁ ἄγγελος ὁ λαλῶν ἐν ἐμοὶ ἔτι. The translators seem to have borrowed the words from ver. 14 (such is the common practice of the LXX., comp. p. 9).

LXX.

Between the first revelation to Zechariah (i. 1—6), and the series of visions, &c. contained in Zech. i. 7—vi. 15, Haggai had received the revelations of Hag. ii. 10—23. Therein God had foretold "I will shake the heavens, and the earth: and I will overthrow the throne of kingdoms, &c." The people were, no doubt, in eager expectation, waiting for this promised overthrow of their enemies. The object of this vision was to assure the prophet (and through him the people) that, though this overthrow had not yet commenced, God's eyes were open, and He was (as it were) sending forth His angel-scouts to reconnoitre, and that, consequently, He was preparing to perform His word. From the grammatical considerations mentioned above it is certain that "the man who stood among the myrtles," and "the Angel of the Lord" are identical. We need not, therefore, enter into the controversies, which have arisen on the subject. With regard to the colours of the horses, since "bay" is first mentioned, it is hardly probable that *s'ruqqim* means another shade of "red." I should, therefore, either render it conjecturally "starling-grey," following the LXX., or suggest that it is a corruption of *s'chōrim*, "black." Since the angel-interpreter gives us no clue to any symbolical meaning of the colours, and therefore all interpretations of this kind must needs be merely conjectural, it seems best to suppose that these colours were mentioned, as those most commonly found among horses, for the purpose of making the picture more realistic (or, because they so appeared to the prophet in the vision). The variety of the opinions of those, who attach symbolical meanings to the colours, is in itself sufficient to show how little dependence can be placed on such interpretations. The following are specimens of such interpretation, (1) that of KEIL: The riders on *red* horses are to cause war and bloodshed, those on *pale-grey* (*s'ruqqin*) to cause hunger, famine and pestilence, those on *white* go to conquest. But this explanation takes no account of the single horseman on the red (bay) horse. Moreover victory implies bloodshed, as much as does war, so that there is no practical distinction made between the *red* and the *white* horses. (2) EWALD deprives "the man standing among the myrtles" of his horse, then he renders the colours of the horses *bright-red*, *brown*, *grey*, and supplies *dark-red* (from his interpretation of vi. 3). Having thus arranged the colours to his fancy, he compares this vision with that of the chariots in chap. vi., and sees in the

Remarks. Verses 8—17.

colours the mission of the riders to the four quarters of heaven. The *red* denotes the East, the *brown* (=black of chap. vi.) the North, the *grey* (i.e. *lâbhân*) the West, the *dark red* the South! (3) VITRINGA interprets the three colours as follows: *red* times of war, *varicoloured* times of varying distress and prosperity, *white* times of complete prosperity, which were sent on the Jewish people. (4) KLIEFOTH considers the colours to denote the different lands in which the riders discharge their mission, viz. Babylon, Medo Persia, and the Græco-Macedonian empire. (5) RABBI MOSHEH ALSHEKH, the cabbalist, interprets *red* of the company of Gabriel which inclines to Strict Justice, *s'ruqqim* of that of Raphael (who is the angel of *healing after smiting*, that is Justice tempered with Mercy), *white* of that of Michael who inclines to Free Grace. But enough has surely been said to show the futility of such methods of interpretation. We will only add that, while the author of the Revelation undoubtedly borrows the idea of the different coloured horses from Zech. and gives them such meanings as suit his purpose, it would be most uncritical to interpret Zechariah by means of the book of Revelation. The mystical interpretation of the words *myrtles* and *the hollow* are equally fantastic. By some the myrtles are said to represent the Pious, by others the Theocracy, or the Land of Judah; and *the hollow* is said to symbolize Babylon, or the Degradation into which the Theocracy, or Judah, had fallen. But what need of such far-fetched ideas? A hollow place where there would be water, and shade of trees, is, of course, a most natural place for a troop to be represented as halting at. Whether there was actually such a place near "The Horse-Gate," well known at that time, we cannot say.

(CHAPTER II. in the Hebrew.)

E. V. CHAP. I. 18—21, and CHAP. II.

(Hebr. II. 1) 18 Then lifted I | up mine eyes, and saw, and behold four horns.

SECOND VISION. THE FOUR HORNS AND THE FOUR SMITHS.

On the form וָאֶרָא see on i. 9. קֶרֶן "a horn," like the name of most things which usually are found in pairs, is ordinarily used in the *dual* instead of the *plural*. In this case there are two forms, viz. קְרָנַיִם (Amos vi. 13, Hab. iii. 4), and קְרָנַיִם (Daniel viii. 3, 6, 20). The construct of both is קַרְנֵי; if from the former the *sh'va* under the ר is quiescent, if from the latter it is moving; but since נ is not a *BeGaDCeFaTh* letter there is no means of discovering which is the case here. The plur. קְרָנוֹת (constr. *qa-r'nôth*) is used only of the *altar*-horns, or (Ezek. xxvii. 25) other *artificial* horns (compare פְּעָמוֹת the artificial feet Ex. xxv. 12, 1 Kings vii. 30); or *figuratively* as in Ps. lxxv. 11, and here.

Verse 1. Words.

ZECHARIAH II. 2—4.

(Hebr. II. 2) 19 And I said unto the angel that talked with me, What be these? And he answered me, These are the horns which have scattered Judah, Israel, and Jerusalem.

(Hebr. II. 3) 20 And the LORD shewed me four carpenters. (Hebr. II. 4) 21 Then said I, What come these to do? And he spake, saying, These are the horns which have scattered Judah, so that

---

זָרוּ (accentuated, of course, on the last syllable, viz. under the ר) is the Pi'el of זָרָה.   *Verse 2. Words.*

Observe that אֵת is prefixed to Y*'hūdāh* and to Y*isrāēl*, but not to Y*'rūshālāim*. In Post-captivity language (comp. Mal. ii. 11) "Judah," and Israel-*cum*-Jerusalem, seem to have been an exhaustive expression for "the whole nation." LXX. [i. 19] supplies κύριε from ver. 9. *Constructions.*

חָרָשׁ is a substantive of the form גַּנָּב a thief (not of the form דָּבָר, plur. דְּבָרִים). The *qāmāç* under the *chēth* stands for *pathach* followed by *dagesh forte*, and is therefore immoveable; thus the constr. is חָרַשׁ, as in חָרַשׁ אֶבֶן (Ex. xxviii. 12) "an engraver of precious-stones," חָרַשׁ בַּרְזֶל (Is. xliv. 12) "a worker in iron," חָרַשׁ עֵצִים (ibid. 13) "a carpenter": and the plur. is חָרָשִׁים, constr. חָרָשֵׁי (Is. xlv. 16), with *metheg* under the *chēth*. (Excurs. II. A. 1.) *Verse 3. Words.*

"And the LORD shewed me," sometimes, as in iii. 1, it is not said who was the person who showed. Perhaps this verse may afford the correct clue. *Remark.*

בָּאִים should be without a dagesh in the בּ (see Excurs. III.).—לִידוֹת is infin. constr. Pi'el of יָדָה. The verb only occurs once in the Qal, viz. Jer. l. 14, יָדוּ אֵלֶיהָ "shoot ye at her." In the Pi'el it always, elsewhere, means to cast a lot, גּוֹרָל (Joel iv. 3, Obad. 11, Nah. iii. 10), or in the form וַיַּדּוּ־אֶבֶן (for וַיְיַדּוּ) "and they cast a stone (or stones)," in Lam. iii. 53.—לְזָרוֹתָהּ is, of course, the infin. Pi'el of the word זָרָה (above), with the pron. suff. 3rd fem. objective. *Verse 4. Words.*

no man did lift up his head: but these are come to fray them, to cast out the horns of the Gentiles, which lifted up *their* horn over the land of Judah to scatter it.

Constructions. זרו must be taken as an actual Past, and not as a Prophetic Perfect, because the Perf. Tense נשא, in the subordinate clause, thus limits its meaning.—The expressions כְּפִי, לְפִי, עַל פִּי, "in proportion to," are, in any but Post-captivity books, only used with a noun (or pronominal suffix as in Job xxxiii. 6) following. In Lev. xxvii. 8 עַל פִּי אֲשֶׁר תַּשִּׂיג יַד הַנֹּדֵר, "in proportion to *what* (= *that* which) the ability of the vower may be able to compass," is no exception; for, the relative אֲשֶׁר (or the antecedent understood in it) is the noun after עַל פִּי. But in Malachi iii. 9 we do find כְּפִי governing a relative clause כְּפִי אֲשֶׁר אֵינְכֶם שֹׁמְרִים "because that (or since) ye do not keep," like the more modern Hebr. לְפִי שׁ. Now, כְּפִי in the passage before us is put for כְּפִי אֲשֶׁר (comp. יַעַן and יַעַן אֲשֶׁר, &c.), only not in the sense in which it is used in Malachi, but as meaning "so that," Fr. *de sorte que*, modern Hebr. בְּאוֹפֶן שׁ. Thus, in the only two biblical passages in which we have כְּפִי (אֲשֶׁר) as a relative particle it means "*because* that" (introducing the cause), and "*so that*" (the effect).—הַנֹּשְׂאִים "which lifted up," not "which do lift up": since the tense of the participle depends on the context, and it is here already settled by the Perfect נשא.

LXX. [i. 21.] After the words τὰ διασκορπίσαντα τὸν Ἰούδα follow καὶ τὸν Ἰσραὴλ κατέαξαν, because in ver. 2 (i. 19 LXX.) Israel, as well as Judah, was mentioned.—כִּי simply καί.— *L'hachă̄riḍ ōthā́m l'yaddṓth* τοῦ ὀξῦναι αὐτὰ εἰς χεῖρας αὐτῶν, reading לְיָדוֹת as לְהַחֲרִיד (as Hiph. of חרד) and taking לִידוֹת as = לְהַחֲרִיד! They insert τέσσαρα before κέρατα, and read יְהוּדָה as יְהוָה, Κυρίου.

Remarks on ii. 1–4. The first vision had revealed to the Prophet, that God was about to fulfil His promise of breaking up the self-complacent security of the Gentile world. The second vision is intended to give him additional assurance, by showing how God had already destroyed some of those, who had in time past scattered His people, and by declaring that He would continue to do so. We have already shown in our note on the expression "so that no man *did* lift up his head," that the scattering of Israel referred to must be that of the past. We must, therefore, at once reject the interpretation, which would make the four horns refer to the Assyrian, Babylonian, Medo-Persian, and Græco-Macedonian

(E. V. II. 1, Hebr. II. 5) I lifted up mine eyes again, and looked, and behold a man with a measuring line in his hand. (Hebr. II. 6) 2 Then said I, Whither goest thou? And he said

Empires, because the latter had not yet come into existence. For the same reason we must, still more emphatically, repudiate the notion that they refer to the four Empires of the prophecies of Daniel, viz. the Babylonian, Medo-Persian, Grecian, and Roman. EWALD, and HITZIG, again have recourse to the four quarters of the heavens, and interpret the horses of Edom and Egypt (S.), Philistines (W.), Moabites and Ammonites (E.), and Syrians, Assyrians, and especially the Chaldeans (N.). But an objection to this view is that the greater number of these nations had no real hand in the dispersion of Israel and Judah. Having disposed of these theories, we have little hesitation in interpreting the *four horses* as symbolizing the *Assyrian, Babylonian, Egyptian,* and *Medo-Persian* Empires. For, though it is true that it was under the patronage of this last-mentioned Empire, that they were carrying on the rebuilding of the Temple, and that it was Cyrus who first passed a decree for the return of the Jews, yet the intervening kings had listened to the accusations of their adversaries, and had decreed the cessation of the work of restoration, and may well be reckoned among the oppressors of the Nation. This vision, therefore, assures the Prophet that, as the horn of the power and hostility of Assyria, Babylonia, and Egypt had been broken, so should that of Persia be cast down, that nothing might be left which could hinder the people from consummating the work of restoration. With regard to the four workmen WRIGHT goes so far as to identify them with *Nebuchadnezzar* who shattered the power of Assyria, *Cyrus* who broke down the pride of Babylon, *Cambyses* who finally subdued Egypt (which had been but humbled by Nebuchadnezzar) and *Alexander the Great* who in his turn levelled the might of Persia in the dust. But KOEHLER supposes that they merely refer to the means in general, whereby God's Providence overthrows the enemies of His people.

THIRD VISION. THE MAN WITH A MEASURING-LINE.

אָ֫נָה, "whither?" is compounded of אָן = אֵי "where," and ה (unaccentuated) a remnant of the acc. case-ending denoting "towards" (see above, note on *láy'lah*, i. 8). The ב has the *símán ráphêh* (see Excurs. III. and II. A. 5).—לִמֹד is the infin. constr. of מָדַד "to measure," with ל prefixed. When ל is prefixed to a monosyllabic infin., or to one from פ"י or פ"נ verb (not in construction), it takes *qāmāç*, thus לָדַעַת to know, לָשֶׁבֶת to sit, לָמֹד to measure (but this is *not* the case with the prefixes ב and כ). As far as form is concerned לְמֹד might be the infin. absol. of לָמַד "to learn."—כַּמָּה denotes "how much?" of quantity, length, time, &c., either in the *oratio recta*

Verse 6. Words.

unto me, To measure Jerusalem, to see what *is* the breadth thereof, and what *is* the length thereof.

(Hebr. II. 7) 3 And, behold, the angel that talked with me went forth, and another angel went out to meet him,

(Hebr. II. 8) 4 And said unto

---

or *obliqua* (as here); or "how much!" i.e. ever so much, or many, as in vii. 3; or (in accordance with the custom, so common in languages, of using a question to imply a negation) it is used (Job xxi. 17) in the sense of "*How often* [how seldom! if ever] is the lamp of the wicked extinguished?"

Verse 7. Words. All infinitives are nouns substantive. Most of them in Hebrew are of a masc. form, as פָּקֹד, constr. פְּקֹד. But some (especially from verbs פ"י and פ"נ, e.g. לֶדֶת, and לֵדָה, "to bring forth," שֶׁבֶת "to sit") are fem. in form: thus לְאַהֲבָה אֶת־שֵׁם י"י "to love the name of the Lord" (from אָהַב), וּלְיִרְאָה אֹתוֹ "and to fear Him" (from יָרֵא). And so from קרה, "to meet," we have an infin. of a fem. (but always of a *construct*) form, viz. לִקְרַאת י"י "to meet the Lord," לִקְרַאתְכֶם "to meet you," לִקְרָאתוֹ (ver. 7) "to meet him"; in which it will be noticed that (1) an א is introduced, as though the root were קרא, (2) the vowel is always thrown back on the ר, and the א is quiescent, thus לִקְרַאת is for לִקְרָאת (compare מְלַאכְתּוֹ "his work" for מְלָאכְתּוֹ), (3) before another noun, or the heavy suffixes כֶם and כֶן, the form is קְרַאת, but before the other suff. it is קְרָאת.

[ii. 3.] ὁ ἄγγελος ὁ λαλῶν ἐν ἐμοὶ εἱστήκει, either reading נִצָּב for **LXX.** יֹצֵא, or giving what they conceived to be the general meaning.

The *u* of רִין is long, it is merely *shûriq* written *defective*, so too the **Verse 8. Words and constructions.** *u* of וְנָסוּ (ver. 10); see note on i. 3. נַעַר denotes a male, from infancy (as Moses in the ark of bulrushes, Ex. ii. 6) to the prime of life (as Isaac, when his father was about to sacrifice him at the age of thirty, Gen. xxii. 5—15).—The full form of הַלָּז is

| him, Run, speak to this young man, saying, Jerusalem shall be inhabited *as* towns without walls for the multitude of men and cattle therein: | (Hebr. II. 9) 5 For I, saith the LORD, will be unto her a wall of fire round about, and will be the glory in the midst of her. |

הַלָּזֶה, which latter is always masculine, while the former is used once as fem. (2 Kings iv. 25). A fem. form הַלֵּזוּ occurs once (Ezk. xxxvi. 35). The word הַלָּזֶה is compounded of the def. article הַ, an intensive demonstrative element לְ, and the ordinary demonstrative pronoun זֶה, thus *ha-llā-zeh* exactly corresponds with the Arabic *al-la-dhī*, which, from being originally a demonstrative, has passed into a relative pronoun "who," "which"; comp. Engl. "that," Germ. "der, die, das."— פְּרָזוֹת "plains," then "unwalled-towns," "suburbs" (comp. Arab. *farz*, "a plain"). The word may be taken as used adverbially, or as the accusative of limitation (these being but two different ways of speaking of one and the same construction); compare notes on i. 2.— The verb יָשַׁב means not only to "sit," "dwell," "remain," "inhabit," but also "*to be inhabited,*" as here (comp. Is. xiii. 20); such is also the case with the verb שָׁכַן (ibid.). LXX.—[ii. 4] κατακάρπως, freely, for *p'rāzōth.*

On the *dagesh* in the ל of *eh'yeh-llāh* see Excurs. III.—*Sābhībh* is a substantive meaning "circuit," it is used here (comp. Ps. iii. 7) in the accusative (but without any distinctive termination) as an adverb "round about."—In the first half of the verse the verb "to be" is followed by the acc. *chōmáth ésh*. We may assume that this is the acc. (and not the nominative as it would be in Latin) from the fact that in Arabic the verb *kāna* "to be" (together with the verbs of like meaning) takes the acc. after it. In the second half of the verse the same verb is followed by ל, as by the Dative in the Latin example "*Exitio* est avidis mare nautis." The former construction may be illustrated by such a passage as ver. 13, or Gen. xii. 2 וְהָיֵה בְּרָכָה "And be thou (i.e. and thou shalt be) a blessing"; and the latter by Zech. ii. 15, or Ex. iv. 16 יהיה לך לפה ואתה תהיה לו לֵאלֹהִים: both constructions are very common.—בְּתוֹכָהּ comes from תּוֹךְ "midst," constr. תּוֹךְ (there is also a word תֹּךְ Ps. x. 7, lv. 12, lxxii. 14, compare תְּכָכִים Prov. xxix. 13, meaning "deceit," "oppres-

Verse 9: Words and constructions.

(Hebr. ii. 10) 6 Ho, ho, *come forth*, and flee from the land of the north, saith the LORD: for I have spread you abroad as the four winds of the heaven, saith the LORD.

---

sion," from an unused verb (תכך). There are two other common words of the form תּוֹךְ, viz. אָוֶן "emptiness," "iniquity" (e.g. אוֹנָם Ps. xciv. 23), and מָוֶת "death," constr. מוֹת.

הוֹי is often equivalent to אוֹי "woe!" "alas!" as in Is. i. 4 הוֹי גּוֹי חֹטֵא "woe to (or alas for) a sinful nation!"

Verse 10. Words and constructions. But here (as in Is. xviii. 1, 2 ...הוֹי אֶרֶץ צִלְצַל כְּנָפָיִם, and Is. lv. 1 הוֹי כָּל צָמֵא לְכוּ לַמַּיִם) it is simply a particle of exhortation and calling. Thus הוֹי may be correctly rendered "Ho! come ye!" It is practically equivalent to an Impert. There is, consequently, no need to understand a verb בּוֹאוּ, or צֵאוּ (as E. V. *come forth*) before וְנֻסוּ.—The *u* in the middle of וְנֻסוּ is long and accentuated, it is merely *written* defectively (comp. note on i. 3).—כְּאַרְבַּע. A few MSS. have בְּאַרְבַּע, but this reading is of no importance (there is *no* reading לְאַרְבַּע). The form אַרְבַּע is absl. and constr. *fem*. Either the *absol.* or the *constr.* may precede its noun.—The Pi‘el פֵּרֵשׂ occurs in all *nine* times in the Hebrew Scriptures. Once (Ps. lxviii. 15 בְּפָרֵשׂ שָׂרַי מְלָכִים) it seems to mean "to scatter." Seven times it is used of stretching forth the hands (Is. i. 15, xxv. 11 bis, lxv. 2, Jer. iv. 31, Ezek. xvii. 21, Ps. cxliii. 6): here it seems to be used in the sense of "spreading abroad," i.e. "multiplying greatly," in which sense פָּרַץ with יִן is used, *intransitively* however (Gen. xxx. 30, Hos. iv. 10, Job i. 10). The verb must be rendered as the Prophetic Perfect "I will spread you abroad as the four winds of heaven."

[ii. 6.] **LXX.** They seem to have understood *pērástī* in a bad sense "I will scatter"; then, feeling the difficulty of such an expression being made use of to the people on their return from captivity, they deliberately altered the passage into ἐκ τῶν τεσσάρων ἀνέμων τοῦ οὐρανοῦ συνάξω ὑμᾶς.

Remarks on ii. 5—10. The man with the measuring-line seems to be simply a figure in the drama, and is not to be regarded as an angel (as in i. 8): for, he has no message to deliver, and is implicitly rebuked for his folly in endeavouring to measure the city. There is little need to discuss the question whether "is" or

(Hebr. II. 11) 7 Deliver thyself, | O Zion, that dwellest *with* the daughter of Babylon.

"should be" or "shall be" is to be supplied with the expression "how great its width, &c." The Vision refers, no doubt, to the future of Jerusalem, beginning from the time then present. The Interpreting Angel "goes forth," i. e. leaves the Prophet's side, and another angel "comes forth," i.e. appears on the scene, and goes to meet him. In ver. 8 the speaker must be the "other angel," otherwise he appears for no object or purpose. "This young man" is by many commentators understood of the Prophet; but, to us it appears much more probable that it refers to the "man with the measuring-line." He is forbidden to measure the city, not because it was to become too great to be measured, but because it was to extend beyond its boundaries, whatever they might be, on account of the multitude of its inhabitants, &c. This promise was literally fulfilled: for Josephus (*Bell. Jud.* v. 4 § 2) speaking of Jerusalem in the time of Herod Agrippa says: πλήθει γὰρ ὑπερχεομένη κατὰ μικρὸν ἐξεῖρπε τῶν περιβόλων, καὶ τοῦ ἱεροῦ τὰ προσάρκτια πρὸς τῷ λόφῳ συμπολίζοντες ἐπ' οὐκ ὀλίγον προῆλθον, καὶ τέταρτον περιοικηθῆναι λόφον, ὃς καλεῖται Βεζεθά, κείμενος μὲν ἀντικρὺ τῆς Ἀντωνίας, ἀποτεμνόμενος δὲ ὀρύγματι βαθεῖ. Compare the letter of Aristéas to Philocrátes, in which a description of Jerusalem after the restoration is given; and the fragments of Hecatæus (who flourished under Alexander the Great), in which Jerusalem is described as a city fifty stadia in circumference, and inhabited by 120,000 men.

הִמָּלְטִי, although with *ethnāch* (ֽ), is not in the pausal form הִמָּלֵטִי (after the analogy of הִשָּׁמְרוּ' Jer. ix. 3), because _{Verse 11. Words.} the verse being very short (like Gen. i. 1), and the second clause being in apposition with צִיּוֹן in the first clause, the sense does not end with the *ethnāch* sufficiently for the only verb of the sentence to take a pausal form with that accent. Had there been two verbs in the sentence, the first would have had the pausal form; for instance, if the verse had been: הִנֵּה צִיּוֹן הִמָּלֵטִי וְתָנוּסִי יוֹשֶׁבֶת בַּת־בָּבֶל—
"Daughter of Babylon" means *inhabitants of Babylon*, like "Daughter of Zion" in ver. 14.—בָּבֶל means "gate of God," and is a contraction of בָּב אֵל (comp. בָּבַת of the next verse), the old Assyrian name being *Bāb ilu*, which is a Semitic translation of the still older Accadian *ca-dimirra-ci* "Place of the Gate of God" (Sayce).—יֹשֶׁבֶת means "dwelling with," and is here construed with the acc., as (Ps. v. 5) יְגֻרְךָ means יָגוּר עִמְּךָ. The instances יוֹשֵׁב תְּהִלּוֹת (Ps. xxii. 4), יוֹשֵׁב

---

[1] Other 2nd pers. Impert. Niph. which occur are: הֵרָנְעִי, הֵאָסְפִי, הִשָּׁמְרִי, הִנָּקְרִי, only once apiece: and, as it so happens, not one of them in pause.

(Hebr. ii. 12) 8 For thus saith the LORD of hosts; After the glory hath he sent me unto the nations which spoiled you: for he that toucheth you toucheth the apple of his eye. (Hebr. ii. 13) 9 For, behold, I will shake mine hand upon them,

---

הכרבים (2 Sam. vi. 2) or יושב אהלים (Gen. xxv. 27), &c., which are sometimes cited as parallels, are not suitable: for, in them the acc. denotes the thing inhabited, while here it denotes the people *with whom* the dwelling takes place.

LXX. [ii. 7.] *Hóy Çiyyôn* they transl. εἰς Σιών: somewhat similarly in Ezek. xxi. 15 (ver. 10 LXX.) אן is translated εἰς.

Verse 12. Words. For אל־הגוים the Cod. Petropol. reads על־.—בְּבַת עֵינִי is an expression peculiar to this passage. Elsewhere it is [אישון] בַּת עֵין. It seems probable that בְּבַת is a fem. form of בַּב (the masc. of which is common in Arab. and Aram.) in the sense of "gate," "opening," which would be very suitably applied to the "pupil of the eye." (But see the Dictionaries.)

Constructions. אחר is sometimes used as an *adverb of place*, as (Gen. xxii. 13) והנה איל אחר "and lo! a ram *behind*"; or as an *adverb of time* before a verb, as (Gen. xviii. 5) אחר תעברו "afterwards ye shall pass on," or, if before a substantive, with a *disjunctive* accent, as (Ps. lxxiii. 24) ואחר כבוד תקחני "and, afterward, Thou wilt gloriously receive me." When, however, it is put before a substantive with a *conjunctive* accent it is a preposition, meaning "after," as (Gen. ix. 28) אחר המבול "after the flood"; (Ps. lxviii. 26) אחר נגנים "after the players on stringed instruments." So, here, אחר כבוד שלחני means "after glory hath he sent me," i. e. posterior to some glory which had already been manifested; or, preferably, "after, i. e. in quest of, glory," comp. (Lev. xxvi. 33) והריקותי אחריכם חרב "and I will draw the sword *after* you," i. e. to find you out, reach you.

Verse 13. Words. הנני. When two of the same letters come together in the middle of a word, and the first of them be with *sh'vā*, if this *sh'vā* be a compound *sh'vā*, the preceding vowel will (Excurs. II. B. 6) take fixed-metheg, e. g. יללת (xi. 3), but if the *sh'vā* be a *simple* moving

ZECHARIAH II. 14—16.

and they shall be a spoil to their servants: and ye shall know that the LORD of hosts hath sent me. (Hebr. II. 14) 10 Sing and rejoice, O daughter of Zion: for, lo, I come, and I will dwell in the midst of thee, saith the LORD. (Hebr. II. 15) 11 And many nations shall be joined to the LORD in that day, and shall be my people: and I will dwell in the midst of thee, and thou shalt know that the LORD of hosts hath sent me unto thee. (Hebr. II. 16) 12 And the LORD shall inherit Judah his portion in the holy land, and shall choose Jerusalem again.

---

sh'vā as in הִנְנִי no *metheg* is placed. The student will observe that Baer points הִנְנִי without *metheg*, while less correct editions have it with a *metheg*.—The reading of the old editions, and by far the majority of MSS., is לְעַבְדֵיהֶם "to their servants," not l'ŏbh'dhēhem "to those who serve them."—*Sh'lāchánī*, the student is reminded that with the 2nd and 3rd sing. perf. of the verb, while the suffix of 1st pers. *plur.* is always *ā́nū* (in or out of pause), that of the 1st per. *sing.* is *anī́* out of pause (ver. 15), and *ā́nī* in pause: thus we always have the forms קְטָלָ֫נוּ and קְטַלְתָּ֫נוּ; but קְטַלְתָּ֫נוּ, קְטָלָ֫נוּ out of pause, and קְטָלָ֫נוּ, קְטַלְתָּ֫נוּ in pause.

Ronnī́ is the pronunciation of the first word of this verse, for the ־ָ being in a closed syllable without accent or *metheg* (Excurs. II. A. 5) is *ŏ* not *ā*; comp. the Infin. Constr. with *maqqēph* (Job xxxviii. 7) בְּרָן־יַ֫חַד כּוֹכְבֵי בֹקֶר "When the morning stars sang together."—On the accentuation of *v'shācantī́* see notes on i. 3. _{Verse 14. Words.}

When the third root-letter of a verb is a guttural, then in the second pers. sing. perfect instead of *sh'va* (as פָּקַדְתְּ), *pathach* is placed under this letter as יָדַ֫עַתְּ *yadá'at*. This *pathach* is (not *furtive*, i.e. to be read *before* the ע as in הוֹדִי֫עַ *hōdī́a'*, but) merely a helping-vowel, and is to be read *after* the ע, comp. the *pathach* after the ח of וַיִּ֫חַדְּ *vayyíchad* (from חדה) "and he rejoiced." _{Verse 15. Words.}

[ii. 11.] *V'nilvū́*, καὶ καταφεύξονται, a free translation; similarly Jer. l. 5 (xxvii. 5, LXX.). For *lī* they read *lō* αὐτῷ; and for *v'shācantī́* they read *v'shāc'nū́* καὶ κατασκηνώσουσιν. _{LXX.}

The expression *ad'māth haqqṓdesh*, "The Holy Land," occurs only in this passage. _{Verse 16.}

(Hebr. II. 17) 13 Be silent, O all flesh, before the LORD: for he is raised up out of his holy habitation.

Verse 17. Words. *Hás*, "hush!" This is probably the imperative Pi'el of הַסֵה (cf. צַר, הַל, גַל), since we have, not only the plur. הַסּוּ (Neh. viii. 11), but also the Hiph. (Numb. xiii. 30) וַיַּהַס "and he stilled." Some grammarians maintain that it is an interjection, which afterwards became conjugated, like the Arab. *haluma* (Hebr. הֲלֹם "hither"), plur. *halumū* "come ye hither!" At any rate it is an onomatopoetic; the Arab. is *ṣah* "sh...!"—נֵעוֹר is an anomalous form of Niph. participle from עוּר. The normal form of such participles is with *qāmāç* in the first syllable, as נָסוֹג. The Participle נִמּוֹל "circumcised" probably comes from מוּל, but some take it from מלל. Such participles seem to follow the analogy of the Imperf. יָקוּם. In Jer. xlviii. 11 we have the Perf. Niph. נָמַר from מוּר, the root being confounded with מרר.

LXX. [ii. 13.] *Hás, εὐλαβείσθω.* For מִמָּעוֹן they give ἐκ νεφελῶν. Elsewhere the LXX. seem to understand the meaning of *Mā‘ôn*. Here they seem to have read מִמַּעֲנָן, and to have understood מַעֲנָן as a derivative of עָנָן *‘ānān* "cloud."

Remarks. ii. 10—17. It seems more natural to regard this prophetic exhortation as the words of the Prophet, than as those of the Interpreting Angel. The land of the North is Babylonia (Jer. i. 14, &c.). Those, who had not yet returned, are exhorted to flee from the evils which are impending over Babylon, such as the rebellions of this period and consequent vengeance of Darius (see *Records of the Past*, I. pp. 118—125). Observe the continual change of Person; the Prophet speaks in the first person when he gives the very words of God, and in the third when he merely conveys their general meaning; or (as especially in ver. 15) the personality of the Sent is at times merged in that of the Sender. Verr. 11—17 are distinctly Messianic, and were fulfilled in the Birth of Jesus. But we must not look for the literal fulfilment of the mere details of the prophecy, which are but the background of the picture. The Prophet foresaw the Messianic times from an Old Testament standpoint, and expected the literal choosing-again of Jerusalem; while, as a matter of fact, the fulfilment of the prophecy was the commencement of the rejection of Israel. At the same time we may believe, on the authority of S. Paul, that God hath not cast off His own people, and that a time will come when all Israel shall be saved.

CHAPTER III.

AND he shewed me Joshua the high priest standing before the angel of the LORD, and Satan standing at his right hand to resist him.

FOURTH VISION.—JOSHUA THE HIGH PRIEST ARRAIGNED BEFORE THE ANGEL OF THE LORD.

For the probable subject of *vayyar'ēnī* comp. ii. 3.—The first *'ōmēd* denotes the state, or circumstances, of the person seen, as (Ex. ii. 11) וירא איש מצרי מכה איש עברי "And he saw an Egyptian man *smiting* a Hebrew man." (Comp. i. 18, and see notes on iv. 7.)—The second *'ōmēd* stands for היה עמד "was standing."—*Haśśāṭān* lit. "The Adversary." The word is used, as a Proper Name, with def. art., here and in Job i. ii., without the art. in Ps. cix. 6, 1 Chron. xxi. 1.—לְשִׂטְנוֹ *l'si-ṭ'nō* "to act as adversary towards him." This verb occurs nowhere else in the Inf., so that from it we can deduce no rules as to the use of *ĭ* instead of *ŏ* in the first syllable. But, the following facts will show how incorrect is the remark of Gesenius (§ 61), "The Inf. of the form שְׁכַב becomes with suffix שָׁכְבָה." Even as far as this one verb is concerned, he is in error: for though the constr. infin. is always שְׁכַב, there is only one passage (Gen. xix. 33, 35) in which it takes *ĭ* in the first syllable with suffixes, while in Deut. vi. 7, xi. 19, Prov. vi. 22 (בְּשָׁכְבְּךָ) and in Ruth iii. 4 (בְּשָׁכְבוֹ) it has *ŏ*. Then again, from לִבְלֹעַ (Jon. ii. 1), which is the only form of the Infin. of this verb, we get בָּלְעִי (Job vii. 19). Similarly the verb שָׁכַן (and שָׁכֵן), which has only the Infin. in *ō* (Gen. xxxv. 22) בְּשָׁכֹן (comp. Numb. ix. 22, 1 Kings viii. 12, Job xxx. 6, Ps. lxviii. 19, lxxxv. 10, 2 Chr. vi. 1), in the only two passages in which it occurs with suffix, takes in one *ŏ* לְשָׁכְנִי *l'sho-c'nī* (Ex. xxix. 46), and in the other *ĭ* לְשִׁכְנוֹ *l'shi-c'no* (Deut. xii. 5).

Verse 1. Words and constructions.

2 And the Lord said unto Satan, The Lord rebuke thee, O Satan; even the Lord that hath chosen Jerusalem rebuke thee: *is not this a brand plucked out of the fire?*
3 Now Joshua was clothed with filthy garments, and stood before the angel.

4 And he answered and spake unto those that stood before him, saying, Take away the filthy garments from him. And unto him he said, Behold, I have caused thine iniquity to pass from thee, and I will clothe thee with change of raiment.

The name יְהוֹשֻׁעַ became יוֹשֵׁעַ and יֵשׁוּעַ (Mishn. Jer. 38ª. 13 &c.), LXX. then יֵשׁוּעַ (Ezr. ii. 2), then יֵשׁוּ, which in Greek was written Ιησου: then, by adding the nominative-ending ς, it became Ἰησοῦς. Other corruptions of the name are אִיסִי (T. B. *Shabb.* 6ᵇ), אִיסָא (T. Y. *T'rumoth*, Hal. 1, ed. Krot. 40ᶜ), Arab. *'īsā*.

The ו of *v'yig'ar* means "yea," as (Ps. xxvii. 14) קַוֵּה...וְקַוֵּה (comp. Verse 2. Constructions. Zech. vi. 10); sometimes ו may be rendered "even" (e.g. Ex. xxv. 9, Zech. vii. 5), or "namely" (Ex. xxxv. 12). The usual construction of גָּעַר in the sense of "rebuking" is with בְּ; contrast Mal. iii. 11, in the sense of "destroying," with the acc. (ibid. ii. 3); at least, this is the distinction made by R. David Qimchi (Ps. ix. 6).—*Habbōchēr is, of course, to be referred to YHVH.*

Lābhúsh is merely written *defectivè* (comp. i. 3).—צוֹאִים occurs only Verse 3. Words and constructions. in this chap. as an adj. "filthy." Elsewhere we have צֵאָה and צֹאָה as a substantive "filth," "stercus." Verbs which take a double accusative in the active, are able to retain one in the passive, so that it is not necessary to put *lābhúsh* into the constr.; but that construction is also admissible, e.g. (Ezk. ix. 11) לְבֻשׁ הַבַּדִּים "who was clothed in fine linen." The Qal *lābhēsh*, and *lābhúsh*, means to "put on," "be clothed with," with acc. of the thing put on (once with בְּ, Esth. vi. 8). In the Hiph. it denotes "to clothe another," and is generally used with two acc. e.g. (Ex. xxviii. 41) וְהִלְבַּשְׁתָּ אֹתָם אֶת־אַהֲרֹן "And thou shalt clothe Aaron with them."

V'halbēsh is the Infin. Absl. Hiph. used emphatically, with the Verse 4. Words and constructions. omission of the finite verb (comp. נָתוֹן אֹתוֹ Gen. xli. 43), the full construction would be וְהִלְבֵּשׁ הִלְבַּשְׁתִּי.— *Mach"lāçóth* "a change of garments" (only again in Is. iii. 22): it is

5 And I said, Let them set a fair mitre upon his head. So they set a fair mitre upon his head, and clothed him with garments. And the angel of the LORD stood by.

used in the plural, probably, because it consisted of several different articles of dress (comp. note on vi. 11).

*V'halbḗsh ōth'cā mach*ᵃ*lāçṓth* καὶ ἐνδύσατε αὐτὸν ποδήρη, reading the verb in the Imperative plur., and for *ōth'cā* reading *ōthṓ*. LXX.

Vā'ōmár, the *first* person is *mit'ra'*, but the *third* person *vayyṓmer* (ver. 4, iv. 14, v. 6) is *mil'ʿél* (see note on i. 9).—*Yāsímū* "let them place."—*Çănîph* "turban," but the technical term for the High Priest's turban is מִצְנֶפֶת (Ex. xxviii. 4, &c.); both words, and also three consecutive words in Is. xxii. 18, are from the same root which means to "fold," "wind." The article in *haççănîph haṭṭāhṓr* is definite, denoting "*the* clean turban" requested above.—The participle *'ōmḗd* here denotes "kept standing (where he was)."

Verse 5. Words, &c.

There is a great variety of opinion among commentators with respect to the capacity, in which Joshua is represented as standing before the Angel of the LORD. THEODORET, among early expositors, and HENGSTEN-BERG, among moderns, maintain that Joshua is seen in the Sanctuary engaged in the work of his priestly office *before* the Angel of the LORD. Against this view may be urged, that, however high may be the dignity of the Angel of the LORD, it is hardly in accordance with the spirit of the Old Testament to represent the high priest as ministering before him, as if before God. Observe, too, how in i. 12, 13 the Personality of the Angel of the LORD is distinct from that of the LORD Himself. EWALD imagines that at this time the high priest was actually accused, or was dreading an accusation, at the Persian court, and that a defamation and persecution of this kind may be discerned as underlying this vision. But there is no historical trace of any such *personal* accusation, nor could Joshua be looked upon as the people's *representative* before the *Persian Court*, since Zerubbabel was their *civil* representative. KOEHLER regards Joshua as standing before the judgment-seat of the Angel, while Satan stands at his right hand (Ps. cix. 6) to accuse him. But, while this interpretation is in the main correct, it must be remembered that no formal judicial process is described in the vision, nor is there any mention of a judgment-seat. WRIGHT's explanation seems to us the best: " The high priest was probably seen in the vision, busied about some part of his priestly duties. While thus engaged, he discovered that he was actually standing as a criminal before the angel, and while the great Adversary accused him, the truth of that accusation was but too clearly seen by the filthy garments with which he then perceived that he was attired."—The filthy garments denote sin (Is. lxiv. 5, comp. iv. 4, Prov. xxx. 9). This sin cannot have been that of marrying strange wives (Ezr. x. 18) as TARG., QIMCHI, &c. suppose, for those marriages took place some sixty years later. Nor is KOEHLER right in referring it to the neglect to rebuild the Temple. For, as KEIL

iii. 1—5. Remarks.

6 And the angel of the LORD protested unto Joshua, saying, | 7 Thus saith the LORD of hosts; If thou wilt walk in my ways, and

remarks, had this been the accusation, it would have been rather late, since the active resumption of the work of rebuilding had taken place five months previously (comp. Hag. i. 15 with Zech. i. 7). The view of WRIGHT is almost correct: "The fourth vision (chap. iii.) is connected with the coming of the LORD recorded in chap. ii., in a way similar to that in which the purification of the sons of Levi, spoken of by Malachi, stands related to the prophecy of the coming of the Angel of the Covenant predicted by that prophet (Mal. iii. 1—4).... The high priest was the representative of the priesthood, and the priests representatives of the people of Israel, who were 'a kingdom of priests, &c.' (Ex. xix. 6). Joshua's sin is therefore spoken of in ver. 9 as 'the sin of the land,' whereby the whole people was defiled." It is true, that the priesthood had fallen under special condemnation, "Her priests have violated my law, and have profaned my holy things" (Ezek. xxii. 26), so that the sins of the priesthood may well be especially referred to here. But, at the same time Joshua, as the people's representative before God, may be looked on as, in a sense, laden with their sins, as well as with his own and those of the priesthood in particular. We do not, therefore, entirely agree with the last remark we quoted from C. H. H. Wright.—For instances of "standing before" being used of the defendant see Numb. xxxv. 12, Deut. xix. 17, Josh. xx. 6.—With ver. 2 comp. Jude 9.—The persons referred to in ver. 4 are, doubtless, the angels of grade inferior to that of the Angel of the LORD. In this verse the Prophet is assured that the iniquity of Joshua is taken away. He seems to have feared that this might be only a personal absolution, hence his anxiety about the "mitre" (ver. 5). Upon the *Miçnéphheth* was the *Çiç*, on which was inscribed *Qôdesh l'Adōnāy*, and it was to be always on the forehead of the high priest, "that he might bear the iniquity of the holy things" (Ex. xxviii. 36—38). By the granting of his request, that a clean mitre might be placed on the head of Joshua, he is assured that the high priest is not pardoned only personally, but also in his official capacity.—There is nothing in the word *'ōmēd* to justify Ewald's statement that the angel, "having risen from the judgment-seat," now lingers, &c.

Verse 6. Words, &c.
Vayyá'ad is the apoc. Imperf. Hiph. of עוּד. The *pathach* in the last syllable is on account of the ע; the normal form of this tense from verbs with medial *vāv* quiescent, is וַיָּקֶם with *segōl*. This verb, when construed with בְּ, denotes to "call another to witness against" (Deut. iv. 26), but also "to testify *to*," as here; see Jennings and Lowe on Ps. l. 7 (for other meanings and constructions consult the Dictionaries).

Verse 7. Words and constructions.
Observe that *v'im-eth-mishmartí* takes no *ga'yā* because it is with a conjunctive accent (Excurs. II. B. 4). On the form *mishmartí* see note on xi. 3.—The apodosis to *im* "if," is introduced by וְגַם "then indeed." Simple וְ would have been sufficient to introduce the apodosis (e.g. xiv. 18), but וְגַם is added

if thou wilt keep my charge, then thou shalt also judge my house, and shalt also keep my courts, and I will give thee places to walk among these that stand by.

8 Hear now, O Joshua the high

---

to intensify the declaration, as in a simple sentence like (Job xviii. 5) גַּם אוֹר רְשָׁעִים יִדְעָךְ "the light of the wicked shall *indeed* be extinguished": comp. (Gen. xlii. 22) וְגַם דָּמוֹ הִנֵּה נִדְרָשׁ "therefore his blood &c.": also observe, that גַּם introduces an interrogative apodosis in Zech. viii. 6. אַתָּה is also emphatic. The second וְגַם is used in quite a different sense, it means merely "and also." Had וְגַם...גַּם meant "also...and," we should have expected the following collocation, וְאַתָּה גַּם תָּדִין...וְגַם תִּשְׁמֹר. Some commentators consider the second וְגַם to be a mere repetition of the former one, for greater emphasis. In this case there is no "and" before the second clause: and so we must render, "Then shalt... : then shalt..."—*Châçêr* "a court" has two plurals, חֲצֵרִים (e.g. Lev. xxv. 31), and חֲצֵרוֹת (e.g. Ezk. xlvi. 22): this latter takes the suffixes in two different ways, viz. (Ps. xcvi. 8) חַצְרוֹתָי, and (Ps. c. 4) חֲצֵרֹתָיו (comp. 1 Chron. xxviii. 6).—*V'năthattî* (on the accentuation see note on i. 3) is dependent on the futures of the preceding clause.—מַהְלְכִים is a plur. subst. meaning "places to walk in." There is a substantive which occurs only in the sing. *constr.* מַהֲלַךְ (Ezk. xlii. 4, Jon. iii. 3, 4) and with suff. מַהֲלָכְךָ (Neh. ii. 6). Had our word been the plur. of this, we should have expected מַהֲלָכִים. It appears, therefore, that it must be from an unused word מַהְלֵךְ, and that its plur. is formed like מַסְמְרִים (Is. xli. 7), from an imaginary מַסְמֵר, and like the plurals of מִזְבֵּחַ and מַעֲשֵׂר which are מִזְבְּחוֹת and מַעְשְׂרוֹת. The supposition of Ewald, that it is a Hiph. Partic. (of what he calls Aram. form) for מוֹלִיכִים = מַהְלִיכִים "leaders," would require מִבִּין instead of בֵּין to follow.

Mahl'cim ἀναστρεφομένους, reading probably מַהְלְכִים. LXX.

מוֹפֵת is from the Rt. אפת, with which some comp. Arab. *'ift* "a sign," comp. מוֹסְרוֹתֵיהֶם (Ps. ii. 3) from אסר.—*An'shê mōphêth* lit. "men of sign (portent)," i.e. not men to be wondered at (E.V.), or men standing by as witnesses of the promise (Ewald);

priest, thou, and thy fellows that sit before thee: for they *are* men wondered at: for, behold, I will bring forth my servant the

BRANCH.

9 For behold the stone that I have laid before Joshua; upon one stone *shall be* seven eyes: behold,

---

but rather, either men for whom miracles are wrought, or men used to interpret prophetic portents. LXX. has ἄνδρες τερατοσκόποι.—"They" probably includes Joshua. For such a change of person comp. Zeph. ii. 12, "Also *ye* Cushim slain by my sword are *they*."—The *Cî* before *hin'nî* is not to be translated, it merely introduces the *oratio recta*, like ὅτι in the New Test. &c. (comp. Gen. xxix. 33).—*Mēbhî'* can only be taken as a Prophetic Participle, denoting the Future (and so too *m'phattḗach* in the next verse, which is followed by the Perfect with strong vāv *umashtî* "and I will remove"), comp. xii. 2, *hinnêh ānōcî śām*. In such cases there is nothing but the context to guide us to decide, whether the time referred to is near at hand, or distant. Thus, the last-cited passage appears to refer to a distant future; while הִנְנִי לֹקֵחַ (Ezk. xxiv. 17) is shown by the next verse to be the imminent future (comp. Hag. ii. 6).

Çĕmach Ἀνατολήν. Syr. *Denchō* "sunrise," the word *Çĕmchō* in Syr. denoting "shining of the sun." In Is. iv. 2 *Yih'yéh Çĕmach YHVH* is rendered by LXX. ἐπιλάμψει ὁ θεός.

LXX. &c.

✓ There is a difficulty in this verse which is so obvious, that one would have thought that it would have occurred to any chance reader of it, whether in the Hebr., or in a translation. And yet it has not been generally mentioned by commentators; indeed we have, as far as we have observed, found it touched on by Arnswald[1] only. It is this: if the Prophet meant by *hā'ébhen* "*the* stone," i.e. some particular stone, why does he afterwards say, "on *one* stone [shall be seven] eyes," and not rather, "on *that* stone," or "on *this* stone"? Arnswald evades the difficulty by paraphrasing *ébhen 'achâth* by הָאֶבֶן הַזֹּאת; but this is surely not admissible. Accordingly we propose to render *hā'ébhen* "*the* stones," viz. the materials for rebuilding the Temple. It is true that, while אֶבֶן *ébhen* is commonly used for "[precious] stones" (e.g. Ex. xxviii. 17, xxxix. 10), אֲבָנִים is generally used for "*building* stones" (e.g. Zech. v. 4), still we do find *ébhen* in this latter sense, e.g. (Gen. xi. 3) וַיְהִי לָהֶם הַלְּבֵנָה לְאָבֶן " so they had

---

[1] בִּאוּר עַל תְּרֵי עָשָׂר.

| I will engrave the graving thereof, | remove the iniquity of that land |
| saith the LORD of hosts, and I will | in one day. |

bricks instead of stones." But the question still remains: how are we to take על אבן אחת, can it mean "on *each* stone"? It is quite possible that it may, for the Prophet could not have written שבעה עינים שבעה עינים (the ordinary distributive phrase[1]), since that would have denoted seven *different* eyes on each stone. But, why did he not use another form of distributive, which would have avoided the repetition, viz. על כל אבן ואבן שבעה עינים, which would have been quite admissible (comp. Esth. ii. 11, iii. 14, iv. 3, viii. 11, 1 Chron. xxviii. 14—18)? This objection can only be answered by calling attention to the fact, that in iv. 2, xii. 12 he does not use the more ordinary distributives. But, should it be thought that this interpretation is not satisfactorily supported by usage[2], we propose another, and render: "Behold the stones, which I have laid before Jehoshua, upon one particular stone [are] seven eyes." For this use of the numeral "one" comp. xiv. 7. Practically this latter is much the same interpretation, as that adopted by most commentators, viz. that the Prophet speaks of some particular stone (be it the foundation stone which had been laid in the time of Cyrus, or the stone on which the Ark had formerly stood, or the head-stone, or chief corner-stone); but, we have, we think, explained to our readers the reason why he said "on *one* stone" instead of "on *this* stone," while others have evaded the difficulty.—Observe that here (as in iv. 10) עינים is construed with a masc. numeral.—The expression *pattēₐch* is used of engraving precious stones (Ex. xxviii. 9), gold (ibid. ver. 36), and of carved work (Ps. lxxiv. 6), or sculpture (2 Chron. ii. 13).—On the accentuation of *umashtî* see note on i. 3, on the absence of *metheg* see Excurs. II. 1, note. It is impossible to take "And I will remove, &c." as the sentence engraved on the stone, as many have done; for such an inscription could not possibly commence with *vāv* conversive and the Perfect. Job xix. 25, "Yet I know, my Vindicator liveth" is in no sense a parallel case (see Delitzsch in loc.).

---

[1] שנים is actually used (Gen. vii. 2) for the שנים שנים of ver. 9; but, then, the preceding שבעה שבעה sufficiently secures the distributive force of שנים. Ewald is mistaken (*Lehrg.* § 313) in taking מטה אחד (Numb. xvii. 18) as "a rod apiece"=מטה אחד מטה אחד. The words imply merely that there should be *one rod* for the whole family of Levi, although they were divided into Priests and Levites; see Rashi (xi[th] cent.), Ibn Ezra (xii[th] cent.), and Ramban (Nachmanides, xiii[th] cent.) in loc.

[2] But see Ezek. i. 6, x. 14.

10 In that day, saith the LORD of hosts, shall ye call every man his neighbour under the vine and under the fig tree.

Versions. *Hinnî m'phattē'ch pittuchâh*, LXX. ἰδοὺ ἐγὼ ὀρύσσω βόθρον, either reading פָּתַח "an opening," or פָּתַח "a trench."—Aq. διαγλύφω ἀνοίγματα αὐτῆς.—Symm. γλύψω γὰρ τὴν γλυφὴν αὐτοῦ.—Syr. "I will open its gates."—For *umashtî* LXX. has καὶ ψηλαφήσω, confounding מוּשׁ "to remove" (generally "to give way") with מוּשׁ = מָשַׁשׁ "to grope after."

Verse 10. The verb *qārā'* in the sense of "calling a person to one," is very frequently followed by לְ of the person called, e. g. Ex. xii. 31 *vayyiqrā l'mōshēh ul'ah°rōn* "and he called Moses and Aaron." On *îsh l're'ēhû* see note on vii. 10.—*El-tachath* "to under" is a *constructio prægnans*, denoting "to come and sit under."

iii. 6—10. Remarks. The Angel of the LORD now proclaims to Joshua a fourfold promise: (α) the confirmation of his official authority, and the elevation of his own spiritual nature; (β) the mission of the Saviour; (γ) God's providential care for the House, which was being rebuilt; (δ) the peace and prosperity of the nation.—Observe in ver. 7 the introverted parallelism "if thou wilt *walk*...and *keep*," "then shalt thou...*keep*...*places to walk*." "Walk in my ways" refers to personal holiness, "keep my charge" to the faithful discharge of his official duties. So, on the other hand, "judge my house" and "keep my courts" refers to his spiritual authority as high priest, and "walks among those that stand by" denotes spiritual access among the angels of God's supernal courts.—Though Zerubbabel is certainly called "my servant" (Hag. ii. 23), the use of the participle, "behold I bring" renders it impossible to interpret the expression "my servant Branch" of him. It can only be referred to the promised Saviour of Israel, or "Branch of the LORD" (Is. iv. 2), a "Righteous Branch," "Branch of Righteousness" (Jer. xxiii. 5), "a Righteous-one my servant" (Is. liii. 12), "my servant David" (Ezek. xxxiv. 23). See further Remarks on chap. vi. 11—15, and comp. Remarks on ii. 14—17.—On ver. 9 refer back to the notes. EWALD supposes the "seven eyes" to have been engraved on the stone, and thinks that they represent the seven Spirits (Rev. i. 4). But, it seems in every way best to understand the seven eyes as denoting God's special, yet all-embracing Providence, which is being directed towards the stone to watch and protect it. Various symbolical meanings have been given to the stones. The only one of them, which is at all reasonable, is this, that it typified the Messiah (comp. Ps. cxviii. 22, Is. xxviii. 16). But, we prefer the interpretation which we gave above in the notes.—"In one day" cannot refer to "the day of Golgotha" (HENGSTENBERG), for how could ver. 10 be applied to that day? How could xii. 10 sqq., and ii. 9, 10, be possibly referred to the same event? The meaning seems to be simply this, that the completion of the work of rebuilding would be the seal of the people's forgiveness, and restoration to favour.—The wording of ver. 10 is a reminiscence of 1 Kings iv. 25, Mic. iv. 4, &c. It is a renewal of the promise contained in Jer. xxxiii. 6, and a declaration of its speedy fulfilment.

CHAPTER IV.

A ND the angel that talked with me came again, and waked me, as a man that is wakened out of his sleep,

---

FOURTH VISION. THE GOLDEN CANDLESTICK.

On the form *vayyáshobh* see notes on iii. 5. The simplest rule for deciding the vocalization of a word with a suffix, like וַיְעִירֵנִי, is the following: when by the addition of a suffix (or accentuated syllable) the accent is drawn towards the end of a word, count back three vowels from this new accentuated syllable (both inclusive), and remove (α) the third vowel if it can be removed; if it cannot, remove (β) the second; (γ) in some cases none of the vowels can be removed. E.g. (α) The Imperf. Hiph. of עוּר is יָעִיר *yā'ír*, when the suffix is added the accent falls on ...*rḗnī:* now *yā* is the third syllable from *rḗ*, therefore remove the *qāmāç* and put *sh'va*, and you get יְעִירֵנִי, similarly חָפֵץ *cháphḗç* plur. חֲפֵצִים *ch^{a}phēçím*. (β) תְּנַפֵּץ *t'nappéç* "thou wilt break in pieces," when it takes the suffix *ḗm*, cannot lose the third vowel from the accent, viz. *pathach*, because it is supported by *dagesh*, therefore remove the second vowel *çērē*, and you get תְּנַפְּצֵם, and similarly all Pres. Partic. Qal which have ō in the first syllable (which is characteristic of the Partic. and is immoveable) lose the second vowel, as עֹמֵד *'ōmḗd* plur. עֹמְדִים *'ōm'dím*. As an instance of (γ) take כּוֹכָב *cōcábh* plur. כּוֹכָבִים *cōcābhím*, and comp. note on ii. 3.—עוֹר is the Niph. Imper. of עוּר (of the form of יְקוּם), the *chiriq* under the *yūd* being changed into *çērē* by way of compensation, since the ע cannot be doubled.—Since שֵׁנָה "sleep" comes from Rt. יָשֵׁן, it loses its first vowel when it takes a suffix, comp. עֵדָה "congregation," עֲדָתוֹ, while עֵדָה "testimony" (which comes from עוּד) retains its vowel, thus עֵדָתוֹ. Consequently there is no difference between *sh'nāthô* "his sleep" from *shēnáh*, and *sh'nāthô* "his year" from *shānáh*.

2 And said unto me, What seest thou? And I said, I have looked, and behold a candlestick all of gold, with a bowl upon the top of

Verse 2. Words and constructions.

The C°thîbh וַיֹּאמֶר seems to have arisen from the fact that the words, which follow, *rā'îthî v'hinnêh*, which generally mean "I looked, and behold!" are more appropriate to narration, than as the answer to the question: What seest thou? As answer we should have expected הִנֵּה רָאִיתִי "lo! I see," or אֲנִי רֹאֶה (v. 1) "I see." The "*vayyômer*" of the C°thîbh must be looked on as parenthetical, thus: "I looked (said he) and behold," &c., comp. v. 6, 8, and the common introduction in Arabic of *qâla* "said he" in narration. Taking the Q°rî "and I said," we must understand *rā'îthî v'hinnêh* in the sense of "I see, and lo," &c.—גֻּלָּהּ "its bowl" might be explained as from a ἅπ. λεγό. גֹּל, or as standing for גֻּלָּתָהּ (from *gullâh* ver. 3), as כְּתֻבֻנָם (Hos. xiii. 2) is for כתבונתם. But, apart from considerations of the difficulty of explaining גֻּלָּה, I regard גֻּלָּה (with the *Hē r°phûyâh*) as the right reading. For, it will be observed that things which must of necessity belong to a candlestick such as "top," or which belonged to the Candlestick of the Tabernacle, viz. "the seven lamps," are marked by the pronon. suff. to denote that they were *proper* to it, "its top," "its seven lamps," but, when other points are mentioned which would not naturally have been expected, such as the "pipes," the "olive-trees," the "spouts," they are without the pron. suff. Now this "bowl" was not a thing to have been expected: not a thing, in fact, which could be called "*its* bowl." Therefore, in accordance with some MSS., we read וְגֻלָּה "and a bowl." For the absol. form of numeral before a defined substantive comp. (Josh. vi. 4) שִׁבְעַת הַנֵּרֹת; for the constr. (Numb. viii. 2) שִׁבְעָה שׁוֹפְרוֹת הַיּוֹבֵל. —*Shibh'âh v'shibh'âh mûçâqôth lannêrôth*, it has been disputed whether two numerals joined by ו can be distributive, i.e. whether these words can denote "seven pipes *apiece* to the lamps." It is certain that this is not the usual construction, we should rather have expected *shibh'âh mûçâqôth shibh'âh mûçâqôth lannêrôth* (or *l°nêr eḥâd*), comp. Is. vi. 2. But 2 Sam. xxi. 20 has been aptly cited to the contrary, the passage runs: וַיְהִי אִישׁ...וְאֶצְבְּעֹת יָדָיו וְאֶצְבְּעֹת רַגְלָיו שֵׁשׁ וָשֵׁשׁ עֶשְׂרִים וְאַרְבַּע מִסְפָּר which should be rendered "and there was a man who had six fingers to each hand, and six toes to each foot, twenty-four in all."

it, and his seven lamps thereon, and seven pipes to the seven lamps, | which *are* upon the top thereof:

In 1 Chron. xx. 6 the same passage occurs, but with the following variation, that the words "hands and feet" are not mentioned, it simply says ואצבעתיו שש־ושש עשרים וארבע. Now, those who dispute the distributive sense of שש ושש say, that "six and six" means that his hands had 6 + 6 = 12, and his feet had 6 + 6 = 12, total 24. That is to say, they divide the 24 fingers and toes into two groups of 12 fingers, and 12 toes, each of which groups is represented by שש ושש. But in giving this explanation they overlook the fact that they take שש ושש, which means 6 + 6, as equivalent to "6 + 6 apiece," viz. to hands and feet 12 apiece. They do, in fact, read שש ושש as equivalent to שש ושש שש ושש (see notes on iii. 9). Kalisch and C. H. H. Wright apply this theory to the שבעה ושבעה before us, and say that it means that the seven lamps had two pipes apiece, viz. 14 in all. But their application of the theory is illogical. The *seven* lamps are already mentioned, as in the other case were (according to that theory) the *two* groups, viz. of fingers, and of toes. Distributing 12 to each of the two groups gives 24. Similarly, distributing 7 + 7 pipes to each of the seven lamps gives 98 pipes, not 14. To have expressed (according to their theory) two pipes to each lamp, we must have had after the mention of *seven* lamps (מספר), ארבעה עשר אחד ואחד ומוצקותם i.e. "and their pipes were 1 + 1 (= 2 apiece), 14 in number." Koehler[1] avoids this blunder by saying that the number is "seven and seven," not 14, because one group of seven pipes was for supplying the lamps from the reservoir, and the other group of seven to connect the seven lamps. But, unless the two outer ones are to be connected, it takes only six pipes to connect seven lamps.—Finally, we have not the slightest hesitation in interpreting שבעה ושבעה as "seven apiece" (so too Arnswald).

For *rā'îthî* LXX. gives ἑώρακα, while for *ᵃnî rō'ĕh* (v. 2) it has ἐγὼ ὁρῶ.—LXX. does not express a suffix with *gullâh*, but says simply καὶ τὸ λαμπάδιον ἐπάνω αὐτῆς, but this is no proof that they did not read the word with a suffix, since for נֵרֹתֶיהָ עָלֶיהָ they give λύχνοι ἐπάνω αὐτῆς. Nor does the Syr. express the suffix in either case.—LXX. Syr. Vulg. E.V. Ewald &c. get over the difficulty of the expression שבעה ושבעה by cancelling the first שבעה, καὶ ἑπτὰ ἐπαρυστρίδες τοῖς λύχνοις τοῖς ἐπάνω αὐτῆς. Hitzig, on the other hand,

Versions and emendations.

---

[1] *Die Nachexilischen Propheten*, II. 141.

3 And two olive trees by it, one | upon the right *side* of the bowl, and the other upon the left *side* thereof.

---

cancels the שִׁבְעָה before נֵרֹתֶיהָ, and construes the שִׁבְעָה, which follows עָלֶיהָ, with that clause, and renders thus, "and its lamps upon it were seven." This construction is natural enough in Ex. xxv. 37, xxxvii. 23, where the candelabrum is first described, but here "and *its* seven lamps upon it" is the collocation we should expect. (See above.) —Pressel has made a clever suggestion, viz. that "seven" is repeated on account of its importance as corresponding to "the seven eyes of the LORD." He would render: "seven (was) the number of its lamps above the same—seven—and seven the number of its pipes." But, our objection to Hitzig's translation applies also to this: and, moreover, had this been the meaning of the prophet, it is hardly likely that he would have written שִׁבְעָה in such an equivocal collocation, but would rather have written שִׁבְעָה מִסְפָּר "seven in number."—Nêr is correctly construed with a *masc.* numeral (comp. Prov. xx. 27, xxiv. 20, and my *Fragment of P'sachim*, p. 40, note).—מוּצָקוֹת in the sense of "pipes" is a ἅπ. λεγό. Gesen. and Fuerst are wrong in calling it a *fem.* substantive as the numeral here shows. It is to be considered as a subst. formed from the *Hiph.* of יצק (וְצַק) viz. *marçâq = mauçâq = môçâq* and then = *mûçâq* (comp. מוֹסָד, and מוּסָד "foundation"). The interchange of *o* and *u* is not uncommon, thus we have נְבוּכָה (Esth. iii. 15), and נְבֻכִים (Ex. xiv. 3); קָרְבָּן, usually *Qorbân*, is in Neh. x. 35, xiii. 31 *qurbân;* the Biblical לוּז makes in Rabb. the plur. לוּזִין; Rabb. פְּרוֹזבּוּל is pronounced *Pruzbul*, and *Prozbol;* in old Jewish epitaphs we find NEPVS for *nepos*, APOSTVLI for *apostoli*, MAIVRES for *majores*, and ΦΑΟϹΤΙΝΙ for *Faustini*[1].

Verse 3. '*âlèhā* "by its side," as עַל יָם "by the sea" (Ex. xiv. 2), comp. '*al- s'mōlāh* "at its left hand." LXX. has ἐπάνω αὐτῆς.— The student should observe that when מִן is prefixed to a word beginning with י, the *yūd* quiesces in the *chiriq*, and no compensation is made for the loss of the נ, therefore we have מִימִין; for this use of מִן see note on v. 3, and comp. ἐκ τοῦ ἔμπροσθεν στῆναι (Xen. *Cyr*. 2. 2). The construction is different in ver. 11.

---

[1] "Atti del IV congresso internazionale degli orientalisti," Firenze 1880, 8vo. Vol. I. pp. 290—293.

4 So I answered and spake to the angel that talked with me, saying, What *are* these, my lord?
5 Then the angel that talked with me answered and said unto me, Knowest thou not what these be? And I said, No, my lord.

6 Then he answered and spake unto me, saying, This *is* the word of the LORD unto Zerubbabel, saying, Not by might, nor by power, but by my spirit, saith the LORD of hosts.
7 Who *art* thou, O great moun-

וָאֹמַר. In illustration of our remarks on i. 9 we will now give several instances of the first person imperf. of verbs, which, with strong *vāv*, would throw the accent on the penultimate in the 3rd masc. and fem., or 2nd per. masc. in the singular, but which retain, according to rule, the accent on the ultimate in the 1st person (they all take *metheg* under the וָ): וָאֵדַע "and I knew," וָאֹהַב "I loved," וָאֹחֵז "I seized," וָאֵחַר "I stayed," וָאִירָא "I feared," וָאֹכַל (and *vā'ōcĕl* in pause) "I ate," וָאֵלֵד "I gave birth," וָאֵלֵךְ (and *vā'ēlăc* in pause) "I went," וָאָסִיר "I removed," וָאָעֵד (and *vā'ā'ĕd*) "I testified," וָאָפִין "I scattered," וָאֶקַל "I was despised," וָאָקוּם (and וָאָקֻם) "I arose," וָאָקֻץ "I abhorred," וָאֵרֶד "I went down," וָאֵשֵׁב "I sat," וָאָשׁוּב "I returned" (v. 1), וָאָשִׁיב "I returned (answer)," וָאָשִׂים "I placed."—Here, and in ver. 12, LXX. render, well enough *quoad sensum*, וָאַעַן by καὶ ἐπηρώτησα.

It is necessary that the student should observe that the accent on זֶה, being placed *before* the word, is *dis*junctive, and therefore the ךְ of *d'bhar* retains the *dagesh lene* (see Excurs. III. 1). This accent is called *Y'thībh*. But when it is placed on the tone-syllable as לֹא בְחַיִל it is *con*junctive, and, therefore, the B'GaDC'FaTh letter following is *r'phūyăh*. This accent is called *Mahpac* (comp. p. 3).—The addition of μεγάλη by LXX. is merely a free rendering.

There is no difficulty in the use of מִי "who?" (not מָה "what?") even if we do not regard "the great mountain" as a personal adversary, or as a personification of oppositions generally. For מִי is often used where in English we require "what?" Thus (1 Sam. xviii. 18) מִי אָנֹכִי וּמִי חַיַּי "who am I, and who (what) is my

tain? before Zerubbabel *thou shalt become* a plain: and he shall bring forth the headstone *thereof with* | shoutings, *crying*, Grace, grace unto it.

---

life?" (comp. Ex. x. 8, Judg. xiii. 17, Mich. i. 5).—*Har-haggādōl* "O great mountain"; with the omission of the article before the substantive. "A great mountain" would be *hār gādōl*; "the great mountain" or "O great mountain" would properly be הָהָר הַגָּדוֹל; but the article is *sometimes* omitted with the noun, e. g. יוֹם הַשִּׁשִּׁי "the sixth day" (Gen. i. 31), אִישׁ אֶפְרָתִי הַזֶּה "this Ephrathite" (1 Sam. xvii. 12), for *hā'īsh hā'ephrāthī hazzéh* (comp. Zech. xiv. 10).—לְמִישׁוֹר is most graphic; by one single word is expressed "thou shalt become a plain!" For this use of לְ with the verb "to be" omitted comp. (Lam. iv. 3) בַּת עַמִּי לְאַכְזָר; and for the omission of other verbs for the sake of terseness comp. (Hos. viii. 1) אֶל־חִכְּךָ שֹׁפָר, כַּנֶּשֶׁר עַל־בֵּית יְיָ.—וְהוֹצִיא "he shall bring out." The perfect with strong *vāv* is often used, independently of any foregoing verb, to express a future, the expectation of which is rendered reasonable by the statement of the preceding clause, as (1 Sam. xvii. 36) "Both the lion and the bear thy servant slew, this uncircumcised Philistine shall be (וְהָיָה) like one of them." So here, the statement "Who art thou O great mountain, before Zerubbabel?" "[Thou shalt become] a plain!" prepares the way for the promise "he shall bring out." The וְ is better, as in many cases, left untranslated in English.—הָרֹאשָׁה is a ἅπ. λεγό. (on the *sīmān rāphéh* see Excurs. IV.), it can only be regarded as a fem. formation from רֹאשׁ denoting "head," and must be in apposition with הָאֶבֶן, and the two words together must be rendered "the head-stone." Substantives are sometimes in Hebrew (with or without def. art.) put in apposition, where in Aryan languages we should have a Tat-purusha compound *genitively dependent* as *birth-place, brick-house*: thus (ver. 10) we have הָאֶבֶן הַבְּדִיל "the lead-weight," or "plumb-line," (2 Kings xvi. 14) הַמִּזְבֵּחַ הַנְּחֹשֶׁת "the brass-altar," הַבָּקָר הַנְּחֹשֶׁת "the brass-oxen" (ver. 17), עֵמֶק הַפְּגָרִים וְהַדֶּשֶׁן "the corpse-and-ashes-valley" (Jer. xxi. 40), הָעֲבֹתֹת הַזָּהָב "the gold-wreaths" (Exod. xxxix. 17), שֶׁבַע־שָׁנִים רָעָב "seven-year-famine" (2 Sam. xxiv. 13), מֵי לַחִין "affliction-water" (1 Kings xxii. 27). The same construction is found in Arabic (with the art.) e. g. aç-çanam udh-dhahabu "the gold-image," aç-çulbān ul-khashbu "the

8 Moreover the word of the LORD came unto me, saying,
9 The hands of Zerubbabel have laid the foundation of this house; his hands shall also finish it; and thou shalt know that the LORD of hosts hath sent me unto you.

wood-crosses."—תְּשֻׁאוֹת "with shoutings," it is the acc. of nearer definition, comp. פֶּה אֶחָד "with one mouth" (1 Kings xxii. 13). But one cannot state definitely, whether it is in the *absol.* or the *constr.* state, because (1) such substantives are of the same form in both states, (2) either construction is admissible, viz. apposition, "With shouts, 'Grace! Grace! to it'" (see above in this note); or annexation, "With shouts of 'Grace, Grace! to it,'" as (Ps. lxxxi. 5) שְׂפַת לֹא יָדַעְתִּי אֶשְׁמָע "the saying of 'I know not [the LORD, Ex. v. 2]' I will take cognizance of."—*Chên,* see xii. 10.

It is by no means unusual to find the LXX. treating Hebr. words, as though they were Aramaic: τοῦ κατορθῶσαι is an instance of this. They have taken לְמֵישַׁר as the Aram. infin. of יָשַׁר or אֲשַׁר; the student will understand this, when he is told that לְמֵימַר is the Aram. for לֵאמֹר.—הָרֹאשָׁה τῆς κληρονομίας, reading the word, apparently, הַיְרֵאשָׁה, comp. יְרֵשָׁה (Numb. xxiv. 18) LXX. κληρονομία. Aq. for *hârōshâh* gives τὸν πρωτεύοντα.—ἰσότητα χάριτος χάριτα αὐτῆς, *Lâh* is taken as the simple possessive, thus χάριτα αὐτῆς represents *chên lâh:* ἰσότητα χάριτος represents תְּשֻׁאוֹת חֵן, the first of these two words being pronounced *Tashvîth,* a noun from the verb שָׁוָה *æquavit,* of the form of תַּבְלִית from בָּלָה, תַּכְלִית from כָּלָה. (This noun in Aram. is generally used of the thing smoothed, e.g. pavement, pillow, bed.) Aq. has ἐξισώσει χάριτος, and Syr. and Vulg. refer the word to the same root.

The note attached to תִּבְצַעֶנָה means that it has *pathach* although with *ethnâch.* This form (when from verbs third root-letter ע or ה) always takes *pathach* in this syllable, e.g. תִּבְקָעֶנָה (2 Kings ii. 24), תִּפְלַחְנָה (Job xxxix. 3), תִּשְׁלַחְנָה (ibidem) and even other verbs, which would otherwise have *çērē* (like תְּדַבֵּרְנָה, תִּמָּהַרְנָה, תִּשָּׁבֵרְנָה) take *pathach* in pause, as: תִּנְאַפְנָה (Hos. iv.

10 For who hath despised the day of small things? for they shall rejoice, and shall see the plummet in the hand of Zerubbabel *with* those seven; they *are* the eyes of the LORD, which run to and fro through the whole earth.

13, 14), תִּרְטַשְׁנָה (Is. xiii. 18), : תֵּעָבַסְנָה (Is. iii. 16). On the accentuation of *v'yâda'tâ* see note on i. 3. For the change from the 2nd pers. *sing.* to 2nd *plur.* comp. Lev. xxv. 14, Mich. i. 11. The LXX. has here deliberately put both in the sing.

Verse 10. Words.

בָּז is the 3rd pers. perf. (instead of בַּז from בּוּז) formed as if from בָּזז, comp. מַח (for מַט) Is. xliv. 18 (on confusion of Rts. see p. 30). Since there is no neuter gender in Hebr. the fem. is often used to supply its place either in the sing. as (Numb. xxii. 18) *q'tannâh ô g'dôlâh* "any thing great or small," or in the plur. as here (comp. *qâshôth* Gen. xlii. 7, 30). LXX. gives wrongly ἡμέρας μικράς.

Constructions.

On *hâ'ebhen habb'dîl* see note on ver. 7.—Bunsen translates this verse "For they who have despised the day of small things, they will rejoice and see the lead-stone in the hand of Zerubbabel; these seven are the eyes of YHVH roaming through the whole earth." This rendering is grammatically defensible, comp. Gen. xliv. 9 (quoted in note on xiv. 17), כִּי being used (comp. Ex. xxiv. 14, Judg. vii. 3) indefinitely "whosoever" as equivalent to מִי אֲשֶׁר (Ex. xxxii. 33). But it would be a strange thing for the Prophet to promise joy to mockers. Köhler renders *v'sâm'chû*, &c. "while these seven see with joy," &c.; but this is an impossible translation, since in a clause descriptive of the state or circumstance beginning with *vâv*, the *vâv* is usually prefixed to the subject, e.g. וְהַמַּחֲנֶה הָיָה בֶטַח "the camp being in confident security" (1 Kings i. 40), but never to the Perfect.—The first clause "For, who hath despised the day of small things?" denotes: "surely none (who hopes to achieve great things) ever despised the day of small things!", and so is practically equivalent to a prohibition: "Let none despise the day of small things." After such a clause the perfect with *vâv* denotes the result of compliance with the prohibition, "Then shall they see with joy the plummet in the hands of Zerubbabel, [viz.] these seven." Of the two verbs וְרָאוּ וְשָׂמְחוּ the former is best rendered by the adverbial expression "with joy," comp. (v. 1) וָאָשׁוּב וָאֶשָּׂא "and I lifted up again," וָאַעַן וָאֹמַר might similarly be rendered "and I said in reply." The last half of the verse should be rendered "The eyes of YHVH, they are scouring the whole earth"; or, neglect-

11 Then answered I, and said unto him, What *are* these two olive trees upon the right *side* of the candlestick and upon the left *side* thereof?

12 And I answered again, and said unto him, What *be these* two olive branches which through the two golden pipes empty the golden *oil* out of themselves?

---

ing the interpunctuation, we might render the words "The eyes of YHVH are they, scouring the whole world" (for this constr. of the partic. see iii. 1), comp. LXX. ἑπτὰ οὗτοι ὀφθαλμοί εἰσιν κυρίου οἱ ἐπιβλέποντες. They ought, however, to have omitted the art. before the partic., comp. LXX. of vi. 1. In either case the last half of the verse is a farther description of "these seven." It need hardly be said that *shibh'āh-ēlleh 'ênê YHVH* cannot mean "these seven eyes of YHVH," which would have been שִׁבְעַת (שִׁבְעָה) or עֵינֵי י״י הָאֵלֶּה, or עֵינֵי י״י הָאֵלֶּה שִׁבְעָתָם (comp. Dan. i. 17).

מַה־שְּׁתִּי, see Excurs. IV.—The sing. שִׁבֹּלֶת "a stream" (Ps. lxix. 16), "ear of corn" (Job xxiv. 24), makes plur. שִׁבֳּלִים (comp. צִפּוֹר plur. צִפֳּרִים). The construct (which occurs here only) is pointed שִׁבֲּלֵי (not שִׁבְּלֵי) by one of those irregularities of traditional pronunciation, for which no reason can be assigned. The word seems to mean here "pendent bunches of olives."—It is impossible (with C. H. H. Wright) to render the next clause "which by means of the two channels of gold are pouring forth, &c.," for in that case we should have had מְרִיקִים, not הַמְרִיקִים, since the clause is introduced by אֲשֶׁר.—צַנְתְּרוֹת is a ἅπ. λεγό. meaning probably "spouts" (see Dictionaries); it is masc., as is shown by the numeral. This clause we render: "which are resting in the two golden spouts."—בְּיַד must mean "in the hand of," i.e. resting in; but see note on vii. 7. It can hardly mean "by the side of," for the figurative expression בְּיָדוֹ נָכוֹן "nigh at hand" (Job xv. 23) will not justify the rendering. To express this it would have been rather עַל (ver. 14), לְיַד (1 Sam. xix. 3), בְּעַד יַד (1 Sam. iv. 18), אֶל יַד (2 Sam. xiv. 30), עַל יַד (Josh. xv. 46), or עַל יְדֵי (Judg. xi. 26).—הַזָּהָב is a ἅπ. λεγό. in the sense of "the gold[en oil]." The clause should be rendered "which pour the golden oil out from themselves," grammatically it refers to the spouts, not to the olive-clusters (which are *fem.*).

13 And he answered me and said, Knowest thou not what these *be*? And I said, No, my lord.

14 Then said he, These *are* the two anointed ones, that stand by the Lord of the whole earth.

B'yád, ἐν ταῖς χερσί.—For the ἅπ. λεγό. *Çant'róth* they give μυξωτήρων.

LXX. המריקים מעליהם הזהב— they render τῶν ἐπιχεόντων καὶ ἀπαναγόντων τὰς ἐπαρυστρίδας τὰς χρυσᾶς· to them, as to us, *hazzāhábh* is a difficulty: we solve it by supposing "the gold" to mean "the golden oil"; they by understanding it as "golden pipes (or funnels)" (comp. ver. 2). καὶ ἀπαναγόντων evidently corresponds to מעליהם, which they seem to have read as ומעלים the Hiph. Partic. of *'āláh* "to go up."

Verse 14. Words.
יצהר is a substantive of the same form as the proper name יצחק "Isaac." This word is nowhere else used of oil-for-anointing. It is used to denote oil as the juice of the olive, the produce of the ground, just as *tīrósh* is used of wine as the produce of the vine. But *yáin* is used of wine fermented for drinking, and *shémen* of oil prepared for burning (שֶׁמֶן לַמָּאוֹר), or for anointing (שֶׁמֶן הַמִּשְׁחָה). On the metheg of *hā'ōm'dīm* see Excurs. II. A. 9.—על denotes "by," see on ver. 3.

Remarks.
It can scarcely be doubted, that the prototype of this golden candlestick is the candlestick, which was placed in the holy place of the former Sanctuaries "before the Lord, as an everlasting statute for their generations on behalf of the children of Israel" (Ex. xxvii. 21). This Candlestick is not mentioned among the vessels of the Sanctuary brought back from the Captivity. It may be that it was the very lack of this important article of the Temple furniture, that impressed the form of it on the Prophet's mind. Be this as it may, the form of Candlestick of the Vision is evidently based on that of the Temple, and Tabernacle. But, at the same time, that of the Vision differs in several points from the other. In the Candlestick of old the lamps had need to be trimmed every evening, by the Priests, while in this the oil poured itself spontaneously from two olive-clusters, and was communicated to the lamps by such a number of pipes, as in an actual lamp would seem almost impossible. The angel-interpreter declares that the significance of the Vision is this: that all difficulties should subside before Zerubbabel, and that he should complete the building of the Temple, and bring forth the head-stone thereof with shouts of "Grace, grace to it!" But, this was to take place by no human power (such as was used for keeping the lamps of the Candlestick alight in former times), but by the Unction from the Holy One: "Not by might, nor by power, but by my Spirit, saith the Lord of Hosts." "Do not then," says the direct revelation of the Lord, "despise the small beginnings of the work, and then the eyes of God's all-embracing Providence, which are specially directed on this

work of rebuilding (iii. 9), will yet view with benign satisfaction the completion of this material building by the hand of Zerubbabel." But, as though the Lord looked with pity on the weakness of human faith, and to explain the meaning of the *two* olive-clusters, He deigns to reveal to the Prophet the two human instruments by which this work was to be consummated, saying " These (the two olive-clusters) are the two anointed ones," i.e. Zerubbabel the Prince of the House of David, the civil head, and Joshua, the High-Priest, the religious head. Thus should this Building be completed. And, as the Candlestick of old had been a symbol of the diffusion of the light of Divine Truth by the Congregation of Israel, whose duty it was (and ever is) to be witnesses to the Truth of the Unity of God, so should this new Building become the centre, whence should go forth the Light to lighten the Gentiles, and to be the Glory of His People Israel. (Comp. the close connection in ch. iii. between the assurance of God's providential care of the work of building, and the promise of the mission of the Messiah.)

CHAPTER V.

THEN I turned, and lifted up mine eyes, and looked, and behold a flying roll.

2 And he said unto me, What seest thou? And I answered, I see a flying roll; the length thereof *is* twenty cubits, and the breadth thereof ten cubits.

SIXTH VISION.—*a.* THE FLYING SCROLL. *β.* THE WOMAN IN THE EPHAH. *γ.* THE TWO WOMEN WITH STORKS' WINGS.

Translate " and I lifted up mine eyes again," see note on iv. 10.— עָפָה (which we know to be a *participle* from its being accentuated *mil'ra'*, see note on ver. 4, and on xiv. 18) may be taken as merely an epithet, "a flying scroll," or better, perhaps, as denoting the circumstance or state, "a scroll, flying" (comp. iii. 1, vi. 1, 5). *Verse 1.*

LXX. for *M'gillâh* have δρέπανον, understanding the word in the sense of מַגָּל "a sickle." Aquila and Theodotion διφθέρα. Gr. Versions. Symm. κεφαλίς, *var. lect.* εἴλημα.

From the wording of this verse the reader will perceive the force of our note on the *Q'rî* and *C'thîbh* of iv. 2.—The expression באמה "[measured] by the ammah" is common (comp. Ex. xxvi. 8, &c.). עֶשֶׂר (masc. עֶשְׂרָה) is *fem.* to agree with *ammôth* understood in the *bâ'ammâh*. *Verse 2.*

3 Then said he unto me, This *is* the curse that goeth forth over the face of the whole earth: for every one that stealeth shall be cut off *as* on this side according to it; and every one that sweareth shall be cut off *as* on that side according to it.

4 I will bring it forth, saith the LORD of hosts, and it shall enter

---

Verse 3. Translation and Construction.

I would render thus: "For every one that stealeth, on the one hand, shall in accordance therewith be certainly destroyed: and every one that sweareth [falsely], on the other hand, shall in accordance therewith be certainly destroyed." מזה...מזה can, surely, only be taken as contrasted one to the other. In Ex. xi. 1, where *mizzéh...mizzéh* occurs, the construction is so utterly different, that it affords no parallel. For the expression used in the sense of "on this side and on that" comp. Ex. xxxii. 15, Num. xxii. 24, Ezk. xlviii. 7. Arnswald says that *mizzéh...mizzéh* cannot mean "on this and that side of the roll," because *zéh* is masc. while *m'gillāh* is fem. But (Ex. xxv. 19) ועשה כרוב אחד מקצה מזה וכרוב־אחד מקצה מזה מן הכפרת... shows that this reason for rejecting that translation is invalid. We reject it on different grounds, viz. that the words do not express that meaning: to have done so they should have been כל...ככתוב עליה מזה נקה וכל...ככתוב עליה מזה נקה. The explanation of Koehler, &c., that *mizzéh* in both cases means "from hence," viz. from the land (comp. Gen. xxxvii. 17, Ex. xi. 1, Deut. xi. 12), is precluded by the evident contrast between *mizzéh* and *mizzéh* implied by the collocation.

Versions.

LXX. rightly for *hā'ālāh* ἡ ἀρά.—Symm. οἱ ὅρκοι.—Aq. ὡσαύτως, reading, apparently, כְּאָלָה. The last half of the verse is rendered as follows by LXX.: διότι πᾶς ὁ κλέπτης ἐκ τούτου ἕως θανάτου ἐκδικηθήσεται, καὶ πᾶς ὁ ἐπίορκος ἐκ τούτου ἕως θανάτου ἐκδικηθήσεται (Cod. Vat. incorrectly omits ἕως θανάτου in the second case). They, no doubt, read מזה as מָוֶת, as in Is. liii. 8 they read the מן of *lāmō* as מָוֶת. They may have rendered כ as ἕως, comp. 1 Sam. xv. 7 (LXX. Βασ. α'. 15. 7, Tisch. reads ὡς), Ps. lx. 7 כְּמוֹ (cod. Kenn. 15. 6 כִּימֵי), LXX. 61. 7 ἕως ἡμέρας. Or they may have read כמוה as לְמוֹת (see note on LXX. ch. x. 12). With regard to נקה it must be observed that it is not elsewhere used (in the Niph.) of a person being destroyed,

into the house of the thief, and into the house of him that sweareth falsely by my name: and it shall remain in the midst of his house, and shall consume it with the timber thereof and the stones thereof.

though it is found (Is. iii. 25 וְנִקָּתָה, LXX. καταλειφθήσῃ μόνη) of a city being laid waste. The Targ. gives לָקֵי (*vapulans*) "being judicially-smitten," giving practically the right meaning, and preserving to a certain extent, if not the original word, at any rate the sound of it. They may have taken נקה as a Niph. partic.; or as an Imperf. (see *Fragment of T. B. P^esachim*, pp. 1—8); or as equivalent to לקה, cf. לשכה and נשכה, even in Bibl. Hebr. There is no reason for supposing (with Gesen.) that they read the word as נָכָּה. The LXX. give essentially the same rendering, either from the Targum or collateral tradition, or translating in accordance with the context. Symm. δίκην δώσει.

Verse 4. Words.

וּבָאָה...וְלָנָה. These words are both accentuated *mil'êl* (see note on page 16), consequently they are the 3rd pers. fem. Perfect, not the Pres. Partic. (see note on xiv. 18). לָנֶה stands for לָנָה, and this is the only instance of final *āh* becoming *eh* in the Perfect; but, in the Imperf. we have אֶקְרָאֶה (1 Sam. xxviii. 15), יְדֻשְׁנֶה (Ps. xx. 3); in a fem. partic. pass. זוּרָה (Is. xxxix. 5). The case of the substantive צֹנֶה (Ps. viii. 7) is not parallel: for, in the first place, if this stood for צֹאנָה we should have expected it to have been accentuated on the first syllable (see note on *láy'lah* i. 8); secondly, the form צֹנַאֲכֶם (Numb. xxxii. 24) points to a collateral form צֹנֶא or צֹנֶה. Note that while in Arab. *ḍā'in* (ضائن) means "a single sheep," and the plur. *ḍa'n* (ضأن)[1] means "sheep," there is also a verb *ḍana-a* (ضنأ), one meaning of which is (according to Freytag) "multa fuerunt (pecora)."— Since *Báyith* "house" is masc., the suffix of *Cillátta* (3rd fem. Perf. Pi'el of כלה) is masc. to agree with it. The only instances of the

---

[1] It is quite within the bounds of possibility that many Hebr. nouns which we call "collectives" are in reality "broken plurals."

5 Then the angel that talked | me, Lift up now thine eyes, and
with me went forth, and said unto | see what *is* this that goeth forth.

3rd masc. suffix with the 3rd fem. Perfect of verbs quiescent ל״ה are this כִּלָּתִי, and הִטַּתּוּ Hiph. of נטה (Prov. vii. 21). The (usual) form of the 3rd fem. Perfect, with 3rd masc. suffix, in the Qal, Hiph. and Polel, is in *áth-hû*, e.g. גְּמָלַתְהוּ (Prov. xxxi. 12), הֶחֱזִקַתְהוּ (Jer. l. 43), רְמָמַתְהוּ (Ezk. xxxi. 4), but with the Pi'el it is *always* *áttû*, as יִסְּרַתּוּ (Prov. xxxi. 1), וּבְעִתַּתּוּ (1 Sam. xvi. 14), זֵהֲמַתּוּ (Job xxxiii. 20). The full form of the 3rd fem. Perfect is that which occurs in Pause, viz. *gāmālāh*, when this takes the suffix it reverts to its older form in *t*, viz. *gāmālat*. Now observe how, in accordance with the rule given in note on iv. 1, when the accent leaves *má* and falls on *lát*, the vowel third from the accentuated syllable goes away, and we get *g'mālāth'i*. The next example cited, viz. *hech'ziqáth-hu*[1], is an instance of a word in which both the second and third vowels from the accent are immoveable. In all the other cases the third vowel (from the accent) is immoveable, but the second has been removed.

וַיֵּצֵא, contrast the position of the tone in וַיֵּשֶׁב (iv. 1). The reason
<small>Verse 5.</small> of this difference is, that all verbs, whose last *root*-letter is א, retain the tone on the ultimate even with *vâv conversive*, and are, therefore, an exception to the general rule given in our note on i. 9. Thus all such forms from בוא are *mil'ra'*, e.g. וַיָּבֹא (Gen. vii. 7), וַתָּבֹא (viii. 11), and Hiph. וַיָּבִיא (Neh. viii. 2), וַיָּבִיא (Ezk. xl. 3), but commonly וַיָּבֵא; and so וַיָּקֵא (Jon. ii. 11) from קיא. And thus also וַיִּירָא (Gen. xxviii. 17) from ירא, and from יצא, Qal וַתֵּצֵא, וַיֵּצֵא (Gen. iv. and xxx. 16), Hiph. וַיּוֹצֵא (Gen. xv. 5), וַיֵּצֵא (Judg. xix. 15), וַתֵּצֵא (Gen. i. 12).—But forms, which end in א on account of the apoc. of the final ה, are *mil'él* according to rule, e.g. וַיֵּרְא

---

[1] A *sh'va*, be it quiescent or moving, simple or compound, is not a vowel, or a semivowel, nor does it ever count in grammar as a syllable. It is merely a sign to show that there is *no vowel* belonging to the consonant under which it is placed.

6 And I said, What *is* it? And he said, This *is* an ephah that goeth forth. He said moreover, This *is* their resemblance through all the earth.

7 And, behold, there was lifted

(Ps. xviii. 11) from דָאָה, וַתֵּלֶא (Job iv. 5) from לָאָה; also וַיֵּתֵא (Deut. xxxiii. 21), an anomalous form from אָתָה or אָתָא.—"What is this that goeth forth?" would be properly *mah-zzôth hayyōçéth*, our text מָה הַיּוֹצֵאת הַזֹּאת denotes "what is this goer-forth?" in which two sentences there is a distinction of phraseology, but hardly a difference of meaning. "What is this going forth?" would be *mah-zzôth yōçéth*.

LXX. καὶ ἴδε τὸ ἐκπορευόμενον τοῦτο, taking מָה as indefinite (comp. p. 46, and LXX. ix. 17), which is impossible in this collocation.

"And I said: 'What is it?' And he said: 'This is an ephah which is going forth: this (continued he) is their appearance in all the earth.'" The use of the def. art. with *ēphâh* is that which writers on the New Test. call *monadic*. The def. art. in such a case denotes merely *a* chance specimen of *the* known class. Thus *hâ'ēphâh* here denotes "a specimen of the thing, you know so well, viz. the ephah-class." This is a distinct Hebraism. It is common in the Mishnah (see my *Fragment of T. B. P*sachim*, p. 95, note 36), as well as in Bibl. Hebr. In the Talmudim and Midrashim the idiom becomes still more marked, and we have not "the" but "*that*" to denote τις. Thus, while הַהוּא גַבְרָא may mean "that man" (in which sense it is often used to denote "I" (or "thou"), like ἀνὴρ ὅδε, and ὅδ' ἀνήρ, as equivalent to ἐγώ), it very generally stands merely for ἀνήρ τις.—For *vayyômer* used parenthetically comp. ver. 8, and note on iv. 2 *C*thîbh*.—For עַיִן in the sense of "appearance" comp. (Numb. xi. 7) וְעֵינוֹ כְּעֵין הַבְּדֹלַח "and its appearance was like that of bdellium" (comp. Lev. xiii. 55).

Verse 6. Translation and Construction.

For עֵינָם LXX. has ἀδικία αὐτῶν, reading עֲוֹנָם. Jerome observes that if the Hebr. word had *vav* instead of *yod* "recte legeretur onam ut LXX. putaverunt." He seems to have thought that עָוֹן was of the form of אָוֶן, and made constr. עֲוֹן (see note on תֹּךְ p. 25). Symm. paraphrases πρὸς τοῦτο ἀποβλέπουσι.

Versions.

Ciccár is the constr. of Ciccár (which is a contraction of the unused Circár, comp. כּוֹכָב which stands for כַּבְכָּב). The word is fem. see (2 Kings v. 5) עֶשֶׂר כִּכְּרֵי כֶסֶף. It has two plurals כִּכָּרִים in the sense of "talents," and כִּכְּרוֹת לֶחֶם "cakes of

Verse 7. Words, Constr. and Transl.

up a talent of lead: and this *is* a woman that sitteth in the midst of the ephah.

8 And he said, This *is* wickedness. And he cast it into the midst of the ephah; and he cast the weight of lead upon the mouth thereof.

---

bread" (Judg. viii. 5).—נְשֵׂאת must be taken as the Niph. Partic. fem. like נִפְלֵאת (Deut. xxx. 11); and so too must it be in כִּי נִשֵּׂאת (1 Chron. xiv. 2); unless we point the word נְשֻׂאת after the form נִפְלְאָת (Ps. cxviii. 23), comp. נִשְׁבַּחַת (Is. xxiii. 15), נִרְפָּאתָה¹ (Jer. li. 9 *Q'ri*), נִפְלְאָתָה (2 Sam. i. 26).—וְזֹאת may be easily explained, if only we follow the context and the rules of grammar. It cannot be taken as equivalent to הִנֵּה, "[and I looked] and behold one woman," because (1) זֹאת is never so used, (2) throughout the visions זֶה, זֹאת, אֵלֶּה always introduce an explanation of the angel interpreter. This verse, and the first clause of the next one, are merely a continuation of the angel's words. In verse 7 he points out to the Prophet the scene that was passing before his eyes, and in the beginning of verse 8 he explains its import. The angel says, "And behold (i.e. and you may see) a disc of lead being lifted up, and this [which you now see on the removal of the disc] is a woman sitting in the midst of the ephah, and this (continued he) is Wickedness."— *Isshâh acháth* might be rendered "a certain woman" as אִישׁ אֶחָד (1 Sam. i. 1) "a certain man" (*τις*); but such a translation would be unsuitable here. Or it may be taken as "*one* woman." Or *acháth* may be used merely as the indef. article, as (Dan. viii. 3) אַיִל אֶחָד "a ram."

Verse 8.

הָרִשְׁעָה as a very personification of Wickedness, so (2 Chron. xxiv. 7) הַמִּרְשַׁעַת is applied to Athaliah.—וַיַּשְׁלֵךְ, the singl. imperf. of the Hiph. with *vâv conversx.* (as a general rule) takes ē instead of î in the second syllable, comp. וַיַּבְדֵּל (Gen. i. 4), but not so the plur. (usually), thus וַיַּבְדִּילוּ (Ezek. xxxix. 14). The angel-interpreter seems to be the agent.—The use of the def. art. identifies the אֶבֶן הָעוֹפֶרֶת with the כִּכַּר עֹפֶרֶת mentioned above: *ébhen* denotes

---

¹ The *C'thibh* should be read נִרְפָּתָה from רפא=רפה. Stade, *Gramm.* I. p. 211, gives, strangely enough, the vowels of the *Q'ri* with the consonants of the *C'thibh*.

9 Then lifted I up mine eyes, and looked, and, behold, there came out two women, and the wind *was* in their wings; for they had wings like the wings of a stork: and they lifted up the ephah between the earth and the heaven.

10 Then said I to the angel that talked with me, Whither do these bear the ephah?

11 And he said unto me, To build it an house in the land of Shinar: and it shall be established, and set there upon her own base.

---

here "a weight" as in Deut. xxv. 13, Prov. xvi. 11.—The prepositions אֶל and עַל are, in many of their meanings, interchangeable, comp. e.g. Is. xxix. 11, 12; 2 Sam. xx. 23, 1 Sam. xiv. 32, 33, 34.—*Pîhā* denotes "its mouth," viz. of the ephah, comp. פִּי הַבְּאֵר (Gen. xxix. 2).

וְרוּחַ בְּכַנְפֵיהֶם a nominal clause introducing a further fact "and the wind was in their wings," comp. vi. 1. The phrase seems to be the Hebr. equivalent of the English nautical expression "bore down on," i.e. approached sailing before the wind. Observe the *masc.* suffix; comp. הֵמָּה for הֵנָּה (ver. 10); and Ruth i. 8, 9.—*C'naphaim* is the dual (see note on p. 20), לָהֵנָּה for the usual לָהֶן, so we have (Jer. xix. 16) לָהֵמָּה for the usual לָהֶם: the form for 2nd pers. fem. is לָכֵנָה, apparently to distinguish it from לָכֵן "therefore."—חֲסִידָה is "a stork"; in later times to distinguish the fem. of חָסִיד "pious" from *ch'sīdāh* "a stork," the form חֲסוּדָה was used, e.g. (T. B. *C'thubboth* 17ᵃ) וְתִשָּׁנֶה.—כַּלָּה נָאָה וַחֲסוּדָה for וְתִשָּׁאנָה (on the *sīmān rāphēh* see Excurs. IV.).—*Bēn...ūbhēn* (Gen. i. 4) or *bēn...l* (i. 6) "between...and."

Verse 9.

לָהּ is softened for לָה and therefore the בּ of the following word is without *dagesh lene* (see Excurs. III. and IV.).—הוּכַן is the Hoph. Perf. 3rd Pers. *masc.* (from כּוּן) though it agrees with a *fem.* subject (comp. xiii. 8).—From נוּחַ we have two Hiph. forms הֵנִיחַ "he gave rest" (Is. xiv. 3), and הִנִּיחַ "he placed" (ver. 1). The Hoph. Partic. from the latter is מֻנָּח (Ezek. xli. 9). Now the Hoph. Perf. 3rd fem. ought to be הֻנְּחָה, this being pronounced *hunn'chāh* might have passed into *hunnīchāh* (for instances of the common use of י in non-biblical MSS. for moving *sh'va* see my *Fragment of T. B. P'sachim*, p. 8, note 2), and then, on account of the following tonic syllable *shām*,

Verse 11.

became *hunníchāh*. On the other hand we find in Biblical Chaldee such a Hophal as הָקִימַת "she was set up" (Dan. vii. 4), so that those have some ground to stand on who call this a Chaldaism[1]. But I prefer my own explanation, since the Hebrew of the Post-captivity Prophets is especially (and intentionally) free from Chaldaisms.

LXX. καὶ ἑτοιμάσαι, either reading וְהוּכַן as the Hiph. וְהֻכַן; or else taking ת for ה (as in ver. 3), and reading וְתֻכַן, which Root they render in 1 Sam. ii. 3, 2 Kings xii. 12 by the verb ἑτοιμάζω.

Remarks. This is but one vision in three dissolving views. (a) The flying scroll denotes the curse upon sinners against the Words of the Two Tables (Exod. xx.). The dimensions of the scroll are those of the Tabernacle in the wilderness, and of the porch of Solomon's Temple. Some commentators consider its measurement to be symbolical. If so, it is best to understand it as meaning, that transgression is not to be measured by man's standard of right and wrong, but by that of the LORD, who deigned to give a special sign of His Presence in the Sanctuary. With verse 4 may be compared the well-known story of Glaucus, and the Delphic oracle concerning *Oath*, who " hath a son nameless, handless, footless, but swift he pursues until he seize and destroy the whole race and house " (Herod. vi. 86). (β) Next a woman, who is Wickedness personified, appears sitting in an ephah. A leaden disc is cast on the mouth of the ephah to prevent her emerging; then (γ) two women, with strong ample wings (the like of which the prophet may have seen in the grotesque figures of Babylon), bear down on the ephah, and carry it off to the land of Shinar, where it is to be finally deposited. This vision appears to be, not only a confirmation of ch. iii. 9, but also an implicit exhortation to the people to leave in the land of their Captivity (the land where mankind first organized a rebellion against God, Gen. xi. 2) the sins, which had caused their deportation thither.

CHAPTER VI.

AND I turned, and lifted up mine eyes, and looked, and, behold, there came four chariots out from between two mountains;

SEVENTH VISION.—THE FOUR CHARIOTS.

In the singl. we have מֶרְכָּב, and מֶרְכָּבָה (ver. 2), but in the plur.

Verse 1. Words and Constructions. always מַרְכָּבוֹת, by the common interchange of *a* and *e* (comp. notes on ix. 5, x. 9). That this change is not caused by the heavy termination of the plur. (as C. H. H. Wright, quoting

[1] Ewald's (§ 131) word הָרִים (Dan. viii. 11) is imaginary on his part, he has read the vowels of the Q'ri with the consonants of the C'thibh; the word is הֲרִים, or הָרַם.

and the mountains *were* mountains of brass.

2 In the first chariot *were* red horses; and in the second chariot black horses;

3 And in the third chariot white horses; and in the fourth chariot grisled and bay horses.

4 Then I answered and said unto the angel that talked with me, What *are* these, my lord?

Koehler, supposes) is shown by the fact, that the plur. of אֶשְׁכֹּל is אֶשְׁכֹּלוֹת (Song of Songs vii. 8, comp. Gen. lx. 10) while the constr. is equally אֶשְׁכְּלוֹת (Deut. xxii. 32) and אַשְׁכְּלוֹת (Song of Songs vii. 9): similarly we have מַלְקָחֶ֫הָ (Numb. iv. 9) and מֶלְקָחֶ֫יהָ (Ex. xxv. 38), comp. the common Rabbinic form of substantive הֶקְדֵּשׁ "that which is devoted to sacred purposes," which is derived from the Hiph. Infin. הַקְדֵּשׁ (comp. note on LXX. xiv. 17).—*V'hehārîm hārê n'chósheth* is a nominal clause, comp. v. 9.

The last-mentioned horses have two epithets applied to them, בְּרֻדִּים אֲמֻצִּים. The latter of these cannot possibly be understood as applying to all the four different coloured horses, since in that case the prophet could only have written אֲמֻצִּים כֻּלָּם. It is strange that two epithets should be applied to one set of horses here, and only one to each of the other sets, both here, and in chap. i. But the greatest difficulties in this passage are (a) that, while in this verse the *B'ruddîm* are identified with the *"muççîm*, in verses 7 and 8 the two are most unmistakably distinguished : and (β) that no mission of the אֲדֻמִּים is mentioned. The Syr., either having a more correct Hebr. text in this passage, or more probably making a conjectural emendation, omits the word *"muççîm* in this verse, and in ver. 7 substitutes וְהָאֲדֻמִּים for וְהָאֲמֻצִּים. And this reading we are compelled to follow, for the present text commits our Prophet to writing in a meaningless style, such as would not be tolerated for a moment in any secular writer. For LXX. see p. 13. For *B'ruddîm* Symm. and Theodotion give πελιδνοί. For *"muççîm* (ver. 3) Aq. has καρτεροί, but in ver. 7 he has πυρροί as though reading, with Syr., *v'hā"dummîm*; in ver. 7 Symm. has συνεσφιγμένοι, and Theod. ἰσχυροί. In the sense of "strong" אֲמֻצִּים would be a ἅπ. λεγό.; but אַמִּיץ (and אָמֵן) is common in this sense (it would, of course, be possible to point אַמִּצִים

Verses 2, 3.

5 And the angel answered and said unto me, These *are* the four spirits of the heavens, which go forth from standing before the Lord of all the earth.

6 The black horses which *are* therein go forth into the north country; and the white go forth after them; and the grisled go forth toward the south country.

7 And the bay went forth, and sought to go that they might walk

ammiçím). If taken in the sense of "red" it is still a ἅπ. λεγό., and must be taken as equivalent to הַמֻצִים, comp. חֲמוּץ בְּגָדִים (Is. lxiii. 1), so Abu-l-Walīd (col. 57), Qimchi (*Sēfer hashshŏrāshīm*), Ewald, &c. Comp. תָּאָרֶץ (1 Chron. viii. 35) for תִּהְרֵעַ (ix. 41). In both verses the Targ. renders *ᵃmuççím* "ash coloured"; Rashi says that he does not know the meaning of the word; Ibn Ezra on ver. 7 remarks that the "*ᵃmuççím* are the *ᵃdummím*," which is certainly the case, by whatever means the result be arrived at.

Arbá' rūchōth hashshāmáim "the four winds of heaven," denoting

Verse 5. Constructions, &c. God's agents working in all the four quarters, i.e. over all the earth.—*Yōçʾōth*, as in ver. 1, describes the state or circumstance.—מֵהִתְיַצֵּב (on the *metheg* see Excurs. II. A. 2) "from standing"; but LXX. give ἐξεπορεύοντο παραστῆναι.—עַל (comp. iv. 14).

Observe that *yōçʾím* "are going forth" agrees by attraction with *hassūsím*, instead of with the real subject of the sentence

Verse 6. which is מֶרְכָּבָה, understood in the אֲשֶׁר בָּהּ, comp. קֶשֶׁת גִּבֹּרִים חַתִּים (1 Sam. ii. 4).—The reason why we have יָצָא twice in this verse and once in the next, instead of יֹצְאִים, is this: that the scene passed so vividly before the mind's eye of the Prophet, that he passes unconsciously from an account of the Angel's explanation of the vision to his own narration of it. LXX. avoid the difficulty by rendering *yōçʾím*, as well as *yāçʾā*, by ἐξεπορεύοντο.—For the expression אֶל אַחֲרֵי with verbs of motion, comp. 2 Sam. v. 23, and סֹב אֶל־אַחֲרָי "turn thou behind me" (2 Kings ix. 18).—תֵּימָן (from יָמִין) denotes the "south," it is found here only with the def. art. (By the Jews *Tēmān* is understood to denote especially that part of Arabia called *Yemen*.)

וַיְבַקְשׁוּ (on the *metheg* see Excurs. II. B. 3), LXX. καὶ ἐπέβλεπον

Verse 7. τοῦ πορεύεσθαι, *var. lect.* καὶ ἐζήτουν καὶ ἐπέβλεπον τοῦ κ.τ.λ. —On the *metheg* on וְתִתְהַלֵּכְנָה see Excurs. II. B. 4.

to and fro through the earth: and he said, Get you hence, walk to and fro through the earth. So they walked to and fro through the earth.

8 Then cried he upon me, and spake unto me, saying, Behold, these that go toward the north country have quieted my spirit in the north country.

"Then cried he upon me," this is an old English expression for "calling by name," "calling out for," "summoning" (comp. "who *calls* on Hamlet?" Shakespear, *Hamlet*, IV. 2. 3; "to *cry* on, or upon" he uses, however, in a different sense, see *As* IV. 3. 150, *Rom.* III. 3. 101); it is as much stronger than "he called me," as *vayyaz'ĕq ōthî* is than *vayyiqrā lî*. וַיִּזְעַק (on the form see note on v. 8) is used of "summoning," "calling together," in Judg. iv. 10, 13, and other forms of the Hiph. in the same sense in 2 Sam. xx. 4. 5.— הֵנִיחוּ " have given rest to," E. V. rightly "have quieted" (see note on v. 11). רוּחַ "spirit" is here used, as in Judg. viii. 3, in the sense of "wrath." For the phrase "to quiet anger" see Ezek. v. 13, xvi. 42, xxiv. 13. LXX. seem to have read וְהֵנִיחוּ, or perhaps rather וַיָּנִיחוּ, since they give καὶ ἀνέπαυσαν.

Remarks. vi. 1—8.

There is no absolute need, on account of the use of the def. art., to understand the "two mountains" as two mountains well known (see notes on i. 8). Since they are spoken of as being "of copper" it is evident that they are *ideal*, rather than *real* mountains. HENGSTENBERG supposes that they represent the power of God, which shields His people; BAUMGARTEN thinks that they symbolize the two central points of the world-power. But, though they are ideal, they had probably their prototype in reality. Thus PRESSEL takes them as Zion and Moriah; WRIGHT as Zion and the Mount of Olives. This last seems the more probable, because the Mount of Olives is spoken of in Zech. xiv. 4, and Mount Zion is represented as the place from which God executes His judgments (Joel iii. 16), and because between them lay the valley of Jehoshaphat, which Joel describes as the judgment-place of the world (iii. 2).—The four chariots are said to be "the four winds of heaven," that is probably, as EWALD says, "they went forth as swiftly as the four winds of heaven into the four parts of the world, driven along, as it were, by the wind-angels as charioteers" (comp. Ps. civ. 4). From ver. 8 we know that, whatever else they were, they were God's agents in executing His just wrath on the nations.—With regard to the difficulties concerning the colours of the horses, which we have mentioned above, HITZIG ascribes them to the carelessness of the writer. But we agree, rather, with MAURER, who suggests that the use of *ămuççim* in ver. 7 (whence probably it crept into ver. 3) is due to a blunder of an early copyist. WRIGHT tries to get over the difficulty by supposing that the *ădummim* signify the Babylonian Empire, and that they were introduced into the vision for completeness' sake, but that they were most suitably (JEROME) passed over in the interpretation, because the day of the real power of Babylon had passed away. He maintains that the *b'ruddim* (ver. 6) are identical with the *ămuççim* (ver. 7), as

9 And the word of the LORD came unto me, saying,

10 Take of *them of* the captivity, even of Heldai, of Tobijah, and of Jedaiah, which are come from Babylon, and come thou the same day, and go into the house of Josiah the son of Zephaniah;

---

they are in ver. 3, as the text now stands. He supposes that the *bᵉruddim* are represented as going forth as directed to the land of the south, and then because they were *ămuççim*, "strong," as asking for further permission to traverse the whole world. But the text will not bear any such interpretation. The *bᵉruddim* (ver. 6) are evidently distinct from the *muççim* (ver. 7). The text is hopelessly corrupt, and can be made intelligible only by adopting the reading (or emendation) of the Syriac. The horses in the chariots are *bay, black, white,* and *iron-grey*. These colours have no symbolical significance. They are used merely as the common colours of horses, and to distinguish one chariot from another. The chariots may denote kingdoms, but certainly not those of Daniel. They are at all events God's instruments of vengeance. Two are sent to the North (viz. *black,* and *white*) because there were *two* powers there to be overcome, the remnant of the old Asshur-Babylonian, and the Medo-Persian. The *grey* go to the South, i.e. to Egypt, which country revolted from Darius, and was reconquered by Xerxes: then after a series of revolts was finally subdued to the Persian power by Ochos, and was afterwards wrested from the hands of Persia by Alexander the Great. The *bay* seek, and obtain, permission to go through all the earth, signifying probably that Israel's Protector would defend them, not only against their ancient enemies, but also against any who should rise up against them from any quarter whatsoever.

The Symbolical Crowning of Joshua.

Lāqṓₐch is the Infin. Absol. used emphatically, and stands for the Infin. followed by the Jussive, or Imperative (comp. iii. 4).

Verse 10. Constructions, &c.

—מֵאֵת and מ (of *mecheldáy*) are identical in meaning (see examples in note on xiv. 17).—גּוֹלָה is properly the fem. of the partic. גֹּלָה (2 Sam. xv. 19), and so is here rightly used of "exiles"; but it is often used for the abstract "exile," e.g. (Ezra iv. 1) בְּנֵי הַגּוֹלָה. On the other hand גָּלוּת is properly abstract, meaning "exile" (see note on ix. 15), but is often used for the concrete "exiles," e.g. Jer. xxiv. 5.— *Ubhāthā attāh bayyṓm hahū'* "and enter thou thyself that very day." *Ubhāthā* (*mil'ra‘*) is the Perf. with *rāv convers.* (see note on *vᵉāmartā* p. 5), it follows naturally after the Imperative implied in לְקוֹחַ (see pp. 5, 6). The "thou" and "on that day" are emphatic.—וּבָאתָ is, equally with the *ubhāthā* above, the Perfect with *rāv convers.*, but it is accentuated on the penultimate on account of the *dis*junctive accent, *l'bkī"* (see (2) in the note on p. 5). The *ubhāthā* is repeated, because

ZECHARIAH VI. 11.

11 Then take silver and gold, | upon the head of Joshua the son
and make crowns, and set *them* | of Josedech, the high priest;

---

the insertion of the words *attāh bayyôm hahū'* has separated the word too far from בֵּית. In such a case, if we are to translate the idiom of one language into that of the other, the *vāv* would be best rendered into English by "I say": thus, "and thou thyself shalt enter that same day, thou shalt enter (I say) into the house of, &c." (comp. vii. 3, viii. 23, 2 Sam. xiv. 4).—On the *dagesh* in בֵּית see Excurs. III. 1.—On the construction of בֵּית with the verb בּוֹא &c. see note on xi. 13. Grammatically it would be possible to render אֲשֶׁר־בָּאוּ "into which they have entered," viz. the house. But, since "from Babylon" follows, such a rendering would be harsh. It would perhaps be better, therefore, to refer this relative sentence to the persons mentioned in the first half of the verse, and to translate it "who are come from Babylon." But this construction is, also, inelegant.

Mē'ēth haggōlāh...yᵉda'yāh, LXX. τὰ ἐκ τῆς αἰχμαλωσίας παρὰ τῶν ἀρχόντων, καὶ παρὰ τῶν χρησίμων αὐτῆς, καὶ παρὰ τῶν ἐπεγνωκότων αὐτήν, translating the names. חֶלְדִּי they took as a plur. (comp. xi. 17); but why they should have given it the meaning of ἀρχόντων it is difficult to imagine. *Tōbhiyyāh* they read as טוֹבִיָּה and referred the suffix to *gōlāh*: and *yᵉda'yāh* as יְדָעֶיהָ. Field (*Hexapla*) notes that some copies give the words as proper names; but this, no doubt, is to be accounted for as a later attempt to correct the LXX. text from the Hebr.—Aquila gives them as proper names.—ªshér bā'ū LXX. read in the *singl.*, and make it agree with *Yōshiyyāh*, τοῦ ἥκοντος. Might *bā'ū*, perhaps, have been intended to refer to *Yōshiyyāh*, and have been attracted into the plural by the number of the names which precede? <small>Greek Versions.</small>

On the *tone* of *vᵉlāqachtā*, *vᵉ'āsîthā*, *vᵉsamtā* see p. 5.—On the *metheg* on *cèseph-v'zāhābh* see Excurs. II. A. 2.—On the *shᵉva* under the *vāv* of *v'zāhābh* see note on xiv. 4.—Since the Prophet has used no pronoun after *vᵉsamtā* it is impossible to say for certain whether עֲטָרוֹת means "crowns," or a "composite-crown" (comp. *machᵃlāṣôth* iii. 4). The latter seems the more probable conjecture, because (α) but one head is mentioned, on which "*ᵃṭārôth* should be placed, (β) the word is construed (ver. 14) with a *singular* verb following it, and moreover, in Job xxxi. 36 אֲעַנְדֶנּוּ עֲטָרוֹת לִי "I would <small>Verse 11. Words.</small>

ZECHARIAH VI. 12, 13.

12 And speak unto him, saying, Thus speaketh the LORD of hosts, saying, Behold the man whose name is The BRANCH; and he shall grow up out of his place, and he shall build the temple of the LORD;

13 Even he shall build the temple of the LORD; and he shall bear the glory, and shall sit and rule upon his throne; and he shall be a priest upon his throne: and the counsel of peace shall be between them both.

---

bind it me as a crown," it seems to be used of a single crown, or fillet. This word (in the singl.) is sometimes used of a royal crown, e.g. (2 Sam. xii. 30) עֲטֶרֶת־מַלְכָּם "their king's crown" (on the *metheg* see Excurs. II. A. 2). LXX. have here στεφάνους.

Verse 12. Words, &c. אִישׁ not "*the* man," but "a man of distinction" (comp. Is. xxxii. 12, Zech. viii. 23), ἀνήρ (but see note on xiii. 5).—וּ is placed before *mittachtáv* because the preceding clause includes the idea of some such word as בָּא "is coming" (see note on ii. 10).— מִתַּחְתָּיו denotes "from his place," the expression is found again only in Ex. x. 23, comp. *tachtéhā* "in her place" (Zech. xii. 6, xiv. 10).— Observe the intentional use of the verb *yiçmách* with the name *Çémach*. —The verb בנה is used figuratively, comp. (Gen. xvi. 2) אוּלַי אִבָּנֶה מִמֶּנָּה "perhaps I shall be built up of her." The expression *hēcál YHVH* is also used figuratively (see Remarks below), as are also בֵּית י״י (Hos. viii. 1), and בַּיִת (Hos. ix. 15, Numb. xii. 7), viz. of the spiritual community of Israel (comp. οἶκος Θεοῦ Heb. iii. 6, 1 Tim. iii. 15).

Verse 13. Words and Constructions. The וְהוּא is in both cases emphatic, and is used to distinguish *Çémach* from the crowned High-Priest, who merely prefigured him. The verse should be rendered: "Yea *He* will build the temple of *YHVH* [i.e. *He* will be the *true* builder], and *He* will bear majesty, and will sit and rule upon His Throne, and will be a Priest upon His Throne, and a Counsel of Peace will be between Them twain." The expression בֵּין שְׁנֵיהֶם is difficult. We see no way of interpreting it, except of the only two Persons mentioned in the verse, viz. *YHVH* and the Priest-King (but see Versions and Remarks). We should rather have expected the expression בֵּינוֹ וּבֵין אֱלֹהָיו "between Him and His God": as the words stand they must have sounded most enigmatical to the Prophet's hearers. הוֹד, while it is employed in a variety of other significations, is especially used of royal majesty (Ps. xxi. 6, Jer. xxii. 18, Dan. xi. 21).—It seems more natural to take the suff. of *cis'ô* "His throne" as referring to

ZECHARIAH VI. 14.

14 And the crowns shall be to Helem, and to Tobijah, and to Jedaiah, and to Hen the son of Zephaniah, for a memorial in the temple of the LORD.

---

the Subject of the whole sentence, than to refer it to *YHVH*. כִּסֵּא (which seems to have been originally a quadrilateral, comp. Arab. *cursiy*, Syr. *cūrsyō*) means an ordinary seat (1 Sam. i. 9, iv. 13), where it is accidental that it was a High-Priest who is mentioned as sitting on it. But the word is used chiefly of a royal throne, e.g. הַכִּסֵּא (Gen. xli. 40), כִּסֵּא מַמְלַכְתּוֹ (Deut. xvii. 18), &c.—כֹּהֵן sometimes means "a prince" (as in 2 Sam. viii. 8), but the expression "High-Priest" (ver. 11) precludes that interpretation here.—Another rendering of the last half of the verse is grammatically admissible, viz. "And there shall be a priest near his throne, and a counsel of peace shall be between them twain" (comp. LXX.). For this use of עַל comp. iv. 14. This rendering has one advantage over the other, viz. that the interpretation of *bēn sh'nēhĕm* is rendered easier, by supposing the King and the Priest to be different persons. But, on the other hand, since the construction of *v'hāyāh* is exactly the same as that of *v'yāshābh* and *umāshāl*, it seems much more natural to suppose that the subject of *v'hāyāh* is the same as that of the other verbs (see Remarks).

Targum paraphrases ver. 12 thus: "Lo the man, The Messiah His name, is destined to be revealed and anointed [comp. *Targ. Y.*, Lev. iv. 3, &c.], and shall build the temple of *YHVH*." The next verse is literally rendered, as we have done (but there are two readings "and shall be a *High*-Priest," or "and shall be a *ministering* Priest"). Syr. omits the last words of ver. 12 *ubhānāh eth-hēcāl YHVH*, while LXX. omits the first words of ver. 13 *v'hū' yibhnēh eth-hēcāl YHVH*: both translators seem to have regarded the words as dittographed, through their not having observed the emphatic force of וְהוּא.—For the last half of ver. 13 LXX. give καὶ ἔσται ἱερεὺς ἐκ δεξιῶν αὐτοῦ, καὶ βουλὴ εἰρηνικὴ ἔσται ἀνὰ μέσον ἀμφοτέρων, substituting עַל יְמִינוֹ for עַל כִּסְאוֹ, and regarding Ἀνατολή and ἱερεύς as two different persons. *Verses 12, 13. Versions.*

חֵלֶם seems to be simply a corruption of חֶלְדַּי (ver. 10). One of David's heroes was called *Cheldāy* (1 Chron. xxvii. 15), and this name is written חֵלֶד (1 Chron. xi. 30), and חֵלֶב *Verse 14. Words and LXX.*
(2 Sam. xxiii. 29). Here the same name has become חֵלֶם: for the

15 And they *that are* far off shall come and build in the temple of the LORD, and ye shall know that the LORD of hosts hath sent me unto you. And *this* shall come to pass, if ye will diligently obey the voice of the LORD your God.

---

interchange of ב and מ comp. דִּיבֹן (Is. xv. 2) and דִּימוֹן (ver. 9); בְּרֹאדַךְ (2 Kings xx. 12) and מְרֹדַךְ (Jer. l. 2); and the explanation of the name כִּלְאָב (2 Sam. iii. 3), as meaning מַכְלִים "causing shame," given in Talm. Babl. *Brachoth* 4ᵃ.—LXX. render the name by τοῖς ὑπομένουσι, reading it as חֹלִם pres. partic. of הוֹל, in the sense of מְיַחֲלִים, comp. וַיָּחֶל (Gen. viii. 10).—לְחֵן may be rendered, as by LXX.; εἰς χάριτα· or "for *Chén*," another name for *Yôshiyyâh* (ver. 10), so Targ. But Syr. reads as in ver. 10.—For *Ziccárôn* LXX. εἰς ψαλμόν, either translating conjecturally, or reading זכרון as זמרון; similarly the two readings בֶּן־עֶשְׂרִים וּשְׁתַּיִם שָׁנָה (2 Kings viii. 26) and בֶּן־אַרְבָּעִים וּשְׁתַּיִם שָׁנָה (2 Chron. xxii. 2) are supposed to have arisen from a confusion between כ׳ 20, and מ׳ 40.

Verse 15. Constructions. In spite of the contrary opinion being expressed by such Hebr. commentators as Rashi, Qimchi, &c. we maintain that to render וְהָיָה as equivalent to וְזֹאת תִּהְיֶה לָכֶם "and this shall happen unto you" is contrary to the usage of the language. The expression *v'hâyâh im shâmô'a' tishm'ûn* seems to be borrowed directly from Jer. xxxi. 24, where (as in every other passage where a similar expression occurs, viz. Deut. xi. 13, xxviii. 1, Ex. xv. 26, xix. 5, xxiii. 22) there is an *apodosis*. Consequently, unless with Hengstenberg we look on this verse as an abrupt *aposiopesis*, we have no choice but to regard it as a case of a *lacuna* in the text (פִּסְקָא בְּאֶמְצַע פָּסוּק, see Josh. iv. 1, &c.), the existence of which has not been handed down by Tradition.

vi. 9 15. Remarks. Zechariah is now commanded to go to the house of Josiah son of Zephaniah, who was entertaining certain Jews, who seem to have come from Babylon with gifts and offerings for the House of the LORD. From these men he was to take gold and silver, and to cause to be made thereof a composite diadem, with which he was to crown Joshua the High-Priest. We cannot, of course, venture with EWALD to insert the words "and upon the head of Zerubbabel" after the words "upon the head of Joshua"; and to insert the name "Joshua" in the clause "and will be a priest upon his throne." Even if such an arbitrary alteration of the text were admissible, it would be most inappropriate.

For, as Pusey has well remarked, had a crown been placed on the head of Zerubbabel, such an act would have aroused false hopes in the minds of the people of a restoration of the temporal kingdom, which had already been finally abolished (Jer. xxii. 30, Ezek. xxi. 31, 32). The crown was removed "until he should come whose right it is," viz. "the king who shall reign in righteousness" (Is. xxxii. 1) "and prosper," as "a Branch of righteousness" (Jer. xxiii. 5). Since Zerubbabel is not even mentioned in this passage, Joshua himself must have felt that the Prophet's words referred to One greater than himself, and that the building spoken of was a spiritual one, to symbolize which the material building was allegorically introduced.—The interpretations of ver. 13 are various—we will note the chief of them. Hitzig holds that the Messiah and an ideal priest are referred to in the clause "counsel of peace shall be between them both." But we cannot see how the thought of some ideal priest and king, who would coincide in some unity of purpose, could have occurred to the minds of the Prophet's hearers. There would be, moreover, no special reason for speaking of unity as existing between a king and a priest: for, as a matter of history, the priests and kings were seldom at variance, though the prophets and kings were frequently so. Rosenmueller considers that the *offices* of priest and king are alluded to. But "a counsel of peace" could not be spoken of as existing between two abstracts. Keil takes the words as referring to the two *characters* of ruler and priest combined in the person of the Messiah. But in this case the clause would be superfluous. Why should there *not* be unity between two such characters combined in one such person? Koehler thinks that the reference is to the two offices of the Messiah, and that the prophecy speaks of a plan devised by the Messiah in His double character, whereby peace and salvation should be secured to His people. But this is in accord with the modes of thought of neither Old nor New Testament. Such an idea would have been incomprehensible to the Prophet's hearers; and in the N. T. any such unity of design for the salvation of mankind is spoken of as existing between the Father and the Messiah (not between two of the offices of the Latter), e.g. John vi. 38, x. 15—18, iii. 16, 17, Col. i. 19, 20. The opinion of Jerome, Vitringa, Pusey, Wright, &c., is that which we have adopted above in our notes. Seeing that the regal dignity of the Messiah must have been generally recognised in the Prophet's time (see Jer. xxiii. 5, &c.), and that, from Ps. cx. the combination of the priestly with the kingly office in the person of the Messiah must have been expected by his contemporaries, it seems to us that they would have understood the Prophet to have referred to the same person as "sitting and ruling upon his throne," and as "being a priest upon his throne": and that, however they may have taken the words of Isaiah ix. 6, "Wonder Counsellor, *El gibbor, Abhi Olam*, Prince of Peace," such words must have somewhat prepared them for the statement, "the Counsel of Peace shall be between Them twain." To us, who have the advantage of later revelation, there is a fitness apparent in the phraseology, which would have been hidden from them.

CHAPTER VII.

A ND it came to pass in the fourth year of king Darius, *that* the word of the LORD came unto Zechariah in the fourth *day* of the ninth month, *even* in Chisleu;

2 When they had sent unto the house of God Sherezer and Regem-melech, and their men, to pray before the LORD,

3 *And* to speak unto the priests

THE BETHEL DEPUTATION (chaps. vii. viii.).

Verses 1–3. Words and Constructions.

בכסלו " viz. in *Cislêv*." The usual constr. is that of i. 7 הוא חדש שבט "that is the month *Sh'bhát*." *B'cislêv* is in apposition with לחדש, comp. such a construction as לבנו ליוסף (Gen. xlvii. 29), where the noun in apposition is repeated with the *same* preposition that is prefixed to the noun with which it is in apposition. But since the ל of *lachódesh* is used only because it is preceded by the number of the day of the month, *Cislêv* takes ב "in," avoiding the somewhat awkward construction with ל "of."— וישלח "then there sent" seems to denote an event subsequent to the revelation spoken of in ver. 1. Comp. 1 Kings xiv. 5, where the prophet Ahijah receives warning of the coming of the wife of Jeroboam.— *Bēthēl* seems to stand for "the inhabitants of Bethel," just as "Jerusalem" often means "the inhabitants of Jerusalem." שראצר Baer edits correctly with ש (not שׂ); it is mentioned as a name of one of the sons of Sennacherib (Is. xxxvii. 38), and Nergal-Sarezer occurs (Jer. xxxix. 3). The name is Assyrian [*Nirgal*]-*sar-uśur* "May [Nergal] protect the king" (Schrader). Ewald and Koehler take the clause "Sarezer, and Regem-melec and his men" as in apposition with *Bethel*, and look on these persons as being some of the chief inhabitants of Bethel, who sent the deputation. Keil, on the other hand, takes the clause as the acc. after the verb *vayyishlách*, and regards these names as those of the deputation sent. It is true that in the very similar passage (Jer. xxvi. 22), וישלח המלך יהויקים אנשים מצרים את־אלנתן בן־עכבור ואנשים אתו..., the particle את is prefixed to the names of the people sent; but it is not absolutely necessary that it should have been expressed, though certainly the presence of the particle makes the sentence much clearer.—*Vayyishlách* is in the masc. *sing.* agreeing with the subject *nearest to it*, comp. ותדבר מרים ואהרן (Numb. xii. 1).— אנשיו comp. (2 Sam. ii. 3) ואנשיו אשר עמו.—On the whole we pre-

which *were* in the house of the Lord of hosts, and to the prophets, saying, Should I weep in the fifth month, separating myself, as I have done these so many years?

4 Then came the word of the Lord of hosts unto me, saying,

---

for the rendering "The [people of] Bethel, [such as] Sarezer, and Regem-melec and his men, sent to entreat the Lord."—It would be possible grammatically to render *Bēthēl* "to Bethel," comp. מִצְרַיִם in Jer. xxvi. 22 cited above. But no reason can be assigned for such a deputation being sent to Bethel, for we have no reason for supposing that "the priests belonging to the House of the Lord *Çʽbhāʽōth*" (ver. 3) dwelt specially at Bethel.—*Bēthēl*, though it means lit. "House of God," is *never* used to denote the Temple, which is called בֵּית י"י, or בֵּית הָאֱלֹהִים.—The phrase וַיְחַל...פְּנֵי י"י occurs as early as Ex. xxxii. 11. —The first לֵאמֹר should be rendered "to say," it is repeated because of the length of the clause which follows it (see note on vi. 10).—לְבֵית־ means "belonging to the house of," not "in &c."—הַאֶבְכֶּה, the interrog. הַ is pointed with a *pathach* before a guttural or a consonant with *shʽva*. It has metheg in accordance with Excurs. II. B. 2; but it is *unnecessary* to place the metheg to the *right* of the vowel, since this *ha* could scarcely be mistaken for the def. art.—For the 1st pers. *sing*. used by a people speaking comp. Numb. xx. 19 וַיֹּאמְרוּ אֵלָיו בְּנֵי יִשְׂרָאֵל...אִם...נִשְׁתֶּה.—As far as form is concerned הִנָּזֵר אֲנִי וּמִקְנַי וּנָתַתִּי מִכְרָם might be either Niph. Infin. *constr.* as לְהִלָּחֵם (Ex. xvii. 25, &c.), or Infin. *absol.* as הִכָּרֵת תִּכָּרֵת (Numb. xv. 31). But it is evidently the *absol.* here, since that is the form used (without לְ) to express what in Latin would be the gerund in *do*, and in Engl. the pres. partic. "separating myself": comp. Gen. xxi. 16 וַתֵּלֶךְ וַתֵּשֶׁב לָהּ...הַרְחֵק "and she went and sat down, *removing herself.*"—*Zēh* comp. i. 12.—On כַּמֶּה see note on ii. 6. Baer points it here *cammēh*, and in ii. 6 *cammāh*; *Cod. Petrop.* has in both passages *cammāh*.

B'cislēv, ὅς ἐστι Χασελεῦ, following the ordinary construction.— For *Rēgem mēlec* Ἀρβεσεὲρ ὁ βασιλεύς, it seems probable that Αρβεσεερ represents the numeral "fourteen" אַרְבָּעָה עָשָׂר, Aram. *Arbēsar*. The אַרְבַּע is easily accounted for from בְּאַרְבָּעָה above, and the עָשָׂר was perhaps deduced from the אֶצֶר of שַׂרְאֶצֶר. The whole runs thus in LXX.: καὶ ἐξαπέστειλεν εἰς Βαιθὴλ Σαρασὰρ καὶ

LXX.

5 Speak unto all the people of the land, and to the priests, saying, When ye fasted and mourned in the fifth and seventh *month*, even those seventy years, did ye at all fast unto me, *even* to me?

6 And when ye did eat, and when ye did drink, did not ye eat *for yourselves*, and drink *for yourselves?*

7 *Should ye* not *hear* the words which the LORD hath cried by the former prophets, when Jerusalem was inhabited and in prosperity, and the cities thereof round about her, when *men* inhabited the south and the plain?

Ἀρβεσεὲρ ὁ βασιλεὺς καὶ οἱ ἄνδρες αὐτοῦ καὶ ἐξιλάσασθαι τὸν Κύριον λέγων κ.τ.λ.—For *l'bḥêth-* wrongly ἐν τῷ οἴκῳ.—For הַבָּכָה...הַנֵּזֶר εἰσελήλυθεν ὧδε...τὸ ἁγίασμα, reading הַבָּא כֹּה...הַנֵּזֶר. Some copies (Field) add ἢ νηστεύσω, another instance of correction in accordance with the Hebr. In Numb. vi. 11, 12 וְקִדַּשׁ is rendered καὶ ἁγιάσει, and וְהִזִּיר...ἡγιάσθη.—*Zêh cammêh shānîm* ἤδη ἱκανὰ ἔτη.

Cî "when," comp. (Ps. xxxii. 3) כִּי הֶחֱרַשְׁתִּי "when I kept silence."

Verses 5—7. Words and Constructions.

וְסָפוֹד—may be taken in two ways, either as the absol. Infin. emphatic for וְסָפוֹד סְפָדְתֶם "and did mourn" (comp. note on iii. 4), or *sāphôd* means "mourning," see note on *hinnāzêr* (ver. 3), and the ו denotes "even," or "yea," as in וְזֶה which follows (see note on iii. 2); according to the latter explanation we should render *v'sāphôd* "yea mourning": comp. (Hag. i. 6) וִידַעְתֶּם הַצּוֹם צַמְתֻּנִי אָנִי—הַרְבֵּה וְהָבֵא מְעָט is very well rendered by the E. V.—With צַמְתֻּנִי comp. (Ezek. xxix. 3) וַאֲנִי עֲשִׂיתִנִי "and *I* made it *for* myself," (Is. xliv. 21) לֹא תִנָּשֵׁנִי "thou shalt not be forgotten *by* me" (ἐπὶ being for *lî*; on לְ denoting the agent after a passive see on Ps. cxi. 2); גְדֵלַנִי (Job xxxi. 18) "grew up *with* me" should rather be compared with Ps. v. 5 (see p. 27, last line). For the emphatic repetition of the pronoun in the separate form after a *datival* suff. compare לָכֶם אַתֶּם (Hag. i. 4), and with *gám* לָשֶׁת גַּם הוּא (Gen. x. 21).—*V'cî thô'clû* "and when ye eat," comp. (Ps. viii. 4) כִּי אֶרְאֶה שָׁמֶיךָ "when I look at the heavens."—*Ha'lô attêm hā'ôc'lîm* "are ye not the eaters," *v'attêm hashshôthîm* "and yourselves the drinkers?" i.e. do ye not eat, and drink unto yourselves? (For the opposite principle comp. 1 Cor. x. 31, εἴτε οὖν ἐσθίετε εἴτε πίνετε εἴτε τι ποιεῖτε πάντα εἰς δόξαν Θεοῦ ποιεῖτε).—אֶת הַדְּבָרִים. There is no need to supply a verb here such as "should ye not hear?" "should ye not do?" or "do ye not know?" For, in view of (2 Kings vi. 5)

8 And the word of the LORD came unto Zechariah, saying, 9 Thus speaketh the LORD of hosts, saying, Execute true judgment, and shew mercy and compassions every man to his brother:

10 And oppress not the widow, nor the fatherless, the stranger, nor the poor; and let none of you imagine evil against his brother in your heart.

ואת־הברזל נפל אל־המים there can be no doubt about את being used for emphasis before the subject of a verb (even when not a passive): moreover in viii. 17 we have an exact parallel. In the verse before us we have (h⁽ă⁾lô) eth-hadd⁽e⁾bhārím "(are not they) the very things?", and then follows the relative governed directly by a verb "shér qārā' "which He proclaimed." So in viii. 17 we have (cî) eth-col-êlleh "(for) all these very-things (are they)," and then follows "shér sānêthí "which I hate."—B⁽e⁾yád "by means of," as (Is. xx. 2) דִּבֶּר יְיָ בְּיַד יְשַׁעְיָהוּ.—

Two renderings, both of which are equally admissible, have been proposed for the following clauses, viz. "when Jerusalem was inhabited, and at peace, and her cities round about her: and the South, and the Lowland was inhabited": and "when Jerusalem was dwelling in security, and her cities round about her: and the South, and the Lowland dwelling (similarly)"; but see p. 15. V⁽e⁾hannégebh stands for וּבִהְיוֹת הַנֶּגֶב.— Observe that the predicate yōshḗbh is in the *masc. sing.*; comp. (Prov. xxvii. 9) שֶׁמֶן וּקְטֹרֶת יְשַׂמַּח־לֵב "oil and perfume rejoice the heart."— The Négebh is the southern district of Judah extending to Beersheba (Josh. xv. 21 *sqq.*).—The Sh⁽e⁾phēlāh (Σεφηλά 1 Macc. xxii. 38) is the Lowland district of Judah, towards the west (Josh. xv. 33 *sqq.*).

Ç⁽e⁾bhā'ôth τῶν δυνάμεων.—V⁽e⁾zéh shibh⁽ʻ⁾ím καὶ ἰδοὺ ἑβδομήκοντα. There is also in ver. 3 a reading ἰδοὺ for ἤδη (Field).—H⁽ă⁾lô eth-hadd⁽e⁾bhārím οὐχ οὗτοι οἱ λόγοι;—Hann⁽e⁾bhî'ím hārîshōním rightly here τῶν προφητῶν τῶν ἔμπροσθεν (see p. 7). LXX.

Mishpát ⁽e⁾méth "true judgment": in viii. 16 we have ⁽e⁾méth unishpát shālôm "truth, and justice which tends to peace," comp. ⁽e⁾çáth shālôm (vi. 13).—Sh⁽e⁾phóṭū is the correct pausal form of shiphʻṭū (viii. 16).—ísh eth āchív "with one another" (see next verse). Verse 9.

al-tā⁽ă⁾shóqū on the methegs see Excurs. II. B. 3 and A. I. 6.—The expression וְרָעַת אִישׁ אָחִיו אַל־תַּחְשְׁבוּ requires some explanation.—āchív is in apposition with ísh, and ísh means "each," and so ísh āchív in Gen. ix. 3 means "each his brother," that Verse 10.

11 But they refused to hearken, and pulled away the shoulder, and stopped their ears, that they should not hear.

12 Yea, they made their hearts as an adamant stone, lest they should hear the law, and the words which the LORD of hosts hath sent in his spirit by the former prophets: therefore came a great wrath from the LORD of hosts.

13 Therefore it is come to pass,

---

is "each other." But here it does not mean "each *his* brother," but "each *your* brother," i.e. "one another"; because, seeing that no such formula as (רֵעֲךָ or) אִישׁ...אָחִיךָ is used, the expression אִישׁ...רֵעֵהוּ (or אָחִיו) comes to be used for the *second* as well as the *third* person e.g. (iii. 10) וַתִּקְרְאוּ אִישׁ לְרֵעֵהוּ. Now, *ish āchîv* is the objective gen. after *rā'ath*, and so the whole expression *rā'ath ish āchîv* means "evil against one another." In this collocation it is impossible to take *ish* as the nom. (LXX.) καὶ κακίαν ἕκαστος τοῦ ἀδελφοῦ αὐτοῦ μὴ μνησικακείτω. But in the more simple and ordinary construction (viii. 17) וְאִישׁ אֶת־רָעַת רֵעֵהוּ אַל־תַּחְשְׁבוּ, *ish* is the nominative. We need not lay more stress on the expression each his *brother* (either here or in Gen. ix. 3), than to remember that this Hebrew expression, and others like it, arose from the ethical truth of the *brotherhood* of all mankind, which is an essential principle of the Hebrew Scriptures. The idiom was afterwards applied to the brute creation and to things inanimate.

The verb מֵאֵן is, in prose, usually construed with לְ and the Infin.

Verses 11, 12. constr.—The normal form of the Hiph. Infin. constr. is with î as *k'haqshîbh*, and of the *absol.* in ē as *v'halbēsh* (iii. 4).—The expression וַיִּתְּנוּ כָתֵף סֹרָרֶת recurs only in Neh. ix. 29, it means "and offered a recusant shoulder," like an animal refusing the yoke.—The מִן of *mishsh'mōa'* denotes "so as not to," or "in order not to," in both verses, comp. (Gen. xxvii. 1, &c.) מֵרְאוֹת. When, as here, *min* with the Infin. follows a verb denoting a deliberate act, it is equivalent to פֶּן with the Subj. (comp. Is. vi. 10).—*Sāmū*, comp. ix. 13.

LXX. *Vayyitt'nū cātheph sōrāreth* καὶ ἔδωκαν νῶτον παραφρονοῦντα.—*Shāmîr*, explaining the metaphor, ἀπειθῆ.

In the sing. we have always שָׁמַע, but the plural in Pause is always

Verses 13, 14. Words. שָׁמֵעוּ: so too *always* שָׂמַח and שָׂמְחוּ (e.g. x. 7); but, while the partic. of the one is always שֹׁמֵעַ from *shāmôa'*, that of the other is always שָׂמֵחַ from *sāmēach*.—וְאֶסְעָרֵם (on the

that as he cried, and they would not hear; so they cried, and I would not hear, saith the LORD of hosts: 14 But I scattered them with a whirlwind among all the nations whom they knew not. Thus the land was desolate after them, that no man passed through nor returned: for they laid the pleasant land desolate.

---

munach, to which the note ב' טְעָמִים = "two accents" refers, see Excurs. II. B. 9. N.B.) is the *Pi'el* and stands for וָאֲסָעֲרֵם, the א being pointed with a full *çērē*, comp. אֱפוּ (for unused אָפֻוּ) "bake ye" (only in Ex. xvi. 23), אֱתָיוּ (for unused *'thū*) "come ye" (Is. xxi. 12, &c.). This is merely a variation in vocalization, but no Aramaism, though it is true that in Syr. an initial א (when pronounced) has *always* a vowel.— נָשַׁמָּה is the 3rd pers. perf. from שׁמם, the fem. partic. would be נְשַׁמָּה.—*Shammāh* is a subst. meaning "a desolation."

The וַיְהִי of ver. 13 and the *nāshámmāh* of ver. 14 show that אֶשְׁמָע, יִקְרָאוּ and וָאֲסָעֲרֵם are *pasts*. They should be rendered "So they kept calling" (comp. note on i. 5) "and I would not hear...but I scattered them (on several occasions)."—עַל is used, and not בֵּין, because the *countries* of the nations are especially thought of here, comp. (Jer. xvi. 13) וְהֵטַלְתִּי אֶתְכֶם מֵעַל הָאָרֶץ הַזֹּאת עַל הָאָרֶץ "and I will cast you out of this land into a land," &c.— אֲשֶׁר לֹא־יְדָעוּם may be either "whom they knew not," or "who knew not them."—*Mē'ōbhḗr umishshábh.* In Ex. xxxii. 27 we find the Imperatives עִבְרוּ וָשׁוּבוּ "pass ye up and down" (through the camp): in Ezek. xxxv. 7 the participles עֹבֵר וָשָׁב denote "all inhabitants." This latter is the meaning here, "so that there were no inhabitants," the מִן being privative, comp. (Jer. xlviii. 2) מִגּוֹי. In ix. 8 we have exactly the same expression מֵעֹבֵר וּמִשָּׁב, but there the מִן is used in the sense of "on account of," and the expression denotes "on account of him [or the army] that passeth up and down [the country]."—אֶרֶץ חֶמְדָּה is a reminiscence of Jer. iii. 19, and is now looked on as a sort of proper name, hence the omission of the art., comp. Çémach (iii. 8, vi. 12).— The ordinary constr. in prose of יָשִׂים (which may be taken as Hiph., or as Qal like יָבִין) is, as here, with the acc. of the thing made, and לְ of

Constructions.

that into which it is made, as (Gen. xxi. 18) לִגְוֹי גָּדוֹל אֲשִׂימֶנּוּ "I will make him into a great nation."

LXX.   For *vayhī* καὶ ἔσται, reading וְיִהְי, and consequently the other verbs also are put incorrectly in the future.

CHAPTER VIII.

AGAIN the word of the LORD of hosts came *to me*, saying,
2 Thus saith the LORD of hosts; I was jealous for Zion with great jealousy, and I was jealous for her with great fury.

3 Thus saith the LORD; I am returned unto Zion, and will dwell in the midst of Jerusalem: and Jerusalem shall be called a city of truth; and the mountain of the LORD of hosts the holy mountain.
4 Thus saith the LORD of hosts;

On *qinnḗthī* with לְ comp. i. 14.—On the accusatives *qin'āh gḏōlāh* and *chēmāh gḏōlāh* see note on i. 2.—*Shābhtī...v'shācantī*
Verses 2, 3. Constructions and LXX. "I am returned...and will dwell," comp. ii. 14—16 (E. V. 10—12).—*'mĕth* "truth" and *qōdesh* "holiness" being abstracts have, as is often the case, the def. art. prefixed. Thus עִיר הָאֱמֶת means "City of Truth," הַר הַקֹּדֶשׁ "Mountain of Holiness." There is no word in Bibl. Hebr. for "true" (though there is נֶאֱמָנָה "faithful," cf. קִרְיָה נֶאֱמָנָה Is. i. 26), so that if the prophet had wished to say "the true city" he could only have used the expression which he has here. But, on the other hand, there is an adj. "holy," so that had he meant to say "the true city, the holy mountain," he might have written instead of *hár haqqṓdesh* הָהָר הַקָּדוֹשׁ.—LXX. πόλις ἀληθινή...ὄρος ἅγιον.

עֹד יֵשְׁבוּ "there shall yet dwell." In ver. 20 we have a slight
Verses 4, 5. Constructions. variation of construction עֹד אֲשֶׁר יָבֹאוּ "it (shall yet be) that there shall come."—אִישׁ means "each" (see note on vii. 10), and the וְ introduces the clause descriptive of additional circumstances, comp. v. 9, vi. 1.—רְחֹב is a *fem.* noun (Dan. ix. 25), but with the plur. the *masc.* verb is here used (hardly because the fem. is here used as a neut., Böttcher, C. II. II. Wright, but) because the Imperf. 3rd and 2nd *fem. plur.* is but sparingly used in Hebrew, comp. (Ps. cxlv. 15) עֵינֵי כֹל אֵלֶיךָ יְשַׂבֵּרוּ, and on the other hand וְלֹא־

There shall yet old men and old women dwell in the streets of Jerusalem, and every man with his staff in his hand for very age. 5 And the streets of the city shall be full of boys and girls playing in the streets thereof. 6 Thus saith the LORD of hosts; If it be marvellous in the eyes of the remnant of this people in these days, should it also be marvellous in mine eyes? saith the LORD of hosts. 7 Thus saith the LORD of hosts; Behold, I will save my people from the east country, and from the west country; 8 And I will bring them, and they shall dwell in the midst of Jerusalem: and they shall be my people, and I will be their God, in truth and in righteousness. 9 Thus saith the LORD of hosts;

תראינה עיניך (2 Kings xxii. 20, &c. and comp. Zech. viii. 9).—On the vocalization of *mish'antô* see note on xi. 3.—The predicate משחקים is *masc.*, as is commonly the case when a masc. and fem. noun precede, as (Gen. xviii. 11) אברהם ושרה זקנים.

כי denotes "if" as in (2 Kings iv. 29) כי תמצא־איש "if thou meet any one." But the expression *bayyāmîm hāhēm* "in those days" (viz. when the House was first founded), not "in *these* days" (E. V.), shows that we cannot render the first *yippālē'* "it be (or shall be) too marvellous" (LXX. εἰ ἀδυνατήσει ...ἐν ταῖς ἡμέραις ἐκείναις). כי יפלא must, therefore, mean "if it *was* too marvellous (see note on i. 5)." גם stands for הֲגַם comp. (1 Sam. xxii. 7) גם־לכלכם יתן "will he give to all of you?" (see also p. 35). Thus גם יפלא may be rendered "was it, therefore, too marvellous," or since the work was not then completed, it may mean "is it, therefore (or will it, therefore, be) too marvellous, &c." LXX. μὴ καὶ ἐνώπιόν μου ἀδυνατήσει;

Verse 6. Constructions and LXX.

מושיע is the Prophetic Participle followed by the Perfect with *vâv* convers. *v'hēbhēthî*, comp. p. 36. (Baer has accidentally omitted the Fixed Metheg with וַאֲנִי.)—For *v'shâc'nû* LXX. give καὶ κατασκηνώσω, reading וְהִשְׁכַּנְתִּי, and that probably deliberately in order to retain the same subject of the sentence.

Verses 7, 8. Words, Constructions and LXX.

Observe that "in *these* days," and "in *those* days," (ver. 10) are contrasted. "The prophets," viz. Haggai and Zechariah, and perhaps others.—*'shēr* stands for אשר היו.—ביום is the constr. before the finite verb *yussâd* "was founded," comp. ביום דִּבֶּר־י׳ (Ex. vi. 2), and the similar Arab. construction *waqta*

Verse 9. Constructions and LXX.

Let your hands be strong, ye that hear in these days these words by the mouth of the prophets, which *were* in the day *that* the foundation of the house of the LORD of hosts was laid, that the temple might be built.

10 For before these days there was no hire for man, nor any hire for beast; neither *was there any* peace to him that went out or came in because of the affliction: for I set all men every one against his neighbour.

---

statura (Hebraice עֵת הִסְתַּתֵּר) "what time he hid himself." (The case of תְּהִלַּת דִּבֶּר־יְ״י Hos. i. 2 is doubtful, for there is a substantive הַדִּבֶּר Jer. v. 13, comp. R. D. Qimchi's Introd. Poem to his *Comm. on Pss.*).— *Hăkēchâl* is in apposition with *Bêth YHVH*: there is no need, with Hitzig, to regard it as a gloss.—לְהִבָּנוֹת "for the purpose of being built," i.e. when its foundations were laid for this purpose. LXX. give what they conceived to be the sense of the passage, and render freely ἀφ' ἧς ἡμέρας τεθεμελίωται...καὶ ὁ ναὸς ἀφ' οὗ ᾠκοδόμηται. There is no need to suppose that they read מֵהִבָּנוֹת (see p. 3, last line).

Verse 10. Words and Constructions.
Śâcâr "hire" is masc., and with it *nih'yâh* agrees; but אֵינֶנָּה is attracted into the gender of הַבְּהֵמָה (see note on vi. 6).— *Nih'yâh* is the 3rd sing. Perf. masc. of הָיָה (on the *ma"rîc* see Excurs. II. A. 7). The Niph. of this verb occurs only in the Perf. and Partic. It generally means "happened" (Judg. xix. 30), "was caused" (1 Kings xii. 24), "was undone," i.e. "went off" (of sleep, Dan. ii. 1), or (into a swoon, Dan. viii. 27). In Joel ii. 2 לֹא נִהְיָה means "was not," and so here. Observe that the tense of אֵין is decided by the context.—מִן "on account of" (comp. ix. 8).—הַצָּר "the enemy," from צַר (Is. v. 30), Rt. צרר (comp. גַּן from גנן, רַע from רעע), the *qāmāṣ* is on account of the disjunctive accent.—וָאֲשַׁלַּח is the correct reading (not וָאִישׁ). Some of these cases, in which we have *vă* when we should have expected *vā*, may be explained as being the Imperf. of repeated action, as וָאֲגָרֵשׁ (Judg. vi. 9) "and I kept driving them," וָאֲשַׁלְּחֶהָ (xx. 6) "and kept sending her" (comp. Zech. vii. 14). But others can only be explained as instances of anomalous vocalization as וָאֲנַתְּחֶהָ (Judg. xx. 6) "and I cut her in pieces," וָאֲמִתְתֵהוּ (2 Sam. i. 10) "and I slew him." *Vă"shallăch*... *b're'ḥā* render "and I kept letting loose all men against one another."

11 But now I *will* not *be* unto the residue of this people as in the former days, saith the LORD of hosts.
12 For the seed *shall be* prosperous; the vine shall give her fruit, and the ground shall give her increase, and the heavens shall give their dew; and I will cause the remnant of this people to possess all these *things*.

13 And it shall come to pass, *that* as ye were a curse among the heathen, O house of Judah, and house of Israel; so will I save you, and ye shall be a blessing: fear not, *but* let your hands be strong.
14 For thus saith the LORD of hosts; As I thought to punish you, when your fathers provoked me to wrath, saith the LORD of hosts, and I repented not:

ὁ μισθὸς...οὐκ ἔσται εἰς ὄνησιν καὶ...οὐχ ὑπάρξει, not only have they read נהיה as נהנה, from the Rabb. and Aram. הנה "to enjoy," but they have taken the initial נ as the Rabb. or Aram. prefix of the Fut. (comp. p. 51); *Μὴ ἁσσάρ...ἀπὸ τῆς θλίψεως καὶ ἐξαποστελῶ*. LXX.

Cayyāmīm hārīshōnīm denotes "as *in* the former days," since after כ a preposition is often understood, e.g. (Is. ix. 3) כיום מדין "as in the day of Midian."—אני "I am," or as E. V. "I will be"; there is no need with LXX. to supply any such verb as ποιῶ.—כי "for" introduces an assurance in proof of the statement of ver. 11. *Zéraʻ hashshālōm* "the seed [which flourishes only in times] of peace," viz. *haggephen* "the vine." In Jer. ii. 21 the word *zéraʻ* "seed" is used of שׁוֹרֵק (see p. 12) in the expression זרע אמת "genuine seed" (the καλὸν σπέρμα of Matt. xiii. 24). For *cî zéraʻ shālōm* Syr. gives "for the seed shall be in peace." LXX. ἀλλ' ἢ δείξω εἰρήνην, *cî* might possibly stand for כי אם (as in Gen. xxxi. 16 after a negative sentence); but here there is hardly sufficient contrast between the two sentences to justify this rendering. For זרע they read possibly אדע, Hiph. of ידע, which they render by δείκνυμι in Gen. xli. 39, &c. Verses 11—13. Constructions and Versions.

זממתי (comp. i. 6) in the 1st pers. Perf. this verb occurs here only in its uncontracted form, and only in Jer. iv. 28 contracted זמתי.—*V'lō nichāmtī* "and I repented not," LXX. καὶ οὐ μετενόησα, see p. 19.—זממתי שבתי "I have again purposed," comp. (Hos. v. 11) הואיל הלך "he went willingly," (Gen. xxx. 31) אשובה ארעה "I will again feed" (comp. p. 46). LXX. παρατέταγμαι καὶ διανενόημαι (in i. 6 they render זמם by παρατέτακται), Verses 14—17. Words, Constructions and LXX.

15 So again have I thought in these days to do well unto Jerusalem and to the house of Judah: fear ye not.
16 These *are* the things that ye shall do; Speak ye every man the truth to his neighbour; execute the judgment of truth and peace in your gates:
17 And let none of you imagine evil in your hearts against his neighbour; and love no false oath: for all these *are things* that I hate, saith the LORD.
18 And the word of the LORD of hosts came unto me, saying,
19 Thus saith the LORD of hosts; The fast of the fourth *month*, and the fast of the fifth, and the fast of the seventh, and the fast of the tenth, shall be to the house of Judah joy and gladness, and cheerful feasts; therefore love the truth and peace.
20 Thus saith the LORD of hosts; *It shall* yet *come to pass*, that there shall come people, and the inhabitants of many cities:
21 And the inhabitants of one *city* shall go to another, saying,

---

here they may have read חשבתי "I thought," "I intended," for שבתי; or, perhaps, taking *shâbhtī* as "again," they paraphrased the expression by two words of cognate meaning.—את־רעהו (ver. 16) *eth* here means "with."—V*ĭsh eth-rā'ăith rē'ēhū* see note on vii. 10.—*Cĭ eth-col-ēlleh ăshēr ṣânéthī* see note on vii. 7, and add as an example of this construction (Hag. ii. 5) את־הדבר אשר כרתי אתכם בצאתכם ממצרים. LXX. simply διότι ταῦτα πάντα ἐμίσησα.

Verse 19.
LXX. and Constructions.

צום הרביעי "the fast of the fourth [month]." LXX., after the analogy of יום הששי (Gen. i. 31) νηστεία ἡ πέμπτη, and so also with the others. After εἰς χαρὰν is inserted καὶ εὐφροσύνην, and after καὶ εἰς ἑορτὰς ἀγαθάς is inserted καὶ εὐφρανθήσεσθε.—The ו of v'hā'mĕth, like the Arab. *fa*, denotes "therefore," comp. (Ezek. xviii. 32) "For I have no pleasure in the death of him that dieth... וְהָשִׁיבוּ וִחְיוּ therefore repent ye and live." (The ו of v'āmartă (i. 3) might be so taken, as indeed it is by the E. V.) In such a case the ו is usually prefixed to the *verb*; but here the objects *hā'mĕth v'hashshālōm* are put first for the sake of emphasis.

Verse 20.
Constructions and LXX.

עד אשר (comp. ver. 4) stands for עד יהיה אשר, as in ver. 23 יהיה is understood before אשר. In both cases אשר is equivalent to כי "that," comp. (Eccles. v. 4) טוב אשר—. After λαοὶ LXX. insert πολλοὶ from ver. 22.

Verses 21, 22.
Constructions and LXX.

For the expression *ăchath el-ăchath* "one to another" comp. Ex. xxxvi. 10, 12, 13.—אלכה and נלכה (with final ה) are certainly "energetics," or "voluntatives" here (see p. 6).— The absol. Infin. *hālōc*, though put *after* the verb is used for the sake of

ZECHARIAH VIII. 22, 23.

Let us go speedily to pray before the LORD, and to seek the LORD of hosts: I will go also. 22 Yea, many people and strong nations shall come to seek the LORD of hosts in Jerusalem, and to pray before the LORD. 23 Thus saith the LORD of hosts;

In those days *it shall come to pass*, that ten men shall take hold out of all languages of the nations, even shall take hold of the skirt of him that is a Jew, saying, We will go with you: for we have heard *that God is with you*.

---

emphasis, comp. הָלוֹךְ הָלַךְ (2 Sam. iii. 24), שִׁמְעוּ שָׁמוֹעַ "listen attentively" (Job xiii. 17).—*L'challóth* see vii. 2.—The other city answers "I also will go." On this usage of the 1st pers. *sing.* see note on vii. 3. *Gam-ánî* see note on vii. 5.—LXX. καὶ συνελεύσονται κατοικοῦντες πέντε πόλεις εἰς μίαν πόλιν, borrowing the word "five" possibly from Is. xix. 18 "In that day there shall be *five* cities..., one shall be called..."—עֲצוּמִים LXX. πολλά, and so in Gen. xviii. 18 *'āçûm polú*, but the word means "numerous," "strong," not "many."

We find בַּיָּמִים הָהֵם (Gen. vi. 4, &c.), and also בַּיָּמִים הָהֵמָּה as here (comp. Joel iii. 2, iv. 2), see also לְהָנֵה (Zech. v. 9).— Verse 23. On the construction of אֲשֶׁר see note on ver. 20; LXX. ἐάν, taking *'shér* as equivalent to *ci* "if" (ver. 6), and וְ as introducing the *apodosis.* On יַחֲזִיקוּ...וְהֶחֱזִיקוּ see note on vi. 10.—The number *ten* is used for an indefinitely large number (e.g. Gen. xxxi. 7). In the passage (Is. iv. 1), which our Prophet seems to have had in mind, the number *seven* is used in this sense.—The expression *l'shōnóth haggōyim* "languages of the nations" is formed after הַגּוֹיִם וְהַלְּשֹׁנוֹת "the nations and the languages" (Is. lxvi. 18), comp. Dan. iii. 29, vii. 14, &c.—*Cānáph* (constr. *c'náph*) is the name of the corner of the long flowing garment then worn by the Jews. To each of these אַרְבַּע כְּנָפַיִם the צִיצִת was attached (Numb. xv. 38): this was the distinctive visible sign of an אִישׁ יְהוּדִי. *Cí* "that" is omitted after *shāmá'nû* probably because *cí* "for" immediately precedes it; on the other hand we have (2 Kings xix. 8, Is. xxxvii. 8) כִּי שָׁמַע כִּי נָסַע מִלָּכִישׁ "For he had heard that he was departed from Lachish."

This mission took place B.C. 518, in the second year after the resumption of the work of rebuilding the Temple (Hag. i. 15), and about two years before its completion (Ezr. vi. 15).—" Two hundred and twenty-three men of Bethel and Ai" had returned "to Jerusalem and Judah, every one to his own city" (Ezr. ii. 1, 28). The four fasts referred to in viii. 19 are of (17th) Tammuz when a breach was made in the walls of Jerusalem by Nebuchadnezzar in the eleventh year of Zedekiah (Jer. lii. 5—7): (9th) Abh, when the Temple was destroyed by Nebuzar-adan in the 19th year of Nebuchadnezzar (Jer. lii. 12, 13, 2 Kings xxv. 8—10): (3rd) Tishri when Gedaliah was assassinated (2 Kings xxv. 25, Jer. xli. 2—6) B.C. 587: 10th Tebheth, when Nebuchadnezzar began to lay siege to Jerusalem (2 Kings xxv. 1, Jer. xxxix.) in the ninth year of Zedekiah. (The number of the day of the month is placed in brackets, where from the Biblical account there is some doubt as to the exact day.)—The people of Bethel seem to have been the representatives of all the people, at all events the reply is given to the whole nation (vii. 5). Though the mission came in the *ninth* month, no question was asked about the fast of the *tenth* month, but only about that of the *fifth* month. The reason of this appears to be, that the fast in *Abh* being in mourning for the destruction of the Temple, it was natural that, now the rebuilding of it had progressed so far, they should inquire whether that particular fast should be kept. The Prophet in his first reply mentions also the fast of the *seventh* month, which was kept in memory of the assassination of Zedekiah, which took place soon after the destruction of the Temple. The 70 years to which he refers are those between the 7th month B.C. 587 and the 9th month B.C. 518. He does not, even in viii. 19, give a definite answer to their question, but warns them against the sins which brought about the deportation of the nation, and promises that their land shall once more be fruitful and prosperous, and their fasts be turned into feasts, if only they will "love Truth and Peace."—Chap. viii. closes (ver. 20—23) with the promise of a glorious future for Israel, in many nations uniting themselves to them to serve the One Only God; comp. Mic. iv. 2, Is. ii. 2, 3, xlv. 14, and Zech. ii. 10—12, xiv. 16—19. Ver. 23 must not be taken as a direct prophecy of the coming of our Lord, for the expression "a man a Jew" is used in the singular merely for the sake of contrast with the "ten men from all languages of the nations," and in reality denotes not an individual Jew, but the whole Jewish nation (see Is. xlv. 14). At the same time the adoption of Christianity (the true development of Judaism) by the Gentiles was a distinct fulfilment of this prophecy.

CHAPTER IX.

THE burden of the word of the Lord in the land of Hadrach, and Damascus *shall be* the rest thereof: when the eyes of man, as of all the tribes of Israel, *shall be* toward the Lord.

Verse 1. Words.

מַשָּׂא, which first of all means "a burden," comes afterwards to be very commonly used of "an oracle" or "prophecy" (comp. especially Jer. xxiii. 33—40), and that, generally, of a threatening character. The Root is נָשָׂא "to take up"; as a man takes up a burden, so a prophet is said in Hebrew to "take up" his speech, compare (Numb. xxiii. 18) וַיִּשָּׂא מְשָׁלוֹ "and he took up his parable." It is only in the post-exilian prophets (Zech. ix. 1, xii. 1, and Mal. i. 1)

2 And Hamath also shall border thereby; Tyrus, and Zidon, though it be very wise.

---

that מַשָּׂא is followed by דְבַר. In Arabic the conjugation, corresponding to the Hebrew Hiphil, of the verb *nasha-a* means "to lift up," (Hebr. נשׂא) and from it is derived a substantive *inshá*, which means "composing," "reciting," or "composition."—חַדְרָךְ (some MSS. read חַדְרָךְ) is the town and district *Ha-ta-ri-ka*, near Damascus and Hamath, which is mentioned in several Assyrian inscriptions (Schrader).—In מְנֻחָתוֹ the *u* is long, and merely written defectively (see note on i. 13); the metheg is placed in accordance with Excurs. II. A. 1. The word denotes "its (i.e. of the oracle of the Lord) resting-place or goal."— אָדָם denotes "mankind"; there is no need (with J. D. Michaelis) to read אֲרָם "Syria," in which case עֵין אֲרָם would mean "the whole face of Syria"; comp. Ex. xx. 15, Numb. xxii. 5, 11. (Baer has accidently עָיִן).

The בּ of *b'éreç* denotes "against," as (Is. xxi. 13) מַשָּׂא בָעֲרָב "the prophecy against Arabia"; but usually *massá* is put in construction with the noun following, e.g. מַשָּׂא בָּבֶל (Is. xiii. 1).—כִּי לַיְיָ עֵין אָדָם seems simply to mean "for to the LORD shall the eye of men be directed," comp. (Ps. cxxiii. 2) "As the eyes of servants are unto the hand of their masters...so are our eyes unto the LORD (אֶל יְיָ)"; only there it is in expectation and here in amazement, &c. It is true that "eye" is here in the singular; but that is an unimportant difference, comp. (Ps. xxxiii. 18) עֵין יְיָ אֶל־יְרֵאָיו with lxxxiv. 16) וּכֹל־.עֵינֵי יְיָ אֶל־צַדִּיקִים stands for וְעֵין כֹּל יְיָ.

Massá LXX. λῆμμα, comp. 4 Kings ix. 25. Aq. ἄρμα. LXX. usually ὅρασις (Is. xiii. 1), ὅραμα (xxi. 1), or ῥῆμα (xiv. 28). *Chadrác* LXX. Σάδραχ. Δαμασκοῦ the locative "in Damascus." For *m'náchathô thusía*, reading (since the *ú* is written *defectivè*) מִנְחָתוֹ.—διότι Κ. ἐφορᾷ ἀνθρώπους κ.τ.λ. taking אָדָם as the obj. gen. "To the LORD is an eye on man, &c."; so too Kochler, comp. Jer. xxxii. 19.

Observe that תִּגְבָּל־בָּהּ (as also וְתִצְבֹּר־כֶּסֶף in the next verse) has *ga‘yá* (Excurs. II. B. 7).—כִּי is a particle which is capable of various significations (see Dictionaries): here it seems best to take it in the sense of "although," as (Ex. xiii. 17) כִּי הוּא

Constructions.

Versions.

Verse 2. Words.

3 And Tyrus did build herself a strong hold, and heaped up silver as the dust, and fine gold as the mire of the streets.
4 Behold, the Lord will cast her out, and he will smite her power in the sea; and she shall be devoured with fire.
5 Ashkelon shall see *it*, and fear; Gaza also *shall see it*, and be very sorrowful, and Ekron; for her expectation shall be ashamed; and the king shall perish from Gaza, and Ashkelon shall not be inhabited.

קָרוֹב "although it was the nearest."—חָכְמָה is the 3rd pers. fem. Perf. (see Excurs. II. A. 4). With this passage comp. Ezek. xxviii. 12 sqq.

Constructions.
This verse is somewhat elliptical, the style of this passage being highly poetical. The meaning is that "also *against* Hamath Tyre and Sidon is the prophecy"; or that "also Hamath Tyre and Sidon shall be its resting-place." Before *tigbol-bāh* the relative must be understood, thus: "Hamath *which* borders thereon (viz. on Damascus)," as (Gen. xxxix. 4) כָּל־אֲשֶׁר יֶשׁ־לוֹ = כָּל־יֶשׁ־לוֹ (of the next verse).—*Chăc'māh* LXX. plur. ἐφρονήσαν.

Verse 3. Words.
מָצוֹר means (1) distress, (2) siege, (3) earthworks for besieging, (4) *fortification*. Its constr. is מְצוֹר (Ezek. iv. 7) and its Root is צוּר. But in the expression מָעוֹז הַיָּם "fortress of the sea," which is an appellation of Tyre in Is. xxiii. 4, the word מָעוֹז does not lose its *qāmāç* in the construct form because it comes from Root עזז (see Jennings and Lowe on Ps. xxxi. 2). The word *Māçôr* is chosen, of course, on account of its similarity of sound with *Çôr* "Tyre."

Verse 5.
For תֵּרֶא Baer (on MS. authority) reads תֵּרָא (so too וְתֵרָא Mic. vii. 10) like the masc. יִרָא (Gen. xli. 33). Some old grammarians seem not to have distinguished between *çērē* and *accentuated seyōl*, thus Rashi (on Ex. i. 20).—וְתָחִיל seems to be a simple future.—הוֹבִישׁ is grammatically the Hiph. of יָבֵשׁ, and would properly mean "he has made to dry up," as in Josh. ii. 10, or "is dried up," as in x. 11, Joel i. 10. And in this latter sense it *may* be here used "her hope is dried up." But it is better to suppose the root to be used in the sense of בּוֹשׁ "to be put to shame," "be disappointed" (Joel i. 11, &c.), since such interchange of roots with one weak letter is one of the commonest phenomena of the Hebr. language (and indeed of Semitic languages generally, even as early as Assyrian), see pp. 30, 46.

6 And a bastard shall dwell in Ashdod, and I will cut off the pride of the Philistines.

7 And I will take away his blood out of his mouth, and his abominations from between his teeth:

but he that remaineth, even he, *shall be* for our God, and he shall be as a governor in Judah, and Ekron as a Jebusite.

8 And I will encamp about mine house because of the army, because

---

מִבְטָחָה— "her hope (or expectation)," comp. מִבְטָם (Is. xx. 5), Root נבט. The *pathach* of the first syllable is here lightened into *seyōl*, as we find יְדֵכֶם (not יִדְכֶם), אֲבִיתָר (not אֲבִיתָר) *Abiathar*. Comp. notes on vi. 1, x. 9.—לֹא תֵשֵׁב "shall not be inhabited" (comp. vii. 7); or "shall not endure" (comp. Gen. xlix. 24).

Mebbāṭāh wrongly παραπτώματι αὐτῆς "her transgression"; perhaps they took *ḥibbīṭ* in the sense of παροράω "to over-look," "miss," and so equivalent to חָטָא; but *Cod. Alex.* rightly ἀπὸ τῆς ἐλπίδος αὐτῆς, which may, however, be a mere correction. LXX.

מַמְזֵר (on the der". consult the Dictionaries) means here "a mixed race."—וְהִכְרַתִּי 1st pers. sing. perf. Hiph. from כרת (for הִכְרַתִּי, the ת being according to rule assimilated to the ת). On the *tone* see note on i. 3. Verse 6. Words.

Ashdōd rightly Ἄζωτος. The case-ending s may represent the final *d* (pronounced *dh*, then θ, then s), comp. Μαχμάς, for מַחְמָד *Machmad* (Hos. ix. 6); or perhaps, seeing that the ω seems to correspond with the ō, the *sh* and *d* became assimilated into ζ, and os is merely the termination. LXX.

On *vǎḥ°sīrōthī* see Excurs. II. A. 1, and 6, and note on i. 3.—On the form שִׁקְצִין see on נֶחָמִים (i. 13).—שָׁנָיו is the dual, from שֵׁן, שְׁנַיִם.—וְנִשְׁאַר is the perfect (with ו consecutive), the participle would be נִשְׁאָר.—כְּאַלֻּף "as a leader," this is the only place in which אַלּוּף is written defectively *in the singular*, the *u* is, of course, long (see on נְאֻם i. 3). Verse 7. Words.

On the *tone* of *v°ḥănīthī* see p. 5.—לְבֵיתִי means "for the protection of my house," comp. (Ps. cxxiv. 1) לוּלֵי י״י שֶׁהָיָה לָנוּ "if it had not been the Lord, who was *on our side*."—מִצָּבָה "on account of an army," on this use of מן see on ii. 8. צבה stands Verse 8. Words.

of him that passeth by, and because of him that returneth : and no oppressor shall pass through them any more : for now have I seen with mine eyes.

---

for צָבָא (which is in fact the reading of some MSS.), as נִסָּה (Ps. iv. 7) stands for נָשָׂא. Some would point the word מַצֵּבָה "as a garrison," in accordance with 1 Sam. xix. 12, which is, however, the only passage in which the word occurs in the fem. form, elsewhere it is always מַצָּב.

—The מ of the next two words means also "on account of."—For the expression עֹבֵר וָשָׁב compare note on vii. 14.

For מצבה LXX. has ἀνάστημα, reading, probably, מַצֵּבָה "a column."—τοῦ μὴ...μηδὲ, giving to מ the privative sense it has in vii. 14. Possibly they read the words מֵעֹבֵר וּמִשָּׁב. (Cod. Alex. ἀνάστεμα, comp. ἀνάθημα and ἀνάθεμα, σύστημα and σύστεμα, &c.)

Remarks.

It is impossible to discuss all the theories which have been propounded with regard to the time of the composition of different parts of Zech. ix.—xiv. We will content ourselves with mentioning here the chief arguments, which have been adduced to prove the pre-exilian authorship of ix. 1—8. (1) It has been argued, that *Zech. ix.* 1—8 *is so like to Amos i.—ii.* 6 (delivered in the early part of Uzziah's reign, i.e. a few years after B.C. 810), *that it seems impossible that two prophecies so similar should have been uttered at periods so wide apart.* Now, the only similarity between these two passages is, that in both Damascus, Tyre, Gaza, Ashdod, Ashkelon, and Ekron are threatened. The dissimilarity, however, is much greater. (α) In Amos we find the Ammonites, Edomites, and Moabites also mentioned, but not so in Zechariah. And this is most natural, for, while in the time of Uzziah these were still powerful nations, on the return from the captivity they were so weak, that when in the time of Nehemiah "Sanballat and Tobiah, and the Arabians and the Ammonites and the Ashdodites" all conspired to hinder the Jews from rebuilding the Wall of Jerusalem, it was found sufficient to repel them that half of the returned exiles should stand to arms, while the other half went on with the work of building. (β) Amos expressly states that Aram-Damascus should be carried away to Kir, while there is no such intimation in Zech. ix. (γ) Amos speaks of Judah and Israel as separate kingdoms, to be subjected to the same judgments as the other nations, while in Zech. Israel is but one nation (comp. ver. 13 and Remarks there), and is assured of God's protection. (δ) The *style* of the two passages is *not* similar. That of Amos i.—ii. 6 is of a marked character, but we find no echo of that style in Zech. ix. 1—8. (ε) It has been urged that *this oracle speaks of several cities and kingdoms as independent, which had lost their independence, before the period of the return from exile.* Thus Damascus lost its independence when Tiglath-Pileser overthrew Syria in the beginning of the reign of Ahaz, and Hamath was subdued to the Assyrians in the time of Hezekiah. (The reference to Tyre and Sidon is admitted by the objectors to afford no clear indication of the early date of the prophecy.) We may reply simply, that Jeremiah prophesied against Damascus and Hamath even after Nebuchadnezzar had overrun their territories (Jer. xlix. 23—37), and Jeremiah (xxv. 20) and Ezekiel (xxv. 15—17) denounced judgments on the Philistines, so that it is not strange that a post-exilian prophet should speak in general terms of the disasters, which would overtake these nations, when the Medo-Persian empire should be overthrown by the Greeks.—(2) The prophecy has been supposed *to allude to the immunity experienced by Jerusalem during the irruption of Rezin king of Syria and Pekah king of Israel into the territories of Judah* (2 Kings xvi. 5), *as well as during the wars with the Philistines which occurred during that period* (2 Chron. xxviii. 18), and it is further argued that *ch. xi.* 14 *shows that the struggle between Judah and Israel is looked on as already begun, at this time when the Prophet threatens Damascus* (*ix.* 1). *The denunciations against Tyre are to be viewed as naturally arising out of the sale of the Israelite captives at that period by Phoenician merchants* (Joel iii. 4—6). But (a) if this were the case it would be most difficult to account for the omission of any notice of the far more important enemies of Judah at that period, viz. Ammon (2 Chron. xxvi. 8, xxvii. 5), Edom and Moab (Amos i. 11—15, ii. 1—3), and Arabia (2 Chron. xxvi. 7). (β) The dissolution of the brotherhood between Israel and Judah is in xi. 14 (see Remarks) distinctly spoken of as in the future. If, then, that passage refers to the revolt under Jeroboam, it must have been written at a time prior even to 975 B.C., when Damascus was still included in the kingdom of Solomon, and such threats against Syria would have been meaningless.—But the strongest argument against such theories is, that to no period of history does this prophecy (ix. 1—8) apply so exactly, as to the conquests of Alexander the Great in 333 B.C. The chief points of the prophecy are, judgments on Syria and Philistia, and the burning of Tyre; the removal of the king from Gaza, the desolation of Ashkelon, the introduction of a mixed race into Ashdod, and the eventual fusion of the Philistines with the Jews; the protection of Israel amid their confusion. Now, when Alexander had completely shattered the might of Persia, in the battle of Issus, he marched into Syria. He sent a strong detachment under Parmenio to operate against Damascus, and himself with the main body marched against Tyre. And this mighty stronghold, which had stood a five years' siege from the Assyrians, and a thirteen years' siege from the Chaldæans, was taken by Alexander in seven months, and then (as Q. Curtius says) "having slain all save those who fled to the temples, he ordered the houses to be set on fire." No special mention, it is true, is made of Ashkelon and Ekron in the accounts of the march of Alexander, but Gaza fell after a siege of five months, and Hegesias (a contemporary of Alexander) especially mentions that "the king of Gaza was brought alive to Alexander. The breaking up of petty nationalities and the fusion of races was part of the policy of Alexander." But no mention is made of any great conversion of the Philistines to the Jewish religion at this period. While, as late as 1 Macc. x. 83, we hear of a temple of Dagon at Ashdod being destroyed by Jonathan, after that time the Philistines disappear as a separate people, and the name of their country "Palestine" became used as the designation of the whole land. It seems best, therefore, to adopt the view of KOEHLER, that "the prophecy does not merely delineate the events connected with the triumphal progress of Alexander, but predicts the general events which followed the Greek conquest of Palestine, inclusive of the various wars which occurred in the latter days of

9 Rejoice greatly, O daughter of Zion; shout, O daughter of Jerusalem: behold, thy King cometh unto thee: he *is* just, and having salvation; lowly, and riding upon an ass, and upon a colt the foal of an ass.

---

the Grecian supremacy" (comp. Remarks on ver. 9—17). The word *Yebhusi* seems to be parallel with *alluph*, and not contrasted with it: therefore, one would suppose it to mean either "Jebusite," in reference to the fact that "they dwelt with the children of Judah in Jerusalem" (Josh. xv. 63); or "Jerusalem itself," in which sense the word is also used (Josh. xviii. 63); and not as equivalent to "Gibeonites" or "Nethinim" who held a servile position (Josh. ix., Neh. x. 28, 29, Ezr. viii. 20, &c.). The promise of protection to Israel given in ver. 8 was signally fulfilled, when Alexander, according to the well-known story (see my *Memorbook of Nürnberg*, p. 20), spared Jerusalem, and granted the Jews special favours. The meaning of the words "no oppressor (task-master) shall pass through (*or* over) them any more" is, that the nation would not be again reduced to the position of slaves, as they were by the Babylonians and Persians. And such was the case, for God's protecting care was over them, in fulfilment of the assurance "now have I seen with mine eyes": so that neither did Alexander, nor any of the Seleucian dynasty, ever succeed in enslaving them.

Verse 9. Words. גִּילִי (the 2nd pers. fem. of imperative Qal of גִּיל) would according to rule be accentuated on the first syllable. But there are many exceptions to the rule (caused perhaps by considerations of euphony), thus Is. li. 9 we have עוּרִי עוּרִי '*úrí* '*úrí*, and so too in the first sentences of Judg. v. 12 '*úrí* '*úrí*, and Is. xxi. 2 צֻרִי *çúrí*; while in the second sentence of Judg. v. 12 the accentuation is regular '*úrí* '*úrí*, as also in *shábhá* (ver. 12).—הָרִיעַ is "to cry aloud," הָרַע "to do harm."—נוֹשָׁע, the Niph. partic. of יָשַׁע, can only mean "saved." —חֲמוֹר is a "he-ass," אָתוֹן a "she-ass."

Constructions. The וְ of וְעַל does not mean "and" as though he were to come riding on two animals; but "even," "namely," "yea," as Ex. xxv. 9 וְכֵן תַּעֲשׂוּ "*even* so shall ye do."—בֶּן־אֲתֹנוֹת means lit. "son of she-asses," i.e. such a foal as she-asses in general are in the habit of bearing, comp. כְּפִיר אֲרָיוֹת "cub of lions" (Judg. xiv. 5).

LXX. &c. κήρυσσε is not a good rendering of *harí'i*. Tischf. mentions no reading ἀλάλαξον. Just. Mart. (*Tryph.* 53) ἀλάλαξον κήρυσσε, but (*Apol.* i. 35) only κήρυσσε.—Cod. Alex. right, ὁ βασιλεύς σου. The translation σώζων for *nósha* cannot be justified. πραΰς would

10 And I will cut off the chariot from Ephraim, and the horse from Jerusalem, and the battle bow shall be cut off: and he shall speak peace unto the heathen: and his dominion *shall be* from sea *even* to sea, and from the river *even* to the ends of the earth.

11 As for thee also, by the blood of thy covenant I have sent forth thy prisoners out of the pit wherein *is* no water.

12 Turn you to the strong hold, ye prisoners of hope: even to day

---

be the correct rendering of ʿănāv rather than of ʿănî. Symm. πτωχός. Theod. ἐπακούων. S. Matt. xxi. 5 omits the words δίκαιος καὶ σώζων. S. John xii. 15 omits also πραΰς, but instead of prefixing "rejoice greatly, cry out" he says μὴ φοβοῦ, while S. Matt. puts εἴπατε τῇ θυγατρὶ Σιών, which has been thought to be borrowed from Is. lxii. 11.

Baer edits וְהִכְרַתִּי with the accent on the ultimate (comp. note on i. 3); but some editions have וְהִכְרַתִּי־רֶכֶב, with *maqqēf* (hyphen), which, of course, takes the accent off the word which precedes it (Excurs. II. A. 2).—Three perfects Piʻel דִּבֶּר, כִּבֶּס and כִּפֶּר take *segōl* in the last syllable (as a rule), unless they be in pause.—מָשְׁלוֹ *mo-sh'lō* (Excurs. I. 7. γ) is the infin. Qal with suffix. <small>Verse 10. Words.</small>

καὶ πλῆθος καὶ εἰρήνη, reading the last ר of *dibbér* as a ו, and joining it to the next word: thus making וְרֹב וְשָׁלוֹם out of וְדִבֶּר שָׁלוֹם. For *miyyām* "from the sea" they read מַיִם *mayim* "waters," ὑδάτων. <small>LXX.</small>

The preceding verse concludes with a description of the glory of the King; but the glory was not to be his exclusively, therefore גַּם אַתְּ "even thou" is prefixed as a *nominativus pendens* to recall the attention to Israel, spoken of in ver. 9 under the figure of *Báth Çiyyōn* and *Báth Y'rushāláim*. The ב of בְּדַם denotes "in consideration of," as in (Gen. xviii. 28) בַּחֲמִשָּׁה "in consideration of the five."—Between בּוֹר and אֵין the relative אֲשֶׁר is understood, comp. note on ver. 2. <small>Verse 11. Constructions.</small>

בִּצָּרוֹן is a ἅπαξ λεγό. meaning "fastness" (LXX. ἐν ὀχυρώμασι) from בצר "to cut off," comp. עִיר בְּצוּרָה (Is. xxvii. 10) עִיר מִבְצָר (Josh. xix. 29) "fortified city."—אֲסִירֵי הַתִּקְוָה "ye prisoners of hope," i.e. ye who are still prisoners in Babylon, but have a great hope set before you.—גַּם הַיּוֹם "even to- <small>Verse 12. Words and Constructions.</small>

do I declare *that* I will render double unto thee; and raised up thy sons, O Zion, against thy sons, O Greece, and made thee as the sword of a mighty man.

13 When I have bent Judah for me, filled the bow with Ephraim,

---

day."—מַגִּיד מִשְׁנֶה אָשִׁיב לָךְ lit. "I announce a double [recompense, which] I will render unto you"; for, if we regard the disjunctive accent under *mishnéh*, we cannot render it "I declare, Double will I render unto you." But the two translations afford much the same meaning. As in Hab. i. 5 the participle פֹּעֵל borrows the pronoun of the first person sing. from הִנְנִי of the next verse, so does מַגִּיד here from the דְּרַכְתִּי of ver. 13.—מִשְׁנֶה often means "second"; but here it means "double," as (Is. lxi. 7) מִשְׁנֶה (*bosh-t'cém*) תַּחַת בָּשְׁתְּכֶם "instead of your shame, double."

LXX. καθήσεσθε, reading *shābhū* (from שׁוּב), as *Sh'bhū* (from יָשַׁב).—Instead of "hope" LXX. has τῆς συναγωγῆς, reading מִקְוֵה *miqvéh* or *miqváh* "a gathering together" (1 Kings x. 28, &c., Is. xxii. 11), instead of תִּקְוָה.—Instead of *maggíd* we have (by interchange of י and ו, and of ר and ד) *mágár* παροικεσίας.

Verse 13. דרך is the ordinary verb used of "bending" a bow. But the expression מִלֵּאתִי אֶפְרַיִם is very difficult. In the connection one naturally thinks of the phrase מִלֵּא יָדוֹ בַקֶּשֶׁת (2 Kings ix. 24) "he filled his hand with a bow," i.e. he took a bow in his hand; but the phrases are not parallel. In the absence of any parallel we must be guided by the sense, and take the verb מָלֵא as denoting "filling" the bow with an arrow (as we speak of loading a gun), i. e. setting an arrow on the string (for which the proper expression is כּוֹנֵן חִצָּם עַל יֶתֶר Ps. xi. 2), and render the verse: "For I will bend me Judah as a bow, and set Ephraim in it [as an arrow]." The verbs here (as also *shilláchtī* in ver. 11) are in the Prophetic Perfect.

LXX. For *ṣámti* "I have placed, i.e. rendered, made," reading *máshti* (in transposed order) we have ψηλαφήσω, comp. Gen. xxvii. 12 יְמֻשֵּׁנִי *y'mushshénī* ψηλαφήσῃ με.

14 And the Lord shall be seen over them, and his arrow shall go forth as the lightning: and the Lord God shall blow the trumpet, and shall go with whirlwinds of the south.

15 The Lord of hosts shall defend them; and they shall devour, and subdue with sling stones; and they shall drink, *and* make a noise as through wine; and they shall be filled like bowls, *and* as the corners of the altar.

עֲלֵיהֶם יֵרָאֶה "will reveal himself on their behalf," comp. (Ps. xliv. 23) עָלֶיךָ הֹרַגְנוּ "for thy sake we are killed."—The words וַאדֹנָי יְהוִה are read *vadōnāy 'lŏhīm* (see note on i. 1).—סַעֲרוֹת is constr. plur. of סְעָרָה; the *pathach* under the *sāmec* is a Light Vowel (Excurs. I. 5). This word occurs in the following forms: סְעָרָה and סַעַר, שְׂעָרָה and שַׂעַר.   Verse 14.

ἀπειλῆς αὐτοῦ, reading אֵימָה *ēmāh* "enmity," for תֵּימָן *Tēmān* "South." (*Possibly* also taking the final ן for וֹ and reading *ēmō* = *ēmāthō*, see note on iv. 2.)   LXX.

On צְבָאוֹת י״י see notes on i. 3.—יָגֵן Fut. Hiph. from גנן.—

וְכָבְשׁוּ אַבְנֵי־קֶלַע "and shall trample upon sling-stones," viz. in their valorous onslaught upon the enemy.—Observe וְשָׁתוּ is correctly accentuated on the *last* syllable as the perfect plur. of שָׁתָה; if it had been accentuated on the penultimate it would have been from שִׁית (comp. note on ver. 9).—Baer (p. 83) edits וְהָמוּ which (and not הָמוּ) is the reading here and in Jer. v. 22, li. 55.—כְּמוֹ־יַיִן (not "as wine," but) "as with wine," comp. x. 7, and note on viii. 11.—מִזְרָק the bowl into which the blood was received, and whence it was sprinkled.—זָוִיּוֹת "corners" only occurs here, and in Ps. cxliv. 12; but it is a well-known word in the Semitic languages, thus (sing.) Chald. *zivytha*, Syr. *zāvīthā*, Arab. *zawiyah*.   Verse 15.

καὶ καταναλώσουσιν αὐτούς, καὶ καταχώσουσιν αὐτοὺς ἐν λίθοις σφενδόνης, καὶ ἐκπίονται αὐτοὺς (*Alex.* το αιμα αυτων) ὡς οἶνον, καὶ πλήσουσι τὰς φιάλας ὡς θυσιαστήριον. הָמוּ is left untranslated, unless they took it as equivalent to הֵמָּה, and that as equivalent to אוֹתָם "them."   LXX.

16 And the Lord their God shall save them in that day as the flock of his people: for *they shall be as the stones of a crown, lifted up as an ensign upon his land.*

17 For how great *is* his goodness, and how great *is* his beauty! corn shall make the young men cheerful, and new wine the maids.

Verse 16. כְּצֹאן עַמּוֹ "his people like a flock"; hardly "as the flock of his people": though either translation is grammatically admissible.—After כִּי we must understand the pronoun הֵמָּה "they are" or "they shall be," comp. Ps. xxii. 29 [הוּא] וּמוֹשֵׁל בַּגּוֹיִם, and so frequently. The Hithpolel הִתְנוֹסֵס (Root נסס, נֵס "a standard") occurs only here and in Ps. lx. 6. With so few *data* it is impossible to be confident as to the exact meaning of the word, but it evidently means here either "to be lifted up" or "to glitter," and in any case to "be in some manner gloriously conspicuous." We would render, therefore, the clause "For [they shall be] as the stones of a diadem set up on high (*or* glittering) over His land."—מִתְנוֹסְסוֹת ought to have *ga'ya* under the מ because of the disjunctive accent (Excurs. II. B. 3).

Abh'nê nêzer is rendered λίθοι ἅγιοι, and so in vii. 3 הַנֵּזֶר is read LXX. *han-nêzer*, and rendered τὸ ἁγίασμα, comp. (Lev. xxi. 12) τὸ ἅγιον ἔλαιον, for *nêzer shêmen*.—*Mithnōs'sôth* they transl. κυλίονται.

Verse 17. The suffix of עַמּוֹ and אַדְמָתוֹ (ver. 16) refers to God, and so one would naturally have understood the suffixes טוּבוֹ and יָפְיוֹ in that sense also. But, since יָפִי (יֳפִי) Ezek. xxviii. 7) "beauty" is never attributed to God, it is better to take the suffix of *ṭubhô* and *yophyô* as referring to "His people." טוּב denotes here "goodliness." מַה is here an exclamation of admiration, as (Gen. xxviii. 17) מַה־נּוֹרָא "how terrible!", (Numb. xxiv. 5) מַה־טֹּבוּ אֹהָלֶיךָ "how goodly are thy tents"; on the *dagesh* after מַה see Excurs. III.—בַּחוּרִים is the plur. of בָּחוּר "a youth"; while בְּחוּרִים is the plur. of בָּחוּר "chosen" (and also means the "age of youth" like זְקֻנִים "old age," נְעוּרִים "childhood," עֲלוּמִים "youth," &c.). The change of the first *qāmāṣ* into *pathach* is remarkable, the nearest parallel that we can adduce is אָח "brother" plur. אַחִים (comp. also Job xxxi. 24 מִבְטָחִי (Baer, not מִבְטָחִי); יְמַח Ps. cix. 13): observe

ZECHARIAH IX.   89

that in all the cases, it is before ה that the shortening takes place.— יְנוּבֵב (only here is the Pōlēl) "shall make to grow (or increase)," comp. חַיִל כִּי יָנוּב "wealth, if it increase" (Ps. lxii. 11, comp. xcii. 15).

מָה is taken in the indefinite sense "whatever" (comp. 2 Sam. xviii. 22, and p. 46), and so the translation runs ὅτι εἴ τι ἀγαθὸν αὐτοῦ καὶ εἴ τι καλὸν αὐτοῦ. Yᵉnōbhḗbh is rendered εὐωδιάζων.   LXX.

This passage is now generally admitted to be Messianic. It falls naturally into two sections. The coming of the King (ver. 9, 10); and the return of the exiles, their glorious victories over the Greeks, and their consequent peace and prosperity (ver. 11—17). Zion is now called on to rejoice in the approaching advent of her long-promised King. And what are His characteristics? He is Righteous (comp. Is. xxxii. 1, liii. 11, Jer. xxiii. 5, 6, &c.), but He is also "afflicted" (comp. Is. lii. 14—liii. 11, Ps. cx. 7), and yet "saved" (see Is. liii. 12, and comp. Ps. cx. 7 with Phil. ii. 7—9, comp. also Acts ii. 23, 24, Eph. i. 19—23, Rom. i. 4). He comes with no military pomp, with neither chariots nor horses, but unostentatiously riding upon a colt of an ass; for, this avoidance of vain display is a mark of the "Servant of YHVH," who "shall not cry, nor lift up nor cause his voice to be heard in the streets" (Is. xlii. 2, comp. Matt. xii. 15—21). At that time the chariot shall be cut off from Ephraim and the horse from Jerusalem (comp. Mich. v. 9, rather than iv. 3 and Is. ii. 4), which seems to imply that the military power of the nation should have ceased, for He is to be a Prince of Peace, speaking peace to the nations, and establishing His spiritual kingdom (in description of which the old terms used of the territory promised to Israel, Ex. xxiii. 31, comp. Ps. lxxii. 8, Ecclus. xliv. 21 are applied) even to the ends of the earth. The prophecy was, doubtless, fulfilled by our Lord, when He rode into Jerusalem on (the day now called) Palm-Sunday. But He fulfilled it more in spirit than to the letter. That He did not fulfil it literally is sufficiently shown by the fact, that the King is here described as already "saved and afflicted," whereas, in the case of our Lord, His entry into Jerusalem took place before His Passion and before He was "saved" by being "raised up from the dead by the glory of the Father" (Rom. vi. 4). But in spirit He most truly fulfilled it, generally by His whole life of humility, and in particular on that day by illustrating, both to friends and foes, by His symbolical act of riding into Jerusalem on an ass, that His kingdom is not of this world.

Remarks ix. 9—17.

But this prophecy was not to be immediately fulfilled. The nation had yet severe sufferings to endure and triumphs to achieve, viz. in those struggles with the "sons of Greece," which render the Maccabean period (B.C. 167—130) one of the most noble pages in Jewish history. Those, who still remained in the land of their exile, are exhorted to come forth (comp. ii. 7—13), confident in the help of the LORD of Hosts, who would wield the reunited Judah and Ephraim (comp. Is. xi. 13) as His weapons of war (comp. Jer. li. 20): He Himself will appear as their champion, with the rolling of the thunder as His war-trumpet, the forked lightning as His arrows, "the wild storm blowing from the southern desert, the resistless fury of His might." And then, when they had fought the good fight, and not before, God promises "the flock His people" the blessings of peace (ver. 16, 17).

[It has been urged as an objection against the post-exilic authorship of this passage that "Ephraim" and "Jerusalem" are mentioned, as though Israel were still separated from Judah. But, on the contrary, Ephraim and Jerusalem are here strictly parallel terms, as are also "Judah" and "Ephraim" (ver. 13), where both are represented as equally opposed to the sons of Javan. The nation was now one (Ezek. xxvii. 22) and known by the names of "Israel" (xii. 1, Mal. i. 1, 5), "all the tribes of Israel" (ix. 1), also the "house of Judah" (x. 3, 6), "house of Joseph" and "Ephraim" (x. 6, 7), besides by those terms mentioned on p. 21. For, now that the "dead bones of the *whole house of Israel*" were revived (Ezek. xxvii. 11), and "my servant David" was about to be "King over them" (ver. 24), the prophecy of Ezekiel (ver. 16—22) was fulfilled, and the staves (*tribes, shibh‘te*) of Joseph and of Judah had become one in God's hand. Hence the interchangeable terms.]

CHAPTER X.

ASK ye of the LORD rain in the time of the latter rain; so the LORD shall make bright clouds, and give them showers of rain, to every one grass in the field.

Verse 1. שַׁאֲלוּ, *pathach* (not *chiriq*) is the proper vowel for the first syllable to the 2nd fem. sing., 2nd masc. plur. of the Imperative of verbs medial guttural, as בַּחֲרוּ, זַעֲקוּ, טַעֲמוּ, רַחֲצוּ, שַׁעֲרוּ; but אֶהֱבוּ, because of the initial א, comp. אֶחֱזוּ.—חֲזִיזִים means "lightnings" (Job xxviii. 27, xxxviii. 25) which precede the rain.—In *um‘tar-géshem*, *Géshem* the consequent, as is usual with two nouns in construction, qualifies the antecedent. Thus *m‘tar-géshem* denotes "a pouring rain," so טִיט הַיָּוֵן (Ps. xl. 3) means "the clayey mud"; in Job xxxvii. 6 we have גֶּשֶׁם מָטָר, and then גֶּשֶׁם מִטְרוֹת עֻזּוֹ.—Instead of לָהֶם one would have expected לָכֶם "to you"; but a sudden change of person is most common in Hebrew, e.g. in Mal. ii. 15.—לְאִישׁ means "for each one," i.e. "for every one" (comp. Gen. xlii. 45 and Zech. vii. 10, viii. 4, 17).

LXX. *B‘éth* is taken as the absolute, καθ' ὥραν: and πρώϊμον καὶ is introduced before *malqŏsh* "latter rain," borrowing, probably, from Deut. xi. 14, Jer. v. 24.—*Ch‘zîzîm* is rendered φαντασίας.

2 For the idols have spoken vanity, and the diviners have seen a lie, and have told false dreams; they comfort in vain: therefore they went their way as a flock, they were troubled, because *there was* no shepherd.

שָׁקֵר חָזוּ, the 3rd plur. perf. חָזוּ being from חָזָה (see note on ix. 15) ought to have been accentuated on the *last* syllable, but it has been drawn back because the next word is accentuated with a great disjunctive accent of the *first* syllable. Observe in this verse the interchange of the Perfect and Imperf., merely for the sake of variety of sound.—יְנַחֵמוּן the Piel imperf. 3rd pers. plur. The ordinary form is יְנַחֵמוּ, in pause יְנַחֵמוּ; but, since here the verb ends in ן and the last syllable thus becomes *closed*, and having a long vowel must needs take the accent (Excurs. I. 8), we get יְנַחֵמוּן with *methey* under the נ in accordance with Excurs. II. A. 1. The form ending in *ûn* is shown by a comparison with the kindred languages to be older than the shortened form in *û*. Hence it is incorrect to call this an additional nun (נון נוספת).—עָנָה in the Qal, Niph'al, Pu'al and Hithpa'el is used in the sense of "to be afflicted."

Verse 2.

T'rāphîm is variously rendered by LXX., here οἱ ἀποφθεγγόμενοι, in Gen. xxxi. 19, 34, 35 by εἴδωλα.—For נָשְׂאוּ ἐξηράνθησαν; but ed. *Compl.* reads ἐξήθησαν, which would represent the Hebr. well enough. For "shepherd" (rō'êh) ἴασις, reading rōphêh רֹפֵה "healer."

LXX.

The first two verses of this chapter seem to be closely connected with the last two of the preceding chapter. In x. 17 it is promised that corn and wine should make the youth of Israel to flourish. Here the people are exhorted to pray to the Lord to send the latter rain. It is probable, since the prophet mentions only the *latter* rain, that he was prophesying between the times of the former rains (*Marcheshvan* and *Cislev*), and the latter rains (*Nisan*). (For the months see p. 10.) Against the post-exilic origin of this passage, and of xiii. 2, it has been objected that, *the mention of idols and false prophets harmonizes only with a time prior to the captivity*. It is perfectly true that after the captivity idolatry was not, as it had been before, the crying sin of the nation. Still, even if the Prophet be not here reverting to sins of the past which had caused the exile, a reference to Ezr. ix. 1, 2, Neh. vi. 10—14, xiii. 23, 24, Mal. iii. 5, 2 Macc. xii. 40, Acts v. 36, 37, xiii. 6, Josephus, *Bell. Jud.* vi. 5, § 2, 3, will clearly show how suitable warnings against idolatry and witchcraft might be, even after the return from captivity. With this passage comp. Jer. xiv. 22.—"Because they had no shepherd" might mean "for want of a good monarch" (comp. Ezek. xxiv. 5, 8);

Remarks. x. 1, 2.

3 Mine anger was kindled against the shepherds, and I punished the goats: for the LORD of hosts hath visited his flock the house of Judah, and hath made them as his goodly horse in the battle.

4 Out of him came forth the corner, out of him the nail, out of him the battle bow, out of him every oppressor together.

5 And they shall be as mighty men, which tread down *their ene-*

---

but it cannot mean "because they had no native king"; for they did not go into captivity because they had no king, but on the contrary, they lost their king because they went into captivity. We think, therefore, that the paraphrase of the LXX. "because they had no healer," i.e. because the True Shepherd of Israel had ceased to guide and protect them, might possibly be defended.

Verse 3. Constructions. Observe the change of tense from *chārāh* to *ephqōd*, which is simply, as we hold, for the sake of variety (comp. note on ver. 2). The difference between *pāqad ʿal* "he punished," and *pāqad* followed by the acc. (as in Ex. iii. 16), is here very decidedly marked.

Verse 4. יַחְדָּו is an adverb, "altogether." It occurs also in the simple form יַחַד, but when it has the suffix it is always וָ , or יָ . Possibly in an earlier stage of the language it was regularly declined. In support of this theory of original declension, we may remark that such words as לְבַד "alone" are actually declined לְבַדִּי, לְבַדְּךָ, לְבַדּוֹ, לְבַדְּהֶן, לְבַדָּן. Similarly in Arabic *dhā* means "this" and *dhāka* "this-there." This latter in old classical Arabic is declined, in speaking to *one man, dhāka;* to one *woman, dhāki;* to *two persons, dhākumā;* to *several men, dhākum;* to *several women, dhākunna*. But as a rule the simple undeclined form *dhāka* is used.

LXX. *Pinnāh* "corner" is read as *pānāh* "he turned," and rendered ἐπέβλεψε (so *p'nōth* (Mal. ii. 13) ἐπιβλέψαι).—*Yāthēdh* "nail," ἔταξε. We saw (ix. 12) that LXX. confound ת and מ, so perhaps they read יָמָד, and understood it as יַעֲמִיד (comp. יָהֵל = אָהֵל Is. xiii. 20) a verb which is translated by the verb τάσσω (2 Chron. xxxi. 2). *Milchāmāh ἐν θυμῷ* reading מִלְחָמָה, and taking מִל as equivalent to לְמִן (xiv. 10), for מִן in the sense of "on account of" (ii. 8).

Verse 5. בּוֹסִים is the pres. partic. of בּוּם, from which we should expect בָּסִים, but we find also קוֹמִים (from קוּם) 2 Kings xvi. 17, and (naturally enough) בּוֹשִׁים (from בּוֹשׁ not בּוֹשׁ) Ezek. xxxii. 30.

mies in the mire of the streets in the battle: and they shall fight, because the LORD *is* with them, and the riders on horses shall be confounded.

6 And I will strengthen the house of Judah, and I will save the house of Joseph, and I will bring them again to place them; for I have mercy upon them: and they shall be as though I had not cast them off: for I *am* the LORD their God, and will hear them.

7 And *they of* Ephraim shall be like a mighty *man*, and their heart shall rejoice as through wine: yea, their children shall see *it*, and be glad; their heart shall rejoice in the LORD.

8 I will hiss for them, and gather

Since בּוּם is elsewhere construed with a simple acc., it will be best here to render: "And they shall be like heroes trampling [*their enemies*] into the mire of the streets."—וְהוֹבִישׁוּ "and shall be ashamed (see notes on ix. 5 and 8).

וְהוֹשַׁבְתִּים is a fusion of הוֹשַׁבְתִּים "I will make them to dwell" (Hiph. of יָשַׁב), and הֲשִׁבוֹתִים "I will make them return" Verse 6.
(Hiph. of שׁוּב ver. 10). The verb is probably intended to have the latter meaning. In Semitic languages the different forms of verbs are often confounded (see notes on ii. 17, iv. 10, ix. 5); nor are we free from such mistakes in English: thus people often say "he lay" for "he laid"; "he flew" for "he fled."—כַּאֲשֶׁר here means "as though" "*quasi*," as (Job x. 19) כַּאֲשֶׁר לֹא־הָיִיתִי "as though I had never been"; more usually it means "as" "*sicut*," or "when" "*quum*" "*postquam*."

רִחַמְתִּים ἠγάπησα αὐτούς, comp. ἀγαπήσω τὴν οὐκ ἠγαπημένην (Hos. ii. 23 [25]); but Hos. i. 6 οὐκ ἠλεημένη. LXX.

From שָׂמַח and שָׂמְחוּ שָׂמֵחַ we may observe that there are two forms of the Perfect of this verb, שָׂמַח and שָׂמֵחַ (comp. p. 70). Verse 7.
In pause all forms from strong verbs take the accent on the second root-letter, unless a long vowel in a closed syllable at the end of the word draw it away (see on ver. 2). יָגֵל לִבָּם "let their heart rejoice." Comp. the exclamation (Ps. xxii. 27) יְחִי לְבַבְכֶם לָעַד.

On the form אֶשְׁרְקָה see p. 6 and note on viii. 21. For this use of the verb comp. Is. v. 26, vii. 18.—וְרָבוּ כְּמוֹ רָבוּ may mean Verse 8.
"and they shall multiply as they did multiply [formerly]," see Ex. i. 12. Or, better, it is to be taken as an idiomatic expression

them; for I have redeemed them: and they shall increase as they have increased.

9 And I will sow them among the people: and they shall remember me in far countries; and they shall live with their children, and turn again.

10 I will bring them again also out of the land of Egypt, and gather them out of Assyria; and I will bring them into the land of Gilead and Lebanon; and *place* shall not be found for them.

"they shall increase as they increase"—i.e. "they shall increase to any extent"; this latter is certainly the meaning of the expression in more modern Hebrew. For the promise comp. Jer. xxiii. 3, Ezek. xxxvi. 11.

Verse 9. Imperfects, which have *pathach* in the second syllable, change it into *qāmāṣ* before a suffix, as אֶזְרָע, אֶזְרָעֵם.—Observe the doubling of the last root-letter in the plur. מֶרְחַקִּים "distant places" (see note on i. 15). The sing. of our word is always מֶרְחָק with *e* in first syllable; but the plur. has also *pathach* in Is. xxxiii. 17, Jer. viii. 9 (see notes on vi. 1, ix. 5).—וְחָיוּ אֶת־ "and shall live with." וְיָשְׁבוּ, the ו is pointed with *qāmāṣ* to prevent the concurrence of two accentuated syllables. This takes place here although *hēm* has a disjunctive accent (*Tiphchā*), comp. (Job iv. 16) : דְּמָמָה וָקוֹל אֶשְׁמָע, while more commonly a preceding disjunctive prevents the *vāv* from taking *qāmāṣ*, as וַיְהִי בָרָד וְאֵשׁ... (Ex. ix. 24).

LXX. ἐκθρέψουσι τὰ τέκνα αὐτῶν, reading instead of *chāyū*, חָיוּ *chiyyū*, the Pi'el.

Verse 10. לֹא־יִמָּצֵא lit. "shall not be found," meaning "there shall not be room enough," comp. Josh. xvii. 16, where, however, הָהָר is the subject of the verb. Some take the verb here as impers., others understand מָקוֹם. In Qal מָצָא לְ means "to reach to" (Is. x. 10), then "to suffice" (Numb. xi. 22), comp. ἱκνέομαι and ἱκανός. (See also note on xi. 6.)

ὑπολειφθῇ taking *yimmāṣē* somewhat in the sense of נִשְׁאַר, or LXX. נוֹתַר "be left," or of נִפְקַד (Numb. xxxi. 49), or נֶעְדָּר (2 Sam. xvii. 22) "be missing," or "left behind."

11 And he shall pass through the sea with affliction, and shall smite the waves in the sea, and all the deeps of the river shall dry up: and the pride of Assyria shall be brought down, and the sceptre of Egypt shall depart away.

12 And I will strengthen them in the LORD; and they shall walk up and down in his name, saith the LORD.

As far as the form of יָם is concerned, it might be the construct, e.g. יָם־כִּנֶּרֶת (Numb. xxxiv. 11), in fact the construct is more commonly יָם־ than יָם. But the def. art. here prefixed to it precludes this interpretation. We must, consequently, translate צָרָה as in apposition with יָם "through the trouble-sea" (comp. p. 44), the passage of the Red Sea being referred to as a symbol of other sufferings and deliverances.—הִכָּה is very usually construed with בְּ.—גַלִּים must be taken as a second object, or "acc. of limitation."—וְהֹבִישׁוּ is intrans. see note on ix. 5.

Verse 11.

For ἐν θαλάσσῃ στενῇ to be correct the Hebrew should be בַּיָּם הַצַּר.
For hūrād these translators give ἀφαιρεθήσεται, and so (Ex. xxxiii. 5) ἀφέλεσθε stands for hōrēd.

LXX.

On the metheg of yithhallācū see Excurs. II. B. 4. Observe that Hithpa'els and Hithpolels take qāmāṣ in pause, not ṣērē, e.g. : תִּתְהַלָּל (Prov. xxxi. 30), הִתְמַגְּנוּ (no ga'yā Excurs. II. B. 4. 3). If the second root-letter be ה, the preceding vowel becomes segōl, as יִתְנֶחָם (Deut. xxxii. 36).

Verse 12.

κατακαυχήσονται for yithhallācū, which they read yithhallālū, לְ being misread for כְ, as in Hos. xiii. 13 בֵּן לֹא is rendered ὁ υἱός σου, as though it were בִּנְכָא, i.e. בִּנְכָה for בִּנְךָ.

LXX.

"The shepherds" (ver. 3) are the native rulers and spiritual guides (as in Jer. ii. 8, xvii. 16, xxiii. 1—4; Ezek. xxxiv. 2, &c.); and not foreign rulers and oppressors (as in Jer. vi. 3, 4, xxv. 34—38, xlix. 19). "The he-goats" are to be identified with "the shepherds," or perhaps rather to be regarded as leaders subordinate to them (comp. Ezek. xxxiv.) "Out of him" means probably "from Judah," i.e. the nation in general, or from Judah as the royal tribe; the latter supposition is hardly probable, however, since the Maccabeans were not of the tribe of Judah, but of Levi. Thus, apparently, "shepherd" is used here in a different sense to that in which it is used in the preceding verse. Similarly, nogēs is not used here in the same sense as in ix. 8. It can here mean

Remarks.
x. 3–12.

only a "native ruler," or "one who will oppress" [or subdue] "the heathen."— "Corner-stone" denotes "a chieftain" (1 Sam. xiv. 38, Is. xix. 13, and so too "nail" (Is. xxii. 23).—The whole of this passage is closely connected with ix. 11—15, the verses ix. 16, 17, x. 1, 2 being only a slight digression.—Vers. 5—7 are parallel with ix. 13—15.—The expression "as though I had not rejected them" seems clearly to point to a time when the captivity had already taken place.—*Ver*. 8—12 *have been looked on as decided evidence in favour of the pre-exilian origin of the passage*. But, (1) the reference in ver. 11 to the passage of the Red Sea shows that, if we please, we may regard the other expressions as figurative, viz., that Egypt is mentioned merely as the typical oppressor of Israel (Hos. viii. 13, ix. 3), as the Exodus is ever looked on as the typical deliverance (e.g. Is. xi. 16); (2) Assyria may be mentioned rather than Babylon or Persia, because thither the ten tribes (Ephraim) had been carried away; or Assyria may actually mean Persia, as in post-captivity times the king of Persia is also often called the king of Babylon (e.g. Ezra vi. 22, 2 Kings xxiii. 29: Judith i. 7, ii. 1, Herod. i. 178—188); (3) it must not be forgotten that but a small portion of the nation had as yet returned under Zerubbabel, and that viii. 8 (not to mention ii. 10—17) is quite as expressive of a restoration *in the future* as this passage, and yet the genuineness of neither ii. 10—17 nor of viii. 8 has ever been called in question (see *Introduction*).

CHAPTER XI.

OPEN thy doors, O Lebanon, that the fire may devour thy cedars.

2 Howl, fir tree; for the cedar is fallen; because the mighty are spoiled: howl, O ye oaks of Bashan; for the forest of the vintage is come down.

Verse 2. Words.

הֵילֵל imperative of יָלַל (see the substantive in next verse). The *singular* imperative only occurs once again, viz. Jer. xlvii. 2, where it is הֵילֵל.—On the names of the trees consult the Dictionaries.—אֲשֶׁר is here (as in Hos. xiv. 4, &c.) equivalent to כִּי "for"; in the latter part of the verse and in verse 3 we actually have כִּי (comp. note on viii. 20).—יַעַר הַבָּצִיר (*q'rî*) means "forest of the vintage," which does not give good sense. יַעַר הַבָּצוּר (*C'thibh*), taking *bâçûr* as a pass. partic., with the article exceptionally prefixed to the epithet only (see note on iv. 7), would mean "the inaccessible forest." Or, we might consider בָּצוּר as a substantive (like כָּבוֹד), in which case the construction would be more regular, and the meaning the same; but the word *bâçôr* does not occur elsewhere.

3 *There is* a voice of the howling of the shepherds; for their glory is spoiled: a voice of the roaring of young lions; for the pride of Jordan is spoiled.
4 Thus saith the LORD my God; Feed the flock of the slaughter;

יְלֵלת constr. of יְלָלָה (Zeph. i. 10), as צִדְקַת from צְדָקָה, the *chīrīq* is "light." On the metheg and לְ see note on ii. 13 (p. 28).—אַדִּרְתָּם, fem. nouns like מִלְחָמָה, יַבֶּשֶׁת, צָעֲרַת which have one syllable followed by ־ָה, ־ֶת or ־ַת, harden the ת in taking the suffixes, as מִלְחַמְתּוֹ: and also nouns which consist *only* of two such syllables as the two last mentioned, as שֶׁבֶת, שִׁבְתּוֹ; דַּלְתּוֹ (2 Kings xii. 10)—instead of the *Q'ri* דַּלְתְּךָ דַּלְתּוֹ, דֶּלֶת, דֵּעָתוֹ, דַּעַת (Is. xxvi. 20), one would prefer the *C'thibh*, and read, as here (ver. 1), דַּלְתֶיךָ.—"The Jordan" is never called the *river* Jordan, but simply הַיַּרְדֵּן "the descender" (on account of its physical peculiarities; comp. Stanley, *Sinai and Palestine*, London, 1875, p. 284). LXX. for *Ya'ar habbāçōr* gives ὁ δρυμὸς ὁ σύμφυτος. שָׁאוֹן φρύαγμα as in Jer. xii. 5.

Verse 3. Words.

These three verses are regarded by BLEEK *as a prophecy of the campaign of Tiglath-Pileser, king of Assyria, against the allied forces of Syria under Rezin, and of Israel under Pekah.* Very similar terms are certainly used by Isaiah in reference to the march of an army, viz. that of Sennacherib (2 Kings xix. 23, Is. xxxvii. 24). But the wording of Zech. xi. 1—3, which in some points reminds one of Jer. xxv. 31—36, is so vague, that, if it refer to an invasion at all, it would be equally applicable to *any* which came from the north, whether Assyrian, Babylonian, Persian, Greek, or Roman. Consequently, although we admit that it would make no perceptible difference to the interpretation of this chapter if this passage were removed, we do not feel that it contains any such internal evidence as would compel us to refer it to pre-exilian times.— Some have looked on these verses as descriptive of a storm bursting over the land from the north.—The Talmudic tradition (T. B. Yoma 39ᵇ) is that the passage refers to the destruction of the Second Temple.—If we are to consider these verses as an integral portion of the chapter, we may say that ver. 1—3 announce in general terms (perhaps under the figure of a storm) the judgment that was coming on the land of Israel, while ver. 4—17 describe the causes which would ultimately bring about this visitation.

xi. 1—3. Remarks.

הַהֲרֵגָה see Excurs. II. A. 6, N.B.—With the expression *çōn hahărēgāh* comp. (Ps. xliv. 23) צֹאן טִבְחָה and (Ps. lxxix. 11, cii. 21) בְּנֵי תְמוּתָה.

Verse 4.

5 Whose possessors slay them, and hold themselves not guilty: and they that sell them say, Blessed be the LORD; for I am rich: and their own shepherds pity them not.

6 For I will no more pity the inhabitants of the land, saith the LORD: but, lo, I will deliver the men every one into his neighbour's hand, and into the hand of his king: and they shall smite the land, and out of their hand I will not deliver *them*.

Verse 5. Words and Constructions.
That קִנְיֻהּ is the plur. here is shown by the verb; but in Is. i. 3 בְּעָלָיו is merely the honorific plural.—יַהֲרֹגְן. On the *metheg* see Excurs. II. A. 1 and 6 NOTE. The final *n* is the 3rd pers. fem. suff.—יֶאְשָׁמוּ. On the *dagesh* see *Massoreth hammassoreth*, ed. Ginsburg, p. 203. The meaning of the word here is "feel themselves guilty," comp. Jer. ii. 3, l. 6, 7.—וְאֶעְשִׁר has the א quiescent after *pathach* (as in לַאדֹנִי); but וָא stands for וְא (not for וָא as it does in וָאֶעֱנֶה 1 Kings xi. 39, or as לָא stands for לְא in לַאדֹנִי). The strict parallel, therefore, is rather to be found in מְלַאכְתּוֹ (which stands for the unused מְלַאכְתּוֹ). The *chîrîq* is merely written *defectivè* (comp. ver. 8): thus the regular form of the word would be וְאֶעְשִׁיר.—Observe the *masc.* suffix. of רֹעֵיהֶם. The sing. לֹא יַחְמוֹל after this plur. denotes that "*each one of them* does not pity," comp. (Ex. xxxi. 14) מְחַלְלֶיהָ מוֹת יוּמָת "those who profane it, each one shall certainly be put to death," and the sing. *yōmar* after *môc'rêhên* of this verse.

LXX.
Lô ye'shāmū οὐ μετεμέλοντο. *Lô yachmōl* "*lehēm* οὐκ ἔπασχον οὐδὲν ἐπ' αὐτοῖς (comp. Ezek. xvi. 5); but in the next verse *Lô 'echmōl* is rendered correctly οὐ φείσομαι.

Verse 6. Words and Constructions.
מָצָא has in *Qal*, among other meanings, that of "to happen to (*acc.*)," e.g. Gen. xliv. 34; whence the *Hiph.* means "to cause to happen to (*acc.*)," Job xxxiv. 11. Again the *Niph.* means "to be present" (Gen. xix. 15); whence the *Hiph.* has the meaning (1) "to present" "to offer to (אֶל)," (Lev. ix. 12); (2) and also "to cause to come to," "to deliver up" into the hand (בְּיַד), as here and in 2 Sam. iii. 8.—אִישׁ בְּיַד־רֵעֵהוּ "into the hands of one another"; similarly in the fem. we have (ver. 9) תֹּאכַלְנָה אִשָּׁה אֶת־בְּשַׂר רְעוּתָהּ "they (*fem.*) shall eat each other's flesh." (Comp pp. 69, 70.)

ZECHARIAH XI. 7.

7 And I will feed the flock of slaughter, *even* you, O poor of the flock. And I took unto me two staves; the one I called Beauty, and the other I called Bands; and I fed the flock.

לָכֵן עֲנִיֵּי הַצֹּאן, the *lācēn* "therefore" cannot refer to the command of ver. 4, since the consequence of that command is already expressed by the וֹ at the beginning of the sentence (see note on viii. 19). The Lesser Massoreth says that לָכֵן stands for לָכֶן (E.V., see also p. 55) i. e. "for you O...," viz. for your protection (comp. ix. 3). Or it would be possible to take לָכֵן as for לְהָכֵן "to establish" as לְמָרֹות (Is. iii. 8) for לְהָמְרוֹת, לְאוֹר (Job xxxiii. 30) for לְהָאוֹר Niph., and לָבִיא (Jer. xxxix. 7, 2 Chron. xxxi. 10) for לְהָבִיא. If *lācēn* is here to have the sense of "therefore," it can refer only to the preceding clause; the meanings "truly" (Qimchi), or "yea verily" (Ewald) assigned to it are questionable. Now, עֲנִיֵּי הַצֹּאן might well after the analogy of צְעִירֵי הַצֹּאן (Jer. xlix. 20, l. 45) mean, not "the afflicted ones of the flock," but "miserable flock." In this case *lācēn* would refer back to the words "flock of the slaughter." Thus, we might understand the clause: "Therefore (וֹ) I fed the flock destined for slaughter, (therefore a most miserable flock)."—But I am inclined (seeing that *cēn* "*niyyē haççōn* recurs in ver. 11) to suppose that the words have been accidentally introduced here from that later passage; but before the time of the LXX., see below. On the *methey* under וָאֶקַּח־לִי see Excurs. II. A. 2, and B. 4 Exception.—מַקְלוֹת *maqlōth* (for *maq-q'lōth*) is the ordinary plural of מַקֵּל (see Excurs. IV.): the *qūph* (as in many words) loses its *dagesh* on losing its vowel; but when it retains the vowel, it does not: as מַקְלְכֶם (Ex. xii. 11).—Here we have אַחַד the *constr.* form instead of אֶחָד the *absol.*, comp. (Gen. xlviii. 22) שְׁכֶם אַחַד, and 2 Sam. xvii. 22; but it may be a rare form of *absol.*

For לָכֵן עֲנִיֵּי הַצֹּאן εἰς τὴν Χαναανίτιν, reading לִכְנַעֲנִיָּה and omitting צֹאן. In ver. 11 they seem to have read לִכְנַעֲנֵי הַצֹּאן. LXX., &c. *Nō'am κάλλος*; Aq. and Symm. εὐπρέπεια.—*Chōbhelīm σχοίνισμα*. The verbs are rendered by futures.

Verse 7.

8 Three shepherds also I cut off in one month; and my soul lothed them, and their soul also abhorred me.

9 Then said I, I will not feed you; that that dieth, let it die; and that that is to be cut off, let it be cut off; and let the rest eat every one the flesh of another.

10 And I took my staff, *even* Beauty, and cut it asunder, that I might break my covenant which I had made with all the people.

11 And it was broken in that day: and so the poor of the flock that waited upon me knew that it *was* the word of the LORD.

---

xi. 4–7. Remarks. The LORD Himself is the Shepherd of Israel (Is. xl. 11, Ezek. xxxiv. 11—16), and the ideal shepherd "my servant David" the Messiah (Ezek. xxxiv. 23, 24) is His representative. The Prophet is now commanded to personate God in this His office of Shepherd, and to feed (i.e. to protect and take care of His flock) the house of Israel, whom their foreign rulers (their owners, sellers, and shepherds) were grinding down, "for," saith the LORD, "I will not pity the inhabitants of the world, but will set mankind one against the other (comp. Ezek. xxvi. 30, 33), and deliver each into the hand of his king, &c.," i.e. He would cause the world to be smitten and broken up with wars and civil tumults: this flock, then, which was "in the world," if it were not to be "taken out of the world," would require special protection to "keep it from the evil" (John xvii. 15). Therefore the Prophet takes two staves "Favour" and "Binders" to symbolize God's gracious protection of His people, and the union which would exist between Judah and Ephraim (Ezek. xxxvii. 16—22).

Verse 8. Words, Constructions and LXX. וָאַכְחִד is only shortened in *appearance*, the *long chīrīq* is merely written *defective*.—אֶת שְׁלֹשֶׁת הָרֹעִים may mean "the three shepherds," and especially so, since אֶת is prefixed; or simply "three shepherds," as שְׁלֹשֶׁת הַחִצִּים (1 Sam. xx. 21); or "three of the shepherds," as חֲמֵשׁ הַיְרִיעֹת "five of the curtains" (Ex. xxvi. 3).—בָּחַל occurs only here, and in the C'thībh of Prov. xx. 21 (in the Pu'al), it seems here to mean "to loathe," בְּחִיל in Syr. means "afflicted with nausea." For *Bāchălāh* LXX. give ἐπωρύοντο "roared."

Verse 9. מֵתָה תָמוּת means *moribunda moriatur*. LXX. τὸ ἀποθνῆσκον ἀποθνῃσκέτω.

Verse 11. Constructions. וַיֵּדְעוּ כִּן... "And they knew that it was so [viz.] that, &c." Comp. אָבִי יָדַע כֵּן "my father knoweth [that it is] so" (1 Sam. xxiii. 17). The rendering "and so (i.e. thus) they knew," would have required the collocation וְכֵן יָדְעוּ.—"niyyĕ haççón see note on ver. 7.

On οἱ Χαναναῖοι see on ver. 7. Here they do not omit הצאן. *Hashshōm'rīm ōthí*, τὰ φυλασσόμενά μοι, they seem to have read הַשֹּׁמְרִים אֹתִי. LXX.

xi. 8 –11. Remarks.

This is one of the passages which by certain commentators have been looked on as conclusive proof of the pre-exilian origin of these chapters. We proceed to give a short *résumé* of the opinions which have been held with regard to it. "One month" has by (α) MAURER been held to be a literal month; (β) QIMCHI takes it to mean an indefinitely short period; (γ) VON HOFFMANN thinks that each day stands for seven years, 210 years in all; (δ) WRIGHT takes "each day for a year" (Ezek. iv. 6), and so understands a period of 30 years to be signified by "one month."—The meaning of the expression "the three shepherds" will, of course, depend on the view taken of the meaning of "one month." Thus (1) CYRIL considers that kings, priests, and prophets are meant, and PUSEY "priests, judges and lawyers," who having "delivered to the cross the Saviour were all taken away (α) in one month, Nisan, A.D. 33." But the rejection of the good shepherd is spoken of by the Prophet as posterior to the cutting off of the shepherds. (2) MAURER would interpret the three shepherds of Zechariah (son of Jeroboam II.), his murderer Shallum who reigned but a month, and a *third unknown usurper* whose downfall speedily took place. But Shallum was certainly murdered by Menahem (2 Kings xv. 10—14), and there is no room for a third unknown usurper. (3) HITZIG would avoid the difficulty by rendering "I removed the three shepherds *which were* in one month" (in support of which construction he refers, and rightly, to such passages as Ex. xxxiv. 31, Is. xxiii. 17, Ezek. xxvi. 20), and takes them to be the kings Zechariah, Shallum and Menahem, who in about the space of one month sat upon the throne of Israel. But the difficulty is really so obviated. Shallum reigned actually "a month of days" (2 Kings xv. 13), and the events referred to occupied much longer. (3) VON HOFFMANN interprets them of the three empires, Babylonian, Medo-Persian and Macedonian, which lasted 215 years from the captivity to Babylon to the death of Alexander the Great. But it cannot be shown that "a day" is ever used to represent "seven years"; nor can the death of Alexander be said to have put an end to the Macedonian empire. (4) QIMCHI explains them as Jehoahaz, Jehoiakim and Zedekiah: (5) ABARBANEL as the three Maccabees, Judas, Jonathan and Simon, but, since the cutting off of the shepherds seems to be looked on by the Prophet as an act of kindness to the flock, which only made their ingratitude the more abominable, it seems better with WRIGHT to understand the 30 years [according to (δ) the "one month"] as those between B.C. 172 when Antiochus Epiphanes desecrated the Temple, and B.C. 141 when the three alien shepherds, *Antiochus Epiphanes, Antiochus Eupator*, and *Demetrius I.*, were cut off, and the last trace of Syrian supremacy was removed by the expulsion of the Syrian garrison from its fortress in Jerusalem.—But the flock were not grateful for this protection, therefore the Prophet cuts asunder the staff "favour," to indicate that God would annul the covenant He had made with the nations in behalf of His people (Ezek. xxiv. 25—28). This was fulfilled in the troubles which overtook the nation, when they became corrupted, at the close of the Maccabean period.

12 And I said unto them, If ye think good, give *me* my price; and if not, forbear. So they weighed for my price thirty *pieces* of silver. 13 And the LORD said unto me, Cast it unto the potter: a goodly price that I was prised at of them. And I took the thirty *pieces* of silver, and cast them to the potter in the house of the LORD.

Verse 12. הָבוּ, plur. Imperative masc. from יהב. This verb is altogether anomalous in its conjugation and accentuation. It occurs only in the Imperative. We have הַב "give thou" (Prov. xxx. 15), and with final הָ, frequently, and accentuated *mil'el* thus הָבָה נִבְנֶה "come (age!) let us build" (Gen. xi. 4), הָבָה תָמִים "give a perfect [lot]" (1 Sam. xiv. 41). The fem. occurs only once (Ruth iii. 15), הָבִי (*mil'el*), but the plur. is (as here) *milra'*, הָבוּ מִקְנֵיכֶם (Gen. xlvii. 16).—חֲדָלוּ is the proper Pausal form of an Imperative which takes *pathach* under the second root-letter, as וְהֲכָמוּ (Prov. viii. 33).—After numerals higher than ten, singular nouns are *generally* used, therefore we have כֶּסֶף "pieces of silver," but not always, e.g. כֶּסֶף שְׁלֹשִׁים שְׁקָלִים (Ex. xxi. 32).

Verse 13. Words. יוֹצֵר must mean "potter" (as in Is. xxix. 16, Ps. ii. 9). When followed by an acc. (as Zech. xii. 2) it retains its participial meaning of "former of."—הַיּוֹצֵר may mean "the potter" or "a potter" (see note on i. 8).—אֶדֶר occurs only here, and in Amos ii. 8: in the latter passage it is equivalent to אַדֶּרֶת (xiii. 4, Josh. vii. 21, &c.) "a cloak." Here in accordance with the ordinary meaning of the Root (xi. 2, 3), it seems to signify "glory" "magnificence."—יְקָר elsewhere means "costliness," "honour," "magnificence," here it undoubtedly means "price." The verb יָקַר elsewhere means "to be precious" originally "to be heavy"; here to "be priced" or "apprized."—מֵעֲלֵיהֶם, this is the only instance we can cite of the use of מֵעַל to signify the agent after a passive; but מִן is not uncommon in this sense, e.g. (Ps. xxxvii. 23) מִי...כּוֹנָנוּ. *Mē'al* generally means "from upon" (*anglicè* "from off"), or "from near." For this modification of its meaning, when applied to denote "by" of the agent, compare Latin *a*, &c.—וָאֶקְחָה, on the termination ה see p. 6, and on the *símān*

14 Then I cut asunder mine other staff, *even* Bands, that I might | break the brotherhood between Judah and Israel.

---

rāphêh, see Excurs. IV. 1 (ϵ)—*ōthô* in the singular, referring to the *sum of thirty pieces of silver.*

אֶדֶר הַיְקָר might be rendered "magnificence of the price!"; or taking the antecedent as qualifying the consequent, as in פֶּרֶא אָדָם (Gen. xvi. 12) "a man as untameable as an onager," we may render it "the magnificent price!"—In either case the expression is ironical.—בֵּית means "into the House of" (without any need of a preposition), as is frequently the case, e.g. (Gen. xii. 15) וַתִּקַּח הָאִשָּׁה בֵּית פַּרְעֹה, comp. xliii. 18, &c. <small>Constructions.</small>

"Cast it to the potter...by them." LXX. has κάθες αὐτοὺς εἰς τὸ χωνευτήριον, καὶ σκέψομαι εἰ δόκιμόν ἐστιν, ὃν τρόπον ἐδοκιμάσθης ὑπὲρ αὐτῶν.—χωνευτήριον, since (1 Kings vii. 15) <small>Versions and readings.</small>

וַיִּצֶר (=וַיֵּיצֶר) is rendered καὶ ἐχώνευσε, it is evident that the LXX. had our reading, but that they took *yōçêr* to mean, not the workman, but the *vessel* in which the metal is fused, as we say a "boiler," "wine-cooler," &c. Καὶ σκέψομαι εἰ δόκιμόν ἐστιν, reading וְאֶרְאֶה הַיְקָר. For Παγγοçêr Symm. also has τὸ χωνευτήριον; but Aq. ὁ πλάστης; Syr. "the treasury," for in Aram. an initial *y* is sometimes read as א, so that (without any alteration of the consonants) they may have read *ōçâr* אוֹצָר. (For an instance of the converse viz. of א read as י see LXX. of xiv. 5.) Three MSS. of Kennicott read אֶל־הָאוֹצָר, and five אֶל בֵּית הַיּוֹצֵר, both readings being, doubtless, derived from the LXX.

Since *maqlî* is defined by the pron. suff. *î, shēnî,* which agrees with it, takes by rule the definite article (see note on v. 6).— <small>Verse 14.</small>

אַחֲוָה "brotherhood" is a ἅπαξ λεγόμενον. אָב and אָח are not from monosyl. roots, their third radicals become apparent in certain circumstances. Thus their constr. is אֲבִי, אֲחִי, and in Aram. the plur. of אָב is אֲבָהָן with the third root-letter ה (which is always interchangeable with ו and י) clearly indicated. In the case before us the third root-letter becomes ו, and we get אַחֲוָה. The fem. אָחוֹת "a sister" stands for אֲחֹת, and in the plur. (with suff.) the third root-letter appears

15 And the LORD said unto me, | of a foolish shepherd.
Take unto thee yet the instruments | 16 For, lo, I will raise up a shep-

---

sometimes as *y*, e. g. (Job i. 4) אֲחִיתִירֶם. The same letters furnish another ἅπ. λεγόμ. אֲחֹוְתִי "my declaration" (Job xiii. 17), which is formed from חוה by means of a prosthetic א.—וּבֵן...בֵּן as in Gen. i. 7, another construction is בֵּין...לְ (ibid. ver. 6).

Vā'eḡdā' καὶ ἀπέρριψα (as in ver. 10). *Hā'aḥăvāh* τὴν κατάσχεσιν reading הָאַחֲוָה. Cod. Alex. has διαθήκην, which appears to be a correction from the Hebrew.

LXX.

The Prophet, still as God's representative, demands his hire of the flock. He receives the miserable sum of 30 pieces of silver (the price of a foreign slave (Ex. xxi. 32). This he is commanded to "cast to the potter." No satisfactory explanation of this phrase can be given. It may be that "to the potter with it" was a proverbial expression for throwing away anything worthless, but it cannot be proved that such was the case. WRIGHT holds that it was thrown to a potter as one of the lowest of the labouring classes. GROTIUS explains it as indicating that God did not value the 30 pieces more than broken potsherds. HENGSTENBERG, trying to show that this prophecy is a renewal of Jer. xviii. 1, xix. 4, in order to justify S. Matthew's quotation of it as from Jeremiah, maintains that "to the potter" means to an unclean place, since the potter of Jeremiah, he holds, had his pottery in the valley of ben Hinnom, which had been made an unclean place by Josiah. KLIEFOTH regards God as the Potter, comp. Jer. xviii. 6 sqq.—The citation in S. Matt. xxvii. 9 is evidently from memory, and a free paraphrase of the original. Though this prophecy may be said to have been fulfilled on every occasion of Israel's ingratitude towards their Protector, it was most signally fulfilled, when the chief priests offered the price of a slave for the betrayal of Him, in whose rejection the ingratitude of the nation culminated.—The breaking of the bond of brotherhood between Judah and Israel is represented as succeeding the rejection of the Good Shepherd. But, as that rejection was not one single act, but the sum of many such acts, so this disseverment of the union between Judah and Israel, while it had its commencement in the confusion which followed the cutting asunder of the staff "Binders" (see above), did not reach its climax until the time of those frightful civil contests, which marked the last winter of Jerusalem before it was taken by Titus (see Joseph. *Bel. Jud.* v.; Milman, *Hist. Jews*, Bk. xvi.); MAURER, HITZIG and EWALD consider the prophecy to refer to the rupture which took place between Israel and Judah, when Pekah (king of Israel) made an alliance with Rezin (king of Syria) and invaded Judah. But history gives no indication of any bond of union existing between Israel and Judah at that period.

*ch. 12–14.
Remarks.*

Verse 15.
Words.

אֱוִלִי is a ἅπ. λεγό., elsewhere we have אֱוִיל "foolish": comp. אֱכָזָר (Lam. iv. 3) and אַכְזָרִי (Prov. v. 9).

ZECHARIAH XI. 17.

herd in the land, *which* shall not visit those that be cut off, neither shall seek the young one, nor heal that that is broken, nor feed that that standeth still: but he shall eat the flesh of the fat, and tear their claws in pieces.

17 Woe to the idol shepherd that leaveth the flock! the sword *shall be* upon his arm, and upon his right eye: his arm shall be clean dried up, and his right eye shall be utterly darkened.

הַנַּעַר. *Ná‘ar* means a "youth," "young man," but is never used of the young of animals. Moreover the mention of the "young" of the flock would not be suitable here, since there would be no need to "seek them," for they would remain with their dams. Hitzig proposes to read נֵעָר (for נִנְעָר) Niph. partic. of נָעַר "to shake out, scatter." The only objection to this is, that all the other participles are in the *fem.*, and this would be *masc.* Perhaps the explanation of Gesenius is the best, viz. that נַעַר is an abstract substantive meaning "scattering," and used for the concrete "that which is scattered" (comp. note on vi. 10).—נִצָּבָה the fem. partic. Niph. denotes "standing firmly," comp. הֶבֶל כָּל אָדָם נִצָּב (Ps. xxxix. 6). —*Y‘calcél*, the *Pilpel* of כּוּל, denotes here (as in Gen. xlv. 11) to "provide with sustenance."—*Uphar‘sêhén* is fem., the sing. being פַּרְסָה, elsewhere the plur. is פְּרָסוֹת, whence we conclude that the *a* under the פ is a "Light vowel" (Excurs. I. 5), and the *sh'vá* under ר consequently moving.—*Y‘phārḗq* "tear off" or "in pieces." Verse 16. Words.

Hanná‘ar rightly τὸ ἐσκορπισμένον. *Y‘calcél* κατευθύνῃ, somewhat similarly it is rendered Ps. cxi. 6 (Heb. cxii. 5) οἰκονομήσει, "will *guide* his words with discretion" (Prayer-Book Version). LXX.

On *hóy* see note on ii. 11.—רֹעִי must mean "my shepherd," if we take אֱלִיל as an adj. "useless": because the latter has the definite article (see note on ver. 13). But if we take אֱלִיל as a substantive "uselessness" (comp. Job xiii. 4, רֹפְאֵי אֱלִיל "physicians of uselessness"), it will be the constr., with the old case ending (see p. 11). From the consideration that the expression "my shepherd" recurs in xiii. 7, we prefer the former interpretation. On the form עֻזְבִי see p. 11.—עֵין יָמִין (1 Sam. xi. 2) means "eye of the right Verse 17. Words and Constructions.

(side)," i.e. "right eye": *ἐν ẏmīnō*, consequently, means "his right eye."

LXX. οἱ ποιμαίνοντες taking the *í* of *rō'í* as equivalent to the plur. termination *ím*, comp. p. 61, and Obad. ver. 12, where, reading *noeŕí* for *noc'rō*, they render ἀλλοτρίων.

Remarks. The "foolish shepherd" seems to denote all the misrulers of Israel from the decline of the glories of the Maccabean period to the time when they willingly proclaimed "we have no king but Cæsar."

According to Ewald's theory, chap. xiii. 7—9 is misplaced, and should come after xi. 17. The passage would then run : "*Woe to my useless shepherd, that forsaketh the flock! A sword [shall descend] upon his arm, and upon his right eye. His arm shall utterly wither, and his right eye shall be utterly dimmed. Sword! awake! against my shepherd, and against a man, my fellow ('tis the utterance of YHVH Çebhā'ōth). Smite the shepherd, and the sheep shall be scattered…… (8) And it shall be in all the land…… (9) … And they shall say: YHVH is my God.*" If this be the true connection, the "third part," which was to be tried and refined, can only be referred to those Jews who embraced the pure religion of Christ, and to those who, laying aside for ever the idolatry of their ancestors, devoted themselves thenceforth to the study of the Law.

CHAPTER XII.

THE burden of the word of the Lord for Israel, saith the Lord, which stretcheth forth the heavens, and layeth the foundation of the earth, and formeth the spirit of man within him.

2 Behold, I will make Jerusalem a cup of trembling unto all the

---

Verse 1. Words and Constructions. *Massâ d'bhár Adōnáy* (see ix. 1).—עַל "concerning," not here, "against" like the בְּ of ix. 1.—*Shāmáyim* is the object after the active partic. *nōṭêh*, and therefore *nōṭêh* is in the absol. form (not in the constr. נֹטֶה). In such a case we are at liberty to use the definite article before the partic. e.g. הַנֹּטֶה כַדֹק שָׁמַיִם (Is. xl. 22), even if the object take the form of a pron. suff. as הָעֹשֵׂהוּ (Job xl. 19) "He who made him."—*Yōçér* (see notes on xi. 13).

Hinnêh ānōçí is more emphatic than simple הִנְנִי. *Sâm* the present

Verse 2. partic. used as a prophetic tense, parallel with אָשִׂים (ver. 3), see p. 36.—*Sáph* "a bowl" (Ex. xii. 22) makes in plur. סִפִּים (Jer. lii. 19), סִפּוֹת (1 Kings vii. 50), comp. צַד "side,"

people round about, when they shall be in the siege both against Judah *and* against Jerusalem.

3 And in that day will I make Jerusalem a burdensome stone for all people: all that burden themselves with it shall be cut in pieces, though all the people of the earth be gathered together against it.

---

plur. צָרִים. With *sáph rá'al* comp. כּוֹס הַתַּרְעֵלָה (Is. li. 17, 22).— Several interpretations of עַל־יְהוּדָה have been proposed. On the whole it seems best to refer the expression to the word *ra'al* in the former clause, and to render the second clause: "And also on Judah [shall fall this reeling] during the siege [which is to take place] against Jerusalem." Others would refer to the opening words of the chapter, and explain "And also concerning Judah [is this burden of the word of the LORD]." The rendering of the E. V. cannot be supported; that of the margin "and also against Judah [shall he be which] shall be in siege against Jerusalem," requires too much to be supplied. The explanation of Ewald "And also upon Judah shall it be [incumbent to be occupied] in the siege against Jerusalem," is grammatically correct, as he shows from the expression עֲלֵיהֶם בַּמְּלָאכָה (1 Chron. ix. 33) "upon them it was incumbent to be occupied in the work." And, if we could understand by it that Judah was to be co-operating *with* (not *against*) Jerusalem in the siege (see ver. 5), this translation would have much to recommend it. No infin. לִהְיוֹת, or לְהִלָּחֵם, is required, any more than an infin. is wanted in the passage cited from Chronicles.

The word *sáph* besides the meaning of "bowl," has that of "threshold" (e.g. Judg. xix. 27), hence the rendering of the LXX. ὡς πρόθυρα σαλευόμενα, and of the Syr. "a gate of fear." LXX. &c. In the last half-verse they understand *'al* as ἐν, a certain support for which rendering might be found in such expressions as that of vii. 4 (see notes). The בּ of *Bammāçór* they seem to take as the so-called *Beth essentiæ*; καὶ ἐν τῇ Ἰουδαίᾳ ἔσται περιοχὴ ἐπὶ Ἱερουσαλήμ.

אֶבֶן מַעֲמָסָה, ἅπ. λεγό. either "a burdensome stone," or "a stone for lifting." כָּל־עֹמְסֶיהָ denotes here, "every one that lifteth it up," comp. Is. xlvi. 3 (where the pass. partic. of *'āmás* is parallel with נָשָׂא), also Gen. xliv. 13 "each *lifted up* [his load] on his ass."—שָׂרַט is the verb used for "cutting the flesh," a custom forbidden to the Israelites by Lev. xxi. 5. *Sārôṭ yiṣṣārēṭū,*

Verse 3. Words and Constructions.

4 In that day, saith the LORD, I will smite every horse with astonishment, and his rider with madness: and I will open mine eyes upon the house of Judah, and will smite every horse of the people with blindness.

5 And the governors of Judah shall say in their heart, The inhabitants of Jerusalem *shall be my*

---

observe that the Infin. absol. *Qal* is often used to emphasize a finite verb in a different voice, e.g. *Niph.* here and (Ex. xxi. 28) סָקֹל יִסָּקֵל, comp. Job vi. 2; *Pu'al*, Gen. xxxvii. 33; *Hoph.* (Lev. xx. 9, 10, &c.).

LXX. λίθον καταπατούμενον...πᾶς ὁ καταπατῶν, since there is a great similarity between the pronunciation of ע and ר׳, it seems that the LXX. took the stem עמס as equivalent to רמס.—For *sārôt yissārêt* they give ἐμπαίζων ἐμπαίζεται, it is possible that they may have read שרק, which is used of "hissing in mockery," Zeph. ii. 5, (LXX. iii. 1 συριεῖ).

Verse 4. Words.
Timmāhôn "astonishment," "terror" occurs only here and once in the constr. (Deut. xxviii. 28) וּבְתִמְהוֹן לֵב, the verb is תָּמַהּ, hence the retention of the ה, while from הרה (with *quiescent* ל״ה) we have הֵרָיוֹן, and contracted הֶרֹנֵךְ "thy conception" (Gen. iii. 16). There are two forms of such words in *ôn*, one disyllabic as חֶשְׁבּוֹן, and the other, like those of this verse, trisyllabic, comp. הִגָּיוֹן. These latter, in construct and with suffix, seem usually to revert to the other (disyllabic) form, thus we have (Is. lvii. 8) זִכְרוֹנֵךְ *zic-rō-nēc*, (Lam. iii. 62) הֶגְיוֹנָם *hey-yōnām*, and constr. חֶזְיוֹן *chez-yôn*, דִּרְאוֹן *dir'ôn*. But from עִצָּבוֹן we have עִצְּבוֹנֵךְ (Gen. iii. 16) *'iç-çbhônēc* (comp. Excurs. II. *in fin.*).

Verse 5. Constructions, Readings and Versions.
אִמְצָה is a fem. substantive of the form of עוֹלָה, כָּבְשָׂה, &c. *Li* is the *dat. comm.* comp. *l'bhêthî* (ix. 8). One of Baer's MSS. reads אַמְּצָה־לִי Imperative Pi'el, this seems to have been the reading of Aquila who renders καρτέρησόν μοι. One MS. gives אָמְצָה־לִי 3rd fem. perf. Qal; but there is no fem. substantive in the sentence with which it could agree. LXX. rendering εὑρήσομεν ἑαυτοῖς

---

[1] Comp., for instance, *Pirqê Rabbi Eliezer* (li.), where for רגלים we have the variant רגלים.

ZECHARIAH XII. 6, 7.

strength in the LORD of hosts their God.

6 In that day will I make the governors of Judah like an hearth of fire among the wood, and like a torch of fire in a sheaf; and they shall devour all the people round about, on the right hand and on the left: and Jerusalem shall be inhabited again in her own place, even in Jerusalem.

7 The LORD also shall save the tents of Judah first, that the glory of the house of David and the glory of the inhabitants of Jerusalem do not magnify *themselves* against Judah.

τοὺς κατοικ. κ.τ.λ. seems to have understood אמצה as equivalent to אמצא, and the singular as used for the plural. Three MSS. do give אמצא. The Targum seems (as frequently) to combine two meanings, viz. that of Rt. מצא, and of Rt. אמץ, and paraphrases "salvation hath been found for the inhabitants of Jerusalem" (reading ליושבי for לי יושבי). Syr. paraphrases "the inhabitants of Jerusalem have been stronger than we." Arab. "We shall find for us," after LXX.

On the *metheg* of כביר see Excurs. II. B. 9.—עמיר (Jer. ix. 21, Amos ii. 13, Mic. iv. 12) = עמר "sheaf." The *qadmā* over the א of אלא stands for *metheg* (Excurs. II. A. 9, N.B.). Since the ō of *s'mōl* is read with the *m*, the ו is not read, but retained (sometimes) merely because an older form of the word was *sam-'ōl*.—סביב adv. "round about" as in Gen. xxiii. 17, such adverbs were originally substantives in the acc.—*Tachtèhā*, lit. "under herself," i.e. "in her place" (comp. note on vi. 12). Verse 6. Words.

In translating כיור by δαλόν (which is their rendering of אוד in iii. 2), some suppose the LXX. to have taken the Hebr. word as used by metonymy for the wood burnt therein. But the rend. may be due to a confusion of letters.—*Tachtèhā* is rendered καθ' ἑαυτήν. LXX.

On the *metheg* under lō *thigdāl* see Excurs. II. A. 1, and for that under *bêth-Dāvîd* see Excurs. II. A. 5. *Dāvîd* is usually spelt דוד (without *yūd*) in the earlier books. Verse 7. Words.

Bārīshōnāh καθὼς ἀπ' ἀρχῆς. Five MSS. are said to read בבראשונה, but none of Baer's MSS. give this reading. The LXX. rendering is, probably, *quoad sensum*, and the prefix ב a later gloss. LXX.

8 In that day shall the LORD defend the inhabitants of Jerusalem; and he that is feeble among them at that day shall be as David; and the house of David *shall be* as God, as the angel of the LORD before them.
9 And it shall come to pass in that day, *that* I will seek to destroy all the nations that come against Jerusalem.

Verse 8.   בְּעַד without prefix or affix is pointed בְּעַד; but with prefix מִבַּעַד, and with suffix בַּעֲדִי, בַּעַדְכֶם; for construction comp. Ps. iii. 4.— *Yōshēv* is used collectively, as may be seen from the *bāhēm* which follows.— *Nichshālīm* means "the weak" as וְנִכְשָׁלִים אָזְרוּ חָיִל (1 Sam. ii. 4), and the בְּ of *bāhēm* means "among" as in Is. v. 27 וְאֵין־כּוֹשֵׁל בּוֹ (and not "against" as in Nah. iii. 3).

LXX.   The expression "as God," or "as Gods," being thought too strong, LXX. paraphrased it by ὡς οἶκος Θεοῦ, comp. a similar proceeding in ver. 10 and xiii. 3.

Verse 9.   The verb בקש *baqqēsh* is used of God only here, and in Ex. iv. 24.

xii. 1—9. Remarks.   These chapters xii.—xiv. are marked off as a distinct section by the recurrence of the expression "Burden of the word of the LORD" (comp. ix. 1, Mal. i. 1). No argument against the post-exilian origin of these chapters can be based on the frequent use of the terms "Judah and Jerusalem," neither is it true that the author of these last chapters "nowhere mentions Israel," as verse 1 is distinctly addressed to "Israel." "Israel" (Zech. xii. 1, Mal. i. 1, 5, ii. 11, 16, Ezr. ix. 1, 4, 15, xi. 10, &c.) is a term constantly used in post-exilian times for the Jewish nation, and as parallel with "Judah and Jerusalem" (Zech. xii.—xiv. *passim*, Mal. ii. 11, iii. 4): so too "all the tribes of Israel" (Zech. ix. 1). Comp. "Ephraim" ix. 10, 13, x. 7, "Joseph" (x. 6), and "Judah" (ix. 8, 13, x. 3, 6), and "Jacob" (Mal. iii. 6, ii. 12) and see p. 21. All these were to a certain extent interchangeable terms in post-exilian times; but "Jerusalem" or "inhabitants of Jerusalem" is used especially of the inhabitants of the metropolis, as distinguished from the rest of the nation, just as a Parisian is distinguished from a Frenchman. PRESSEL considers the prophecy to refer to the repulse of Sennacherib from the walls of Jerusalem. Against this theory it has been rightly urged, that in the days of Hezekiah, when the royal house was foremost in the ranks of religious reformation, it would be strange that a prophet should speak of the house of David as concerned in the martyrdom of one of God's prophets. MAURER places the date of chap. xii.—xiv. between the death of Josiah (xii. 11), and the capture of Jerusalem by the Chaldæans. Chap. xii.—xiii. 6 he supposes to have been written in the fourth year of Jehoiakim, when the prophet expected that the enemy would be driven from the gates of Jerusalem; xiii. 7—xiv. 21, after the

10 And I will pour upon the house of David, and upon the inhabitants of Jerusalem, the spirit of grace and of supplications: and they shall look upon me whom they have pierced, and they shall mourn for him, as one mourneth for *his* only *son*, and shall be in bitterness for him, as one that is in bitterness for *his* firstborn.

battle of Carchemish, when darker fears intruded themselves upon his mind.—But there is a very strong objection against referring xii. 1—xiii. 6 to a time prior to the captivity. For how can we imagine a prophet at the time, when the house of David was the reigning dynasty, making use of such an expression as "that the glory of the house of David and of the inhabitants of Jerusalem may not be magnified over Judah"? We agree, therefore, with WRIGHT in supposing (at any rate) xii. 1—9 to refer to the period between the restoration from the captivity, and the coming of our Lord, when many nations, "Idumæans, Philistines, Arabians, Ammonites, Tyrians, Syrians, and Greeks made various attempts against the Jewish people and against Jerusalem. They are sometimes successful for a short time, but never for any lengthened period. Their attempts were always foiled, often with great loss to themselves, sometimes to their utter ruin." It must be remembered, too, that after the time of Zerubbabel the house of David fell into comparative obscurity, and that the great leaders the Maccabees were of the tribe of Levi, and not of the house of David.

LXX. καὶ ἐπιβλέψονται πρὸς μὲ ἀνθ' ὧν κατωρχήσαντο. Perhaps they read רקדו which means to "leap" (this is the reading of one of Kennicott's MSS.); but more probably they took דקר in the figurative sense of "insulting," as נקב "to pierce" is used of "cursing." Calvin in his Comm. on S. John took this view of the Hebr. verb, and said "metaphorice hic accipitur confixcio pro continua irritatione"; but this sense of the verb is not supported by usage. Besides this passage and xiii. 3, the word occurs only in Numb. xxv. 8, Judg. ix. 54, 1 Sam. xxxi. 4, 1 Chron. x. 4, Is. xiii. 15, Jer. xxxvii. 10, li. 4, Lam. iv. 9, in all of which (except perhaps Jer. xxxvii. 10, where at any rate it means "severely wounded") it denotes "to thrust through" so as to kill. The only passage which could be cited to justify a figurative meaning of the word is Prov. xii. 18, where the substantive *madqrôth* is used, יש בוטה כמדקרות חרב "[the words of] an idler-talker are sometimes like sword-thrusts: but the speech of the wise is healing." But there, the gnomic nature of the composition, and the use of the comparative כ, prepare one for the figurative use of the word. Such is not the case here.—Aq. σὺν ᾧ ἐξεκέντησαν (but then he gives σὺν for the *ēth* of Gen. i. 1!). Theodotion καὶ ἐπιβλέψονται πρὸς μὲ εἰς ὃν ἐξεκέντησαν. Syr. and Vulg. "et aspicient ad me quem confixerunt." All the ancient versions, as we see, read אלי, not אליו

Verse 10. Versions, readings, emendations, &c.

11 In that day shall there be a great mourning in Jerusalem, as the mourning of Hadadrimmon in the valley of Megiddon.

12 And the land shall mourn, every family apart; the family of the house of David apart, and their wives apart; the family of the house of Nathan apart, and their wives apart;

(which is however the reading of *some* MSS., though the great majority, and all the best, read אֵלַי). S. John xix. 37 and Rev. i. 7 cannot be looked on as positive evidence in favour of the reading אֵלָיו, because, not the actual words, but merely the sense of the passage seems to be given in those two places. The reading אֵלָיו has, however, been supported by Kennicott, Ewald, Geiger, Bunsen. For *hayyāchîd* LXX. ἀγαπητῷ, either translating *ad sensum*, or reading הַיָּחִיד.

Remarks. If we are to interpret this verse as it stands, we must certainly understand "the house of David and the inhabitants of Jerusalem" as the subject of the verbs *v'hibbîtu* "and they shall look," and *dāqaru* "they pierced," or rather "thrust-through." So we cannot with Rashi understand the verse to mean, that Israel will look [unto God] in mourning for those slain by the Chaldeans; nor with Ibn Ezra, that all the nations will look unto God to see what He will do to them on account of their having slain the Messiah, son of Joseph (comp. T. B. *Succah* 52ᵃ): for (apart from the question of the subject of the verbs), as Qimchi most sensibly remarks, if Messiah son of Joseph be referred to here (and we may add, in Ezek. xxxviii. xxxix. also) why is he not mentioned? Retaining the reading of the Text *elay* "unto me," some interpret the verb *dāqaru* figuratively "they pierced," i.e. "contemned." The Person might be God Himself, or the Prophet (who seems to have personified the Rejected Shepherd in ch. xi.) looked on as identified (Hitzig) for the moment with Him that sent him. But surely, such a rendering of *dāqaru* (even supposing it to be admissible, which we do not think to be the case) is too weak to account for the strong expressions which follow, "and they shall mourn over him as with the mourning for an only son, &c.," which can only refer to the case of some one actually slain. We must therefore reject this interpretation of *dāqaru*. If, on the other hand, we take it as meaning "they thrust-through," the first person "unto me" presents great difficulties. For it cannot be referred to God Himself, as that would, as Ewald says, "introduce into the Old Testament the absurd notion that persons will bitterly lament over Yahvé (*YHVH*) as over one that is dead." Nor can it be explained, primarily, of the twofold nature of Christ, as that is a notion which could never have suggested itself to a Jew of Zechariah's time. Nor can it be interpreted of the Prophet as representing Him who sent him, for no mention is made of the slaying of such a person, nor is any hint dropped of such a thing even in xi. 13. Ewald would read *elav* "unto him," and says "we can only say, that at that time a distinguished martyr in the cause of Jerusalem and the house of David and the true religion may have fallen shortly before without receiving the just acknowledgment of the capital, and there may be here reference to him." But this "distinguished martyr" exists only in

13 The family of the house of Levi apart, and their wives apart; the family of Shimei apart, and their wives apart;

14 All the families that remain, every family apart, and their wives apart.

the imagination of the commentator. As we see no way of interpreting this passage in its present context, so, at least, as to have been understood by the prophet's hearers, we propose to place it after xiii. 3. See Remarks, p. 114—117.

CHAPTER XIII.

IN that day there shall be a fountain opened to the house of David and to the inhabitants of Jerusalem for sin and for uncleanness.
2 And it shall come to pass in

DESERTION OF IDOLATRY. ZEAL NOT ACCORDING TO KNOWLEDGE. SLAYING OF THE PROPHET. CONSEQUENT MOURNING.

There is, no doubt, a reference here to Numb. xix. 9 לְמֵי נִדָּה חַטָּאת הוּא "for water of purification, a means of removing sin is it." *Chattáth* means "sin," "offering for sin," "means of removing sin" (comp. the use of the verb תְּחַטְּאֵנִי Ps. li. 9, "thou shalt cleanse me," and יִתְחַטָּא Numb. xix. 12, "he shall cleanse himself"). Similarly *niddáh*, while it means especially that sort of ceremonial uncleanness, which requires separation (Lev. xii. 2, &c.), denotes also "the removal of this uncleanness." So we may here correctly render the words *l'chattáth ul'niddáh* "for the removal of sin and uncleanness." Elsewhere the word is חַטָּאת in the absol., and חַטַּאת in the constr.; but here all authorities read חַטָּאת.

Verse 1.
Words.

Maqór πᾶς τόπος, reading מָקוֹם, and taking, apparently, the undefined substantive as meaning "*every* place."—In rendering *l'chattáth* by εἰς τὴν μετακίνησιν, they appear to have taken לְהַטֹּאת as the Infin. Hiph. of נטה (לְהַטּוֹת).—*Niddáh* χωρισμόν, reverting to the primary meaning of the root.

LXX.

that day, saith the LORD of hosts, *that* I will cut off the names of the idols out of the land, and they shall no more be remembered: and also I will cause the prophets and the unclean spirit to pass out of the land.

3 And it shall come to pass, *that* when any shall yet prophesy, then his father and his mother that begat him shall say unto him, Thou shalt not live; for thou speakest lies in the name of the LORD: and his father and his mother that begat him shall thrust him through when he prophesieth.

Verse 2. Words and LXX.
עֲצַבִּים occurs in the plur. only, the form is that of גְּמָל, גְּמַלִּים; the singl., if it occurred, would be 'ăçābh. As a singular in the sense of "idol" we have עֶצֶב in use (Is. xlviii. 5). עֶצֶב and עָצָב "trouble" make in plur. "çābhīm, e.g. לֶחֶם הָעֲצָבִים (Ps. cxxvii. 2) "bread earned by much toil." The expression rû‘ach haṭṭum'āh "the unclean spirit," which occurs here only, is the origin, doubtless, of the common N.T. expression τὸ πνεῦμα τὸ ἀκάθαρτον.— הֶעֱבִיר in the sense of "removing," comp. (2 Chron. xv. 8) וַיַּעֲבֵר הַשִּׁקּוּצִים "and he removed the abominations." LXX. understand "The prophets" correctly as ψευδοπροφήτας.

Verse 3. Words and constructions.
כִּי "if," or "when" (comp. note on p. 73).—וְאָמְרוּ "then shall say unto him his father and his mother": yōl‘dhâv "even they who bare him," is added for emphasis.—וּדְקָרֻהוּ ud‘qārûhū, the rû is long, merely defectively written (comp. xi. 5); the word means "and they shall thrust him through," comp. וַיִּדְקֹר אֶת־שְׁנֵיהֶם "and he thrust them both through" (Numb. xxv. 8).—B‘hinnâbh‘ó might mean "in his act of prophesying," but "because of his prophesying" is better, comp. בְּהִשָּׁעֶנְךָ "because of thy leaning on" (2 Chron. xvi. 7).

LXX.
ud‘qārûhū καὶ συμποδιοῦσιν αὐτόν, translating euphemistically, as in xii. 10 they give for the same verb κατωρχήσαντο.

Remarks.
Here we propose to read chap. xii. 10—14. We admit that we have no authority for so doing, either of MSS., versions, or commentators. Two considerations have suggested to us this rearrangement of the text: (1) We are unable to discover any

intelligible meaning which the words "and they shall look on me (or him) whom they thrust through," in the place in which they now stand in the Hebrew Text, could have conveyed to the Prophet's hearers, and even to us of the present day they seem enigmatical words suddenly introduced without the idea of "thrusting through" having been supplied by the context: (2) If we place them after ch. xiii. 3, in which the "thrusting through" of a son is distinctly mentioned, the words which commentators have taxed their ingenuity in vain to explain, will convey the simplest and most obvious sense. In a section, in which the phrase "on that day," "and it shall come to pass on that day," occurs so often, it is easy to imagine that a confusion of order may have arisen in early times. If our conjecture (and it is but a conjecture) be correct, the whole passage will run as follows:

(iii. 1) In that day shall be a fountain opened, for the house of David and for the inhabitants of Jerusalem, for [removal of] sin and of uncleanness.—(2) And it shall be in that day ('tis the utterance of *YHVH Ç'bā'ôth*) I will cut off the names of the idols from the land, and they shall not be remembered any more; and the [false] prophets and the unclean spirit will I cause to pass away from the land. (3) And it shall be, when a man shall prophesy, then they shall say to him, his father and his mother, they that bare him, "Thou shalt not live, because thou hast spoken lies in the name of *YHVH*;" and *they shall thrust him through*, his father and his mother, they that bare him, on account of his prophesying. (xii. 10) Then will I pour out upon the house of David, and upon the inhabitants of Jerusalem, the spirit of grace and supplication, and they *shall look on him, even him whom they thrust through*, and they shall mourn over him, as the mourning for an only son, and they shall make bitter mourning over him, as one mourneth bitterly for a firstborn. In that day... (14)...and their wives apart.

When, in the blindness of fanaticism, these people should have been led to commit such a crime, as that mentioned xiii. 3, then God would have pity on them, and pour out on them the spirit of grace and supplication, &c. The reader will perceive, that the application of the expression "and they shall look on him whom they thrust through" to our Lord (John xix. 34, 37, Rev. i. 7) is even more appropriate, if the words be taken as we have proposed, than if they were left in their present context. For the passage, as we propose to read it, depicts a Prophet, and a true Prophet, rejected by his own people as a false prophet, and slain by them. What more appropriate passage could be cited relative to our Lord? We must not, however, any more than in xi. 12, 13, confine the application of the prophecy to this single fulfilment, though it is certainly by far the most remarkable and important one.

On the accentuation of *v'shâphactâ* see notes on i. 3. *Chên* seems to denote here "Divine favour," i.e. "grace." *Tách⁰nūnîm* "earnest supplication" as the result of *chên* (but LXX. οἰκτιρμοῦ).—והביטו אלי " And they shall look on me"; but we prefer to read אליו "on him" (see pp. 112, 115).—הביט אל, among other meanings, has that of "to contemplate" as (Ps. cii. 20) מן השמים הביט אל ארץ, (Is. lxvi. 2) ואל זה אביט אל עני ונכה רוח. The nature of the feelings of the contemplator is decided by the context. Here they are, evidently, those of compunction. For the construction את אשר־דקרו אליו(ן) "unto me (or *him*), viz. him whom they thrust through," compare (Jer. xxxviii. 9) לירמיהו הנביא את אשר־השליכו אל־הבור " to Jeremiah the prophet, him whom they cast into the pit."—*Hayyâchîd*, the article is generic, and may be best rendered into English by "a"; in Amos viii. 10 we have כאבל יחיד (where also the next clause contains a derivative of מרר).—*V'hâmêr* is the Infin. Absol. Hiph. and may be taken as used emphatically, for והמר ימירנו (but see note on vii. 5). In the Hiph. this verb is nowhere else used of "mourning bitterly," but in the Pi'el is so used (Is. xxii. 4) אמרר בבכי.—*C'hâmêr* is the Infin. Construct lit. "as the mourning bitterly for."—We can hardly take *v'sâph'dhâ 'âlâv* to mean they shall mourn over it (*ea de re*), viz. the crime committed, as that would materially weaken the force of the expressions which follow, "over an only son," "over a first-born."

Hadadrimmon "is a city," says Jerome, "near Jezreel, now called Maximianopolis, in the field of Mageddon, where the good king Josiah was (mortally) wounded in battle (2 Chron. xxxv. 22—25) with Pharaoh-necho." According to Assyriologists, *Hadar-Ramman* is the proper pronunciation of this word. The fact that a place in the tribe of Issachar was at the time of these prophecies known by an *Assyrian* name is an additional link in the chain of evidence, which proves them to be of post-exilian origin. The mourning for Josiah became, no doubt, proverbial for a great national mourning.

Hᵃdadrimmôn is rendered ῥοῶνος " of a *plantation* of pomegranates," by way of conjecture (*rimmôn* means pomegranate). *M'giddôn* is rendered ἐκκοπτομένον, by reverting to the meaning of the root גדד, comp. (Dan. iv. 11) *gódû*, ἐκκόψατε.

Mishpâchôth mishpâchôth "each family"; for the repetition of the substantive to denote "*each single*," compare עדר עדר לבדו "each flock by itself" (Gen. xxxii. 17); the *plur.* however is not generally used in this manner, but comp. Ezek. xxiv. 6

4 And it shall come to pass in that day, *that* the prophets shall be ashamed every one of his vision, when he hath prophesied; neither shall they wear a rough garment to deceive:

(2 Kings iii. 16, Joel iv. 14, Ex. viii. 10, Gen. xiv. 10 are instances of quite a different use of the repetition of substantives).—*L'bhād* is often used without suffix (e.g. Ex. xxvi. 9). Comp. note on x. 4.

"*Nathan*," not the prophet, but the son of David (2 Sam. v. 14). He represents a subordinate branch of the house of Judah. Remarks.

The patronymic from *Simeon* is הַשִּׁמְעֹנִי (Numb. xxv. 14, Josh. xxi. 4), while that from שִׁמְעִי (*Shemei*) is הַשִּׁמְעִי (Numb. ii. 12). With the construction מִשְׁפַּחַת הַשִּׁמְעִי comp. מ׳ הַחֲנֹכִי, &c. (Numb. xxvi. 5, 6, 12, 13, &c.). Chap. xii. 13. Words, etc.

This *Shemei* seems to be of the house of Gershon (Numb. iii. 17) a subordinate house of Levi; not the Benjaminite (2 Sam. xvi. 5). Observe the particularization of ver. 12, 13, and the generalization of ver. 14. This seems to point to the general, and yet particular nature of the mourning. For the fulfilment in reference to the Crucifixion see Luke xxiii. 48, Acts ii. 37—41. Remarks.

FALSE PROPHETS DISCLAIM THE GIFT OF PROPHECY.

The Imperf. of בּוֹשׁ is יֵבשׁ, with which may be compared אוֹר Imperf. יָאוֹר (unless this latter is to be regarded as a Niph.).—The *mè* of *mĕchezyōnō* denotes "on account of," comp. ii. 8. For the verb *Bōsh* construed with *min*, of the thing to be ashamed of, comp. Ezek. xxxvi. 32. With regard to the form of *Chizzāyōn* with suffixes see note on xii. 4.—*B'hinnābh'ōthō* = *b'hinnābh'ō* of ver. 3. This form with final ת is formed after the analogy of such Infinitives as מַלְאוֹת, שְׂנֹאת, קְרֹאות, חֲטֹאת, מְלֹאת. This is the only instance of a *Niph.* Infin. in ת from a verb quiescent ל״א.— On the construction of *lābhāsh* see note on iii. 3.—On *addēreth* see note on ii. 13.—*L'ma'an* construed with the Infin. construct. is common, compare Amos ii. 7 לְמַעַן חַלֵּל, Deut. xxix. 18, Jer. vii. 10, &c. Chap. xii. 4. Words and constructions.

καὶ ἐνδύσονται δέρριν τριχίνην, omitting לֹא. ἀνθ' ὧν ἐψεύσαντο is simply a mistranslation. LXX.

5 But he shall say, I *am* no prophet, I *am* an husbandman; for man taught me to keep cattle from my youth.

6 And *one* shall say unto him, What *are* these wounds in thine hands? Then he shall answer, *Those* with which I was wounded *in* the house of my friends.

Verse 5. It must be observed that אִישׁ is here, by no means, used to denote a man of importance, as it is when opposed to אָדָם (Ps. xlix. 3). It simply means "an individual:" for, though *ādām* occurs in the next clause, it cannot be said to be opposed to *īsh*. Similarly our Prophet uses גֶּבֶר *gébher*, with no special significance, in ver. 7. *'ōbhēd* a*dāmāh* "an agriculturist," as in Gen. iv. 2.—הִקְנָנִי (on the *sīmām rāphēh* see Excurs. iv.). The verb קָנָה in the Qal means to "originate," "acquire," "possess," but since it occurs nowhere else in the Hiph., there is great difficulty in determining its exact force in this passage. Some take it as a stronger Qal "to purchase"; others "to sell" (as לָוָה in Qal is "to borrow," in Hiph. "to lend," and Aram. *z^ebán* "to buy," Pa'el *zabbén* "to sell"). Others, taking it as a denominative from *miqnēh* "possession," deduce the same meaning "to buy." Qimchi makes it a denominative from *miqnēh* in the sense of "a flock," and understands it as "made me a herdsman." Whatever be the exact meaning of the word (LXX. ἐγέννησέ με), it is clear that the person accused of assuming prophetic powers disavows all such assumption, and claims to be looked on as a simple rustic. Aq. ἔταξέ με, Symm. ἐμέρισέ με, Theod. ἔδειξέ με. On *n^e'urīm* see note on ix. 17.

Verse 6. בֵּין יָדֶיךָ "between thy hands" is an expression which presents great difficulty. Rosenmüller, comparing בֵּין הָרְחֹבוֹת (Prov. xxvi. 13) with בְּתוֹךְ רְחֹבוֹת (xxii. 13), would render it *in manibus tuis*. Possibly this may be the meaning. But, since בֵּין זְרֹעָיו (2 Kings ix. 24) certainly means "in the body," our expression may be taken here to denote "on the chest." (Comp. *Bén 'ēnēcā* Deut. vi. 8, and my *Fragment of T. B. P^esachim*, p. 74, note 4. The expression "between thy hands" in Arab. means simply "before thee," לְפָנֶיךָ; but that meaning is not suitable here; neither is it a Hebrew usage.) *Béth* denotes "in the house of," comp. Gen. xxiv. 23. —*V^e'āmār* "and one will say," i.e. the other will reply, is wrongly rendered by the LXX. καὶ ἐρῶ.

ZECHARIAH XIII. 7.

7 Awake, O sword, against my shepherd, and against the man *that is* my fellow, saith the LORD of hosts: smite the shepherd, and the sheep shall be scattered: and I will turn mine hand upon the little ones.

The "rough garment" was the ordinary dress of the prophets. If one who was not a prophet wore it, it caused him to be taken for such, and was therefore worn "to deceive." The words of ver. 5 are very similar to those of Amos vii. 14, 15; but the purport of the two passages is very different. Amos declares that though he was a herdsman and had never been brought up as a prophet, still he had received a divine mission, which he intended to perform in spite of Jeroboam II., and Amaziah priest of Bethel. But here the false prophet, when accused of exercising the functions of a prophet, utterly denies the charge. The wounds which he is accused of having inflicted on himself (in idolatrous worship 1 Kings xviii. 28, Jer. xlvii. 5, xlviii. 37), he asserts to have been inflicted on him by others "in the house of his friends." ROSENMÜLLER understands that he confesses to have been punished in his parents' house for false prophecies. HENGSTENBERG thinks that he acknowledges, with shame, that he had been so wounded in the house of his friends, i. e. in the idol temples. WRIGHT says that perhaps he may have suggested that these wounds were received by him on the occasion of some carousal with boon companions. <small>Remarks. Chap. xiii. 4—6.</small>

SHEPHERD SMITTEN. FLOCK SCATTERED.

On the accentuation of '*ûrî* see notes on ix. 9, p. 84.—'*ămîthî* "my fellow" is a word which occurs only here, and in Leviticus. There it occurs only with the suffixes ךָ and וֹ. It seems to be a subst. of the form of גָּוִית, זָוִית (ix. 15, in plur.) &c., and to denote "fellowship" "neighbourship" in the abstract, and then to be used (as in Lev.) for the concrete (comp. notes on vi. 10, xi. 16). According to the first meaning *gêbher* would be here the constr. and the expression would mean "the man of my fellowship." According to the second (and current use of the word) '*ămîthî* would be in apposition with *gêbher*, and we should render "a man my fellow."—*Hâc* "smite thou" is in the masc., although '*ûrî* agrees correctly with *chérebh* in the fem.— <small>Verse 7. Words, etc.</small>

וּתְפוּצֶיןָ "that may be scattered." (On this verb see note on i. 17.) The forms of the 3rd pers. fem. plur. Imperf. in ן, instead of נָה, are common; e. g. תֵּשַׁבְןָ (Ezek. xvi. 55), תִּירֶאןָ (Ex. i. 17), תִּמְצֶאןָ (Deut. xxi. 21), תִּקְרֶאןָ (Numb. xxv. 2), תַּשְׁקֶיןָ (Gen. xix. 33). —On the accentuation of *văhăshîbhōthî* see note on i. 3.—The participle צֹעֲרִים does not occur elsewhere: it can scarcely be taken as equivalent

8 And it shall come to pass, *that* in all the land, saith the Lord, two parts therein shall be cut off *and* die; but the third shall be left therein.

9 And I will bring the third part through the fire, and will refine them as silver is refined, and will try them as gold is tried: they shall call on my name, and I will hear them: I will say, It *is* my people: and they shall say, The Lord *is* my God.

---

to צְעִירִים "little ones" (Judg. vi. 15, Ps. cxix. 141): it seems rather to denote "those who make themselves small," "the humble ones." The expression "to turn the hand back upon" is often used to denote anger (Amos i. 8, Ps. lxxxi. 15); but sometimes it signifies loving chastisement (Is. i. 25), and such appears to be its meaning here.

LXX.
To arrive at τοὺς ποιμένας μου LXX. must have read rō'ay instead of rō'î. For "mîthî they give πολίτην μου. The verb t'phūçēnā they considered as active, and rendered ἐκσπάσατε; and to make hác correspond with this, they rendered it also by the plur. πατάξατε (Matt. xxvi. 31 πατάξω).—Haççō'rîm τοὺς μικρούς.

Verse 8. Words.
פִּי־שְׁנַיִם (on the *metheg* see Excurs. II. A. 3) denotes "a double portion" (Gen. xliii. 34), comp. מָנָה אַחַת אַפָּיִם (1 Sam. i. 5): here by the expression *hashsh'lîshîth*, in the second half-verse, it is shown to mean "two thirds."—*Báh* "in it," the flock (çôn).—The verb גָּוַע "to die," like חוּר (: יֶחֱוָרוּ Is. xxix. 22), has the medial ו as a strong consonant, and not quiescent as in קוּם.

Verse 9.
V'hēbhēthî should be so accentuated, as Baer edits; not *v'hĕbhēthî* (see note on i. 3). With the latter accentuation the verb must be looked on as the Prophetic Perfect.—The verb *Qārā'* is construed with בְּ in the sense of "calling upon" the Name of God &c. (Gen. iv. 26), or of Baal (1 Kings xviii. 26).—*āmartî* (on the placing of the accent *pashtā* see page 16) is the Perfect, which preceded, and followed by Futures, may be used as a Future even without *vāv* convers. comp. (Is. xiii. 10) וּכְסִילֵיהֶם לֹא יָהֵלּוּ אוֹרָם חָשַׁךְ הַשֶּׁמֶשׁ בְּצֵאתוֹ וְיָרֵחַ לֹא־יַגִּיהַ אוֹרוֹ: LXX. καὶ ἐρῶ.

Remarks. Chap. xiii. 7–9.
Wright objects to Ewald's theory that these verses form a sequel to chap. xi., that "the removal of foolish shepherds could only be a blessing to the flock, while the removal of the shepherd is here represented as utterly disastrous." But since in xiii. 7—9, the figure of the shepherd and his flock is evidently intended to suggest the notion of a leader and his army,

and the death of the leader, even when incompetent, would involve the scattering of the army (this very figure is used by Micaiah in foretelling the death of the wicked Ahab, 1 Kings xxii. 17), this objection does not seem to us conclusive. But, if we are to reject this suggestion of Ewald, or if we are not to regard this passage as a distinct prophecy by itself (see *Introduction*), "the shepherd" can only mean some prophet of the Lord, who on account of the sins of the people should be taken away by a violent death. After his death a remnant were to be purified and saved. Ver. 7 is quoted by our Lord (Matt. xxvi. 31, Mark xiv. 27).

CHAPTER XIV.

BEHOLD, the day of the Lord cometh, and thy spoil shall be divided in the midst of thee.

2 For I will gather all nations against Jerusalem to battle; and the city shall be taken, and the houses rifled, and the women ravished; and half of the city shall go forth into captivity, and the residue of the people shall not be cut off from the city.

3 Then shall the Lord go forth, and fight against those nations, as when he fought in the day of battle.

ONE DAY, IT IS KNOWN BY YHVH.

Hinnéh yōm bâ lAdōnây "behold a day cometh for the Lord": the expression is exactly equivalent to that of Is. ii. 12, *Yōm lAdōnây* "[there is] a day [coming] for the Lord."— יוֹם לַי" בָּא (comp. Is. xiii. 6, 9) would mean "a day of the Lord's cometh," while יוֹם י" בָּא might mean "a day of the Lord," or "the day of the Lord cometh" (comp. p. 15). LXX. has the plur. ἰδοὺ ἡμέραι ἔρχονται. *Verse 1. Words and constructions.*

Nashássū is the Niph. Perf. of שָׁסַס, the Niph. occurs only once again (also with *habbâtîm*, viz. (Is. xiii. 16) יִשַּׁסּוּ. For תִּשָּׁגַלְנָה¹ we have in the *Q'rî* the more modest expression *tishshācábhnāh*, the four instances of the same substitution are Deut. xxviii. 30, Is. xiii. 16, Jer. iii. 2, and this passage. Similar euphemisms are to be found in the *Q'rî* of 2 Kings xviii. 27, Is. xxxvi. 12, Deut. xxviii. 27, 1 Sam. v. 6, 9, 12, vi. 4, 5. The LXX. has for תִּשָּׁגַלְנָה μολυνθήσονται (there is also a version of the *Q'rî* κοιτασθήσονται): and for "the people" τοῦ λαοῦ μου. *Verse 2.*

C'yōm must be regarded as an acc. "as at the time of" (see notes on i. 8, viii. 9, 11). With the expression *yōm hillâch^amō* comp. (Ezek. xxxix. 13) יוֹם הִכָּבְדִי. On the first *metheg* of *hillâch^amō* see Excurs. II. B. 3. *Verse 3. Words, etc.*

¹ The vowels in the Text belong, of course, to the *Q'rî*.

4 And his feet shall stand in that day upon the mount of Olives, which *is* before Jerusalem on the east, and the mount of Olives shall cleave in the midst thereof toward the east and toward the west, *and there shall be* a very great valley; and half of the mountain shall remove toward the north, and half of it toward the south.

Verse 4. Words and constructions.

‘*Al-pʻnê* " over against," as (Judg. xvi. 3) ‘*al-pʻnê Chebhrŏn* " opposite Hebron."—*Miqqédem* " towards (*or* in) the East," and so, probably, Gen. ii. 8: comp. note on iv. 3, and the expression *mĕcheçyó*, which follows.—*Checyó* denotes here, not "half" (Ex. xxiv. 16, and in the second half of our verse), but "middle" (Judg. xvi. 3) בַּחֲצִי הַלַּיְלָה "at midnight": thus *mĕcheçyó* denotes "in its midst."—מִזְרָחָה וָיָמָּה the *vāv* is pointed with *qāmāç*, because the latter word is accentuated on the *first* syllable (without intervening disjunctive accent): comp. (Gen. xiii. 14): צָפֹנָה וָנֶגְבָּה וָקֵדְמָה וָיָמָּה (see also xxviii. 14); similarly תֹּהוּ וָבֹהוּ (Gen. i. 2) and זָהָב וָכֶסֶף (1 Kings x. 22), which rule ל follows in Gen. i. 6: בֵּין מַיִם לָמָיִם. But, if the second word be *milʻraʻ*, the *vāv* takes *shʻvā* as כֶּסֶף־וְזָהָב (vi. 11). On the final ־ָה of these words see p. 11.—גַּיְא is the *absolute* form. The form גַּיְא as the absolute occurs in Numb. xxi. 20, Deut. iii. 29, iv. 46, 1 Sam. xvii. 3, Jer. ii. 23, Neh. ii. 13, 15, iii. 13, 1 Chron. iv. 39, 2 Chron. xxvi. 9; and, dropping the א, in the form גַּי Deut. xxxiv. 6, Josh. xiii. 11, Mic. i. 4; and even גַּיְא Is. xl. 4. And here only as *Absolute* in the form גַּיְא, which (collaterally with גֵּי) is the ordinary form of the *construct* (as in the next verse). This form of the absolute is not without parallel: thus we have לֵיל distinctly *absol.* at the end of Is. xxi. 11; בְּחַיִל כָּבֵד " with a great host" (2 Kings xviii. 17)[2].—The expression "the Mount of Olives" occurs

---

[1] This seems to be merely a variation of pronunciation. In illustration of the tendency of *ay* to be pronounced as *ē* (*ĭ*) observe that Arab *bayna* (בֵּין) is pronounced *bēna*, and the Syr. suffix *ayca* as *ēca*, and that in modern Greek αι is pronounced *ē* αἷμα *ēma* (with a very slight aspiration).

[2] בֵּית גָּדוֹל (2 Kings xxv. 9) is not included, since it might mean "great-man's house." The expression חֲמָת רַבָּה (absol. חֲמָת) in Amos vi. 2 is not sufficient ground on which to found a statement that the constr. can be used with an epithet, since the word is a proper name, and the expression may be parallel with חֲמָת צוֹבָה (2 Chron. viii. 3).

5 And ye shall flee *to* the valley of the mountains; for the valley of the mountains shall reach unto Azal: yea, ye shall flee, like as ye fled from before the earthquake in the days of Uzziah king of Judah: and the LORD my God shall come, *and* all the saints with thee.

---

here only in the O. T.; for other designations of that hill see 2 Sam. xv. 30, 1 Kings xi. 7, 2 Kings xxiii. 13, Ezek. xi. 23.

Gê' gᵉdōlā́h mᵉ'ōd χάος μέγα σφόδρα.—Umāsh καὶ κλινεῖ, by which word they render also מוֹט (Ps. xlv. 6), and נטשׁ (1 Sam. iv. 2). LXX.

Nās followed by the acc. can only mean "to flee to"; the translation of Luther *vor solchem Thal* is inadmissible. For an instance of the construction found here comp. (Ps. xi. 1) נודו הרכם צפור   Verse 5.

The expression אֶל־אָצַל is difficult. In 1 Chron. viii. 38 we find אָצֵל as the Pausal form of אָצַל (as *pathach* is found often in Pause for *ç̌erē*, e.g. וַיֵּלֶךְ Gen. xxiv. 61 &c.). Supposing, then, that the preposition אֵצֶל is the constr. of אָצֵל (as is probable, comp. גֵּזֶל, Ezek. xviii. 18, as the constr. of גָּזֵל), *el-āçāl* would mean "to nigh," "to very near." *Āçāl* would in this case be used independently (as an adverb), as we have shown (ii. 12) that *achár* is used. The Prophet turns abruptly from speaking of God "*ubhā...'lōhāy*," to addressing Him "*'immāc*": for a similar abrupt transition compare (Song of Songs i. 1) "*yishshāqḗnī...cī-ṭōbhīm dōdḗcā miyyāin.*"

נסתם occurs three times in this verse. According to the Western punctuation it is read נַסְתֶּם (see above), but the Oriental reading is וְנִסְתַּם "and the valley of my mountains *shall be*   Variants and Versions. *closed up*" in the first case, and נַסְתָּם in the two other cases: so, too, the Targum and Rashi, and Ibn Ezra. LXX. in all three cases (Symm. and Hex.-Syr. in the first two) read *nistám*, and render the passage: καὶ φραχθήσεται ἡ φάραγξ τῶν ὀρέων μου, καὶ ἐγκολληθήσεται φάραγξ ὀρέων ἕως Ἰασόδ, καὶ ἐμφραχθήσεται καθὼς ἐνεφράγη ἐν ταῖς ἡμέραις τοῦ συσσεισμοῦ κ.τ.λ.—The word ΙΑΣΟΔ is merely a corruption of ΙΑΣΟΛ (אאצל); some copies of the Hex.-Syr. give Ἀσαήλ. Observe that the transliteration of אצל by Ιασολ (reading א as *ya*) is just the converse

6 And it shall come to pass in | that day, *that* the light shall not be clear, *nor* dark :

---

of the process by which the Syr. gets אָצֵר out of יוֹצֵר (xi. 13). Ἐν ταῖς ἡμέραις is merely a free translation of *mippᵉnê*.—οἱ ἅγιοι μετ' αὐτοῦ, for *qᵉdōshı̂m 'immāc*. One of Baer's MSS. notes that some correct MSS. read קְדֹשָׁיו עִמּוֹ; but, the *Massóreth* states that קְדֹשָׁיו occurs only in Deut. xxxiii. 3, Ps. xxxiv. 10, and, therefore, *qᵉdōsháv* must be looked on as only an emendation. As for עִמּוֹ, it is easy to see how עִמּוֹ might have been written עִמָּן, and that read as עִמָּךְ; but still, the transition from the third to the second Person is so thoroughly in accordance with usage, that one cannot see any reason for doubting the correctness of the reading עִמָּךְ.

<small>Remarks.
Chap. xiv. 6.</small> The earthquake in the days of Uzziah is nowhere mentioned by the sacred historians, and the account given of it by Josephus (*Antiq*. ix. 10 § 4) must be looked on as apocryphal. Still, so great and lasting was the impression made by that event on the popular mind, that it formed an era from which events were dated (Amos i. 1), and is here referred to as a well-known catastrophe. It has been argued that this reference to the earthquake fixes the date of this prophecy to a time shortly after that event. But, as reasonably might it be argued, that an author who used the expression "they fell to a man, as they did at Thermopylæ," had written shortly after B.C. 480!

<small>Verse 6.
Words, etc.</small> The *Cᵉthı̂bh* is יְקָרוֹת יִקְפָּאוּן (for there is no occasion, with Gesen., to invent a Niph. of קפא). The verb is in the masc. although its nominative is fem. comp. חָזוּת קָשָׁה הַגֶּד־לִי (Is. xxi. 2). In Job xxxi. 26 *yāqār* is applied to the Moon, יָרֵחַ יָקָר הֹלֵךְ "the moon, sailing resplendent." So here *yᵉqārōth* seems to denote "the resplendent heavenly bodies." The definite article is omitted before *yᵉqārōth* (as it is before כּוֹכָבִים "the stars" ten times, against nine times in which it is expressed). The verb is that found in Ex. xv. 8 קָפְאוּ תְהֹמֹת בְּלֶב־יָם "the depths became consolidated in the midst of the sea." The meaning, then, of *yᵉqārōth yiqqā'ūn* seems to be "the splendid (heavenly bodies) will contract their splendour," i.e. will wane.—The *Qᵉrı̂* gives the ἅπ. λεγό. וְקִפָּאוֹן (of the form of *timmāhōn* &c. xii. 4) "and consolidation," "coagulation." And the meaning of *yᵉqārōth wᵉqippā'ōn* is perhaps "[there will be] intense-

7 But it shall be one day which that living waters shall go out from Jerusalem; half of them toward the former sea, and half of them toward the hinder sea: in summer and in winter shall it be.

8 And it shall be in that day,

brightness, and then waning," comp. (Job iv. 16) דְּמָמָה וָקוֹל אֶשְׁמָע "[there was] silence, and then a voice I heard." But the first word would perhaps be better pointed יְקָרוֹת "cold" (of the form of קַדְרוּת "darkness" Is. 1. 3), Rt. יקר being taken as equivalent to Rt. קרר "to be cold." Some would read a vāv instead of the first yūd thus וְקָרוֹת וְקִפָּאוֹן and render "but cold and coagulation," making the first vāv adversative. The C͑thîbh appears to us the better reading.

LXX. take יקרות וקפאון והיה יום אחד as one clause, and render καὶ ψύχος (Cod. Alex.) καὶ πάγος ἔσται μίαν ἡμέραν. The reading ψύχη (Cod. Vat.) is a manifest error. On the rendering ψύχος see above.—πάγος (both Targ. and Syr. agree with LXX. in the rendering ψύχος καὶ πάγος) is given as the translation of קפאון from two considerations, (1) it is parallel with the assumed meaning of יקרות, (2) קפא is used (see above) of the consolidation of water: since then, the only natural mode of consolidating water, is by frost, it was surmised that qippā'ôn meant "frost." Versions.

Yōm-echād denotes "a unique day," comp. (Ezek. vii. 5) רָעָה אַחַת רָעָה הִנֵּה בָאָה "an evil, a unique evil, lo! is coming."—הוּא is emphatic.—L͑'ēth "at the time of" (Gen. viii. 11, &c.), on the metheg with l͑'ēth-'erebh see Excurs. II. A. 5. Verse 7. Words, etc.

הוּא is expanded into καὶ ἡ ἡμέρα ἐκείνη. For v͑hāyāh l͑'ēth-'erebh simply καὶ πρὸς ἑσπέραν. LXX.

קַדְמֹנִי denote "eastern" (as in Ezek. x. 19); but it also has the meaning of "ancient" (comp. the meanings of קֶדֶם). In Ezek. xlvii. 8 we find also a fem. קַדְמוֹנָה which presupposes a masc. qadmôn (comp. note on xi. 15). On the fixed-metheg on hā'ach͑rôn, and the absence of ordinary-metheg, see Excurs. II. A. 9.—Haqqadmōnî LXX. τὴν πρώτην: hā'ach͑rôn τὴν ἐσχάτην: in accordance with the primary meanings of the words (comp. LXX. Joel ii. 20).—For "in Winter" they give ἐν ἔαρι "in Spring." Verse 8.

9 And the LORD shall be king over all the earth: in that day shall there be one LORD, and his name one.

10 All the land shall be turned as a plain from Geba to Rimmon south of Jerusalem: and it shall be lifted up, and inhabited in her place, from Benjamin's gate unto the place of the first gate, unto the corner gate, and *from* the tower of Hananeel unto the king's wine-presses.

Verse 10. Words, etc.

It is a disputed point among grammarians whether such forms as יִתֹּם, יָקֹד, יָדֹם, יָסֹב, from verbs with the second root-letter doubled, are to be regarded as Qal, or Niph.—Baer, here and in Is. xxxiii. 9, edits כָּעֲרָבָה without the def. article; but the *Cod. Petropol.* reads כָּ. We prefer this latter reading "like *the* plain," viz. that now called *Al-Ghor*, which extends with some interruptions from the slopes of Hermon to the Elamitic gulf of the Red Sea. If we read כְּ, we must suppose that '*Arābāh* was already regarded as a proper name (comp. note on vii. 14). *Něgebh* "to the south of" as (Josh. xi. 2) נֶגֶב כִּנְרוֹת "*to the south of Cinn'rōth.*"—וְרָאֲמָה is an anomalous 3rd pers. fem. sing. Qal from רוּם. A variant is וְרָאֲמָה, which is after the analogy of וְקָאָם (Joel ii. 6), comp. רָאשׁ "poor" (Prov. x. 4, xiii. 23).—*L'mish-sha'ar*, the prefix לְמִן denotes "from," of place as here (comp. Job xxxvi. 3), or of time as (2 Sam. vii. 19).—*Sha'ar hā-rīshōn* on the article see p. 44.—*Migdāl* stands for *mimmigdāl*, or *l'mimmigdāl*, the *min*, or *l'min*, being understood from לְמִשַּׁעַר, or מִגֶּבַע, which precede. Some MSS. read מִמִּגְדָל (comp. i. 4).—*Yiqbhē*, the *constr.* plur. occurs here only, but it is regularly formed from יֶקֶב.

LXX. κυκλῶν agreeing, one would suppose, with Κύριος of the preceding verse. This rendering of יָסֹב is defensible (though inappropriate). For an imperfect is often used to describe the state or condition of a person (like the participle, see notes on iii. 1, v. 1), especially for the sake of *variety*, e.g. (Is. xl. 30) נֹתֵן לַיָּעֵף כֹּחַ וּלְאֵין אוֹנִים עָצְמָה יַרְבֶּה (compare the use of בָּאָה after תַּעֲלֶה xiv. 18). καὶ τὴν ἔρημον, as a free translation, "compassing all the earth, *as* (it will) the desert," i.e. "all the earth *and* the desert."—'Papá, taking רָאמָה as a Proper Name, which however is always spelt רָמָה.—καὶ ἕως τοῦ πύργου, they carry on '*ad* from '*ad sha'ur happinním*, instead of *min*, as we do.

11 And *men* shall dwell in it, and there shall be no more utter destruction; but Jerusalem shall be safely inhabited.

12 And this shall be the plague wherewith the LORD will smite all the people that have fought against Jerusalem; Their flesh shall consume away while they stand upon their feet, and their eyes shall consume away in their holes, and their tongue shall consume away in their mouth.

13 And it shall come to pass in that day, *that* a great tumult from the LORD shall be among them; and they shall lay hold every one on the hand of his neighbour, and his hand shall rise up against the hand of his neighbour.

Baer edits (not חֵרֶם but) חָרֵם, this is the pointing of the word in every other passage, whether in the sense of "net," or of "ban." Some MSS. read חֶרֶב "sword" (comp. p. 64). The rendering of the Targ. קְטָלָא cannot be said to be conclusively in favour of this latter reading: since "slaughter" may be only a paraphrase of "ban"; LXX. has correctly ἀνάθεμα.   *Verse 11. Words.*

צָבָא עַל comp. Numb. xxxi. 7, &c.—הָמֵק is the Infin. of מקק, it may be taken as the Infin. *Absol.* used emphatically with the omission of the finite verb (comp. xii. 11); or it may be *construct*, and be explanatory "and this shall be the plague, &c." viz. "the rotting of," comp. the second הָמֵר in xii. 11.—The suffix of *b'saró* is distributive, and refers to each of "all the nations," or to each individual of them. The clause *v'hû 'ōmēd 'al-ragláv* denotes the state in which he shall be, when overtaken by the plague (comp. p. 46). תִּמַּקְנָה is the Fut. Niph. 3rd pers. plur. for תִּמֹּקְנָה, comp. Niph. of צלל תִּצַּלְנָה (2 Kings xxi. 13, Jer. xix. 3); the form תְּצִלֶּינָה (1 Sam. iii. 11) is Hiphil.   *Verse 12.*

For *V'hû 'ōmēd* ἑστηκότων, this is correct enough *quoad sensum:* the participle agrees with the persons understood in the preceding αὐτόν.   *LXX.*

וְהֶחֱזִיקוּ אִישׁ יַד רֵעֵהוּ "And they shall seize each other by the hand," to grapple together. *Hĕch'zíq* is generally construed with בְּ before יָד; but compare יְדֵ־עָנִי...לֹא הֶחֱזִיקָה (Ezek. xvi. 49). Some MSS. read here בְיַד.—*V'ál'tháh...'al* "and shall [rise i.e.] be lifted up against."   *Verse 13. Constructions.*

14 And Judah also shall fight at Jerusalem; and the wealth of all the heathen round about shall be gathered together, gold, and silver, and apparel, in great abundance.

15 And so shall be the plague of the horse, of the mule, of the camel, and of the ass, and of all the beasts that shall be in these tents, as this plague.

16 And it shall come to pass, *that* every one that is left of all the nations which came against Jerusalem shall even go up from year to year to worship the King, the LORD of hosts, and to keep the feast of tabernacles.

LXX. *V^e'ăl'tháh...'al...* is freely rendered καὶ συμπλακήσεται... πρὸς....

Verse 14. After the verb נִלְחַם the preposition בְּ generally means "against" (e.g. Ex. i. 10); but it also, after the same verb, denotes the place at which the battle takes place, e.g. (Ex. xvii. 8) וַיִּלָּחֶם עִם־ ישראל ברפידם "and fought with Israel at Rephidim" (comp. Judg. v. 19, 2 Chron. xxxv. 20, 22). The context shows that the latter is the meaning here.—The monosyllable רֹב when לְ is prefixed to it always takes the euphonic *qāmāç*, except once (Est. x. 3) where *rŏbh* is in constr. לְרוֹב אֶחָיו. For the expression לָרֹב מְאֹד (comp. 2 Chr. iv. 18, ix. 9) "in great abundance."

LXX. has correctly ἐν Ἱερουσαλήμ.—καὶ συνάξει, reading, with LXX. different vowels, *v^e'āsāf* instead of *v^e'ussáf.*

Verse 15. The order of the clauses of this verse is inverted, we should have expected וכמגפה הזאת כן תהיה וגו׳. Observe that after all this string of substantives we have not יהיו (or תהיה agreeing with בהמה) but simply יהיה, comp. (Is. lxiv. 10) בית קדשנו מחנים or מחנות...היה...ותפארתנו.—וכל־מחמדינו היה Whether be used, as the plur. of מַחֲנֶה, it is masc. as here, but the sing. is fem. in Gen. xxxii. 9, Ps. xxvii. 3.

Verse 16. והיה...ועלו "and it shall be...that they shall go up," comp. (Lev. v. 15) והיה...והתודה "and it shall be...that he shall confess"; similarly in the past (1 Sam. xi. 11) ויהי הנשארים ויפצו "and it came to pass that those who were left were scattered."—*Middē shānáh bk'shānáh* "every year" comp. (1 Sam. vii. 16) מדי שנה

ZECHARIAH XIV. 17, 18.

17 And it shall be, *that* whoso will not come up of *all* the families of the earth unto Jerusalem to worship the King, the LORD of hosts, even upon them shall be no rain.

18 And if the family of Egypt go not up, and come not, that *have* no *rain;* there shall be the plague, wherewith the LORD will smite the heathen that come not up to keep the feast of tabernacles.

בְּשָׁנָה (comp. also Is. lxvi. 23).—On the first *metheg* of *t'hishtãch°vôth* see Excurs. II. B. 3.—*Mélec* is, doubtless, the absol., and in apposition to *YHVH Ç'bhã'ôth:* so LXX. correctly τῷ βασιλεῖ Κυρίῳ.

The reason why the Feast of *Tabernacles* is specified seems to be as follows. *Passover* is indeed the chief festival (see *Memorbook of Nürnberg,* p. 20), but then it is a distinctly Jewish festival in commemoration of the Exodus. The Feast of *Weeks* again, as the festival of the Giving of the Law, is distinctly Jewish. But the Feast of Tabernacles, being the "Feast of Ingathering," when they rejoice over those things which are provided for the *animal* nature of man, would be a Festival in which the Nations of the World could rejoice and praise the Giver, as well as the Israelite (see also *Introduction*). *Remarks.*

אֲשֶׁר means "whosoever." The וְ of v'ló introduces the apodosis, comp. (Gen. xliv. 9) וָמֵת וְעַבְדְּךָ "with אֲשֶׁר יִמָּצֵא אִתּוֹ מֵעֲבָדֶיךָ whomsoever of thy servants it shall be found, he shall die." *Verse 17. Constructions.*

מֵאֵת "out of" as (Josh. xxi. 16) תֵּשַׁע מֵאֵת שְׁנֵי הַשְּׁבָטִים הָאֵלֶּה "nine [cities] out of these two tribes."

For וְלֹא עֲלֵיהֶם יִהְיֶה הַגֶּשֶׁם LXX. give καὶ οὗτοι ἐκείνοις προστεθήσονται: Köhler supposes they read וְאֵלֶּה עֲלֵיהֶם יֵהֵנוּ נֶגֶשׁ; but, seeing that the Septuagint translators were somewhat acquainted with more modern Hebrew, I should say that they read וְאֵלֶּה עֲלֵיהֶם יִהְיֶה הַגֶּשֶׁם (or more probably simple וַעֲלֵיהֶם) lit. "and to them shall be the-making-to-approach-of-the-others": *heggésh* would be an Hiphilic substantive of the form of *heqqésh* "comparison." *LXX.*

בָּאָה is the pres. partic. fem. Qal of בּוֹא, as (Gen. xxix. 6) ...הִנֵּה

בִּתּוֹ בָּאָה "behold his daughter...coming"; but בָּאָה is the 3rd pers. fem. sing. Perf. Qal, as (ver. 9) וְרָחֵל בָּאָה "and Rachel came." The words can only be rendered "And if the family of Egypt go not up, and cometh not," the participle being used instead of תָּבֹא merely for the sake of variety of sound. We cannot see that there can be any *Verse 18. Constructions.*

19 This shall be the punishment of Egypt, and the punishment of all nations that come not up to keep the feast of tabernacles.

20 In that day shall there be upon the bells of the horses, HO-

---

greater objection to this construction, than to the following (Ezek. xxxix. 8) הִנֵּה בָאָה וְנִהְיָתָה "Lo! it cometh, and shall certainly take place." (The E. V. of Ezek. takes *bā'āh*, as *bā'āh* the perfect, in which case it would have been accentuated בָּאָה (see page 16). LXX. understands the phrase correctly ἐὰν...μὴ ἀναβῇ μηδὲ ἔλθῃ. Von Hofmann has suggested the reading וְלָאֲבָה "then it shall thirst," from the expression אֶרֶץ תַּלְאֻבוֹת (Hos. xiii. 5).—וְלֹא עֲלֵיהֶם, some would supply *yih'yeh haggéshem* from the preceding verse, and render "then upon them shall not be rain." The objection to this interpretation is, that in this case we should require *zōth* (as in the next verse) before *tih'yeh*; "*This* shall be the plague, &c." The rendering "will, then, there not fall upon them the plague, &c.?" (Hitzig, Bunsen and Lange) is better. Here וְ introduces the apodosis (comp. ver. 16, iii. 7), and לֹא is interrogative *nonne?* as, certainly, (Ex. viii. 22) ...הֵן נִזְבַּח וְלֹא יִסְקְלֻנוּ "If we slay...will, then, they not stone us?"

Versions and Variants. וְלֹא עֲלֵיהֶם תִּהְיֶה וְגוֹ, LXX. καὶ ἐπὶ τούτοις ἔσται ἡ πτῶσις κ.τ.λ. simply, omitting לֹא; two Hebr. MSS. omit לֹא, and four omit וְלֹא. We think it quite possible that the לֹא may have crept into the text from the וְלֹא which precedes, or from the וְלֹא עֲלֵיהֶם of the preceding verse. Certainly "Then upon them shall be the plague, with which, &c." is the simplest construction, and affords the best sense.—Some MSS. and many Edd. read *col* between *eth* and *haggōyim*, but it seems to have crept in from אֶת־כָּל־הָעַמִּים (ver. 12), comp. xii. 2. 3.

Verse 19. *Chaṭṭăth* is the constr. of *chaṭṭāth* (see note on xiii. 1). It may mean here "sin," or "punishment" (comp. the frequent use of עָוֹן).

Verse 20. מְצִלּוֹת "bells" is a ἅπ. λεγό. but comp. מְצִלְתַּיִם (1 Chron. xiii. 18): LXX. τὸ ἐπὶ τὸν χαλινόν, which is well enough *quoad sensum*. Both words come from the root of תְּצַלֶּינָה "shall tingle," see note on

LINESS UNTO THE LORD; and the pots in the LORD's house shall be like the bowls before the altar.

21 Yea, every pot in Jerusalem and in Judah shall be holiness unto the LORD of hosts; and all they that sacrifice shall come and take of them, and seethe therein: and in that day there shall be no more the Canaanite in the house of the LORD of hosts.

---

ver. 12 [thus, whatever may be the case in English, in Hebr. the words *tingle* and *tinkle* are the same, viz. צָלַל].—Observe *hāyăh* in the sing. masc. (comp. note on ver. 15); but here, since the verb *precedes* its nominative, it has no need to agree with it: e.g. (Is. xviii. 5) יִהְיֶה נִצָּה, (Gen. i. 14) יְהִי מְאֹרֹת.—*Sîr* in the sing. denotes "a pot" (*masc.* Jer. i. 13, *fem.* Ezek. xxiv. 6), its plur. is סִירוֹת (Ex. xxxviii. 3); in Amos iv. 2 *sîrôth* perhaps means "hooks." But סִירִים means "thorns," e.g. (Eccles. vii. 6) כְּקוֹל הַסִּירִים תַּחַת הַסִּיר "like the crackling of thorns under a pot" (comp. Ps. lviii. 10).

Mēhēm "of them," i.e. "some of them," as many as may be required: comp. (Gen. xxviii. 11) וַיִּקַּח מֵאַבְנֵי הַמָּקוֹם "and he took some of the stones of the place."—כְּנַעֲנִי is used in the signification of "merchant" (Job xl. 30, Prov. xxxi. 24), and so the word is understood here by Aquila, and the Chaldee Paraphrase (Targum), followed by Hitzig, Maurer &c.

<small>Verse 21.</small>

If this be the meaning, the reference must be to traders who sold pots, cattle, &c., for the sacrifices (comp. John ii. 14—16, Matt. xxi. 12, 13). But, though there probably were such in the Temple at this time, it cannot be actually proved that there were. VON HOFMANN understands by Canaanite the Gibeonites and Nethinim, who were employed in the menial services of the Temple. THEODORET, LUTHER, EWALD take it as denoting notorious sinners, devoted to destruction, as were the Canaanites of old. PRESSEL, combining two interpretations, understands by Canaanite, those who traffic in holy things, and the ungodly and profane. But, it seems best on the whole, to suppose that the prophet, having referred above to the Egyptians, fell naturally into the use of the word "Canaanite" (since they were also the enemies of Israel in days of old), and that he meant by it nothing more than "heathen," "infidel."

<small>Remarks.</small>

We almost agree with DE WETTE that this chapter defies all historical explanation. If we attempt to interpret it of the taking of Jerusalem by the Chaldæans, we are met by the following difficulties. (1) Though ver. 1, 2 were only too literally fulfilled on that, and on other occasions, ver. 3—5 were certainly

<small>Concluding Remarks on chap. xiv.</small>

not fulfilled, for God made no demonstration at that time on behalf of his people. (2) While other pre-exilian prophets foretell clearly the deportation, and subsequent return of the people, our prophet mentions neither deportation nor return, but merely speaks of Jerusalem being inhabited in safety (ver. 10—11). But, if it refer to events after the Captivity, what can those events be? It might perhaps refer to the taking of Jerusalem by Ptolemy, a successor of Alexander, in B.C. 321; or more probably to its pillage by Antiochus Epiphanes in B.C. 167. In this latter case, the language of ver. 3—5 might be looked on as prophetic, in a highly figurative manner, of the deliverance of Israel by God through the instrumentality of the Maccabees: ver. 8, 9 might represent the revival of pure and undefiled religion in those days, and ver. 10 and 11 the peaceful prosperity of that period; but still, we could not in reference to the Maccabean era give any satisfactory account of ver. 16—21. We cannot possibly with EUSEBIUS, CYRIL, and THEODORET refer the prophecy directly to the destruction of Jerusalem by the Romans (A.D. 70). For, admitting the truth of Eichhorn's remark "prophets threaten with no people, and promise nothing of any, till the people itself is come on the scene and into relation with their people," one cannot imagine that at a time when the *Greeks* were only just come into prominence in connection with the East, the Prophet should speak of the destruction of Jerusalem by the *Romans*, when Rome was but as yet only an insignificant city, gradually asserting its superiority over the Latin peoples, and still troubled with the dissensions between Patricians and Plebeians. Further, the description of what took place on that occasion, as given by Josephus (*Bel. Jud.* VI. 9 § 2), which is a direct contradiction of the promises ver. 2—6, 12—15, precludes such an interpretation. The above considerations are independent of any hypothesis as to the authorship of the chapter.—We are compelled therefore to interpret the chapter wholly in a figurative and Messianic sense. The Prophet, to whom were known the traditions of the prophetic schools concerning the times which were to precede the Messianic era, foretells the grievous troubles of "that day." Speaking in the language of the Psalms of the Theophany (xcvi.—xcix) he represents God as revealing Himself for the protection of His people. The day of the Messiah is to be one of great Spiritual Knowledge: Jerusalem is to be inhabited in security: not only is the wealth of all nations to flow thereunto, but the nations themselves are come and do homage to The King, the Lord of Hosts, in Jerusalem. As for those that come not up, on them will fall the direst punishments. In "that day" (he does not imply that the Law of Moses shall be literally re-established, still less that it shall be abrogated, but) there shall be such a diffusion of the knowledge of God, that there shall be a general elevation of everything in sanctity מַעֲלָה יתרה בקדש, so that the very bells of the horses shall be engraven with the significant inscription of the Ϛἱς of the High Priest קדש לי״י (*Qṓdesh lAdōnāy*), and idolatry and unbelief shall all but entirely pass away.—The whole scene, which he depicts, is ideal. To some extent it may be said to have been fulfilled in the Christian Church. But the full consummation of "that day" will not take place, until (1 Cor. xv. 28) "God shall be all in all," and the voice of the Angel shall proclaim (Rev. xi. 15):

ΕΓΕΝΟΝΤΟ ΑΙ ΒΑΣΙΛΕΙΑΙ ΤΟΥ ΚΟΣΜΟΥ
ΤΟΥ ΚΥΡΙΟΥ ΗΜΩΝ ΚΑΙ ΤΟΥ ΧΡΙΣΤΟΥ ΑΥΤΟΥ
ΚΑΙ ΒΑΣΙΛΕΥΣΕΙ ΕΙΣ ΤΟΥΣ ΑΙΩΝΑΣ ΤΩΝ ΑΙΩΝΩΝ.

EXCURSUS I.

Rules for Syllable-dividing in Biblical Hebrew.

1. Every vowelless consonant has a *sh^eva*[1] either expressed or understood. If a word end in a *single* vowelless consonant the *sh^eva* is not written, thus כֹּל, or before *maqqeph* כָּל־הָעִיר. If such a vowelless consonant be preceded by a *quiescent* consonant some editors give it without a *sh^eva*, others (as Baer) with *sh^eva*, thus וּבָאתְ or וּבָאת (Mic. iv. 10), וְהַדְקוֹת or וַהֲדַקּוֹת (ver. 13).

2. A *sh^eva* must be either *moving* or *quiescent*. The *sh^eva* under a letter which begins a syllable is called *moving*, all others are quiescent.

3. Every *compound* sh^eva (ֲ, ֱ, ֳ) is moving. Every *simple* sh^eva (ְ) under any of the letters אהחע is quiescent; except the *sh^eva* of הֱ and חֱ in verbs הָיָה and חָיָה, which is always *moving* as in לִהְיוֹת (see Excurs. II. A. 7).

4. (α) When *two* sh^evas fall together *in the midst of* a word, the *first* is *quiescent*, and the *second moving*, as יִקְטְלוּ *yiq-t^elū*.

(β) A *dagesh forte* in a *vowelless* consonant always produces *two* sh^evas [the one quiescent and the other moving, in accordance with (α)]. Thus the *dagesh forte* in the פ of מִפְּנֵיכֶם produces a *quiescent* sh^eva under the first *p*, and a *moving* sh^eva under the second, so that the syllables are *mip-p^enē-cém* (standing for *min-p^enē-cém*).

5. (a) It would be impossible to pronounce two successive consonants both bearing *moving* sh^eva. Consequently, if in the process of altering the vocalization of a word, as it passes from one grammatical form to another, *two moving* sh^evas would fall together, the first is

---

[1] See footnote p. 52.

changed into a *short* vowel. Such a vowel is called a *Light* (by others a *Slight* vowel), in Hebr. תְּנוּעָה קַלָּה. E.g. if the prefix בְּ be put to a word beginning with a consonant bearing *simple moving* sh°va, the sh°va of בְּ becomes a *Light chiriq*[1].

(β) It follows, of course, from this rule, that a sh°va *after* a *Light* vowel is always *moving*.

N.B. When the conjunction וְ becomes וּ it is but a *Light* vowel (though, when it occurs before a labial bearing a vowel, we use that term in a somewhat extended sense). For *grammatical* purposes this וּ is not looked on as a long vowel (see Excurs. II. A. 1 NOTE). In *prosody* (which is not native to Hebrew, but borrowed from the Arabic) it is at times looked on as a *sh°va*, so that וּבָא may have the same value in metre as וְקָם. The case of the conjunction וּ is the only one in which a word can *begin with a vowel* in Hebrew. But the exception is more apparent than real, for *u* merely stands for *wa*, *va*, or *vi*.

6. (a) A syllable that ends in a consonant with *sh°va* either expressed, or understood (see rules 1 and 4), is called *closed*. A syllable that does not end in a consonant with *sh°va* (expressed or understood) is called *open*.

(β) When a consonant is *quiescent*[2], no *sh°va* is understood with it. Consequently an *open* syllable may end, either in a *simple* vowel long, or short (see rule 9), or in a vowel with quiescent consonant (or consonants), such as: אָ, הָ; אַ, הַ (in מָה); אֵ, יֵא, הֵ, יֵ; אֶ, הֶ, יֶ; אִ, יִא, יִ; אֹ, אוֹ, וֹ, הֹ; אוּ, אֻ, וּ.

---

[1] In order to avoid the frequent use of the words "long" and "short," I vocalize most of the names of the vowels in such a manner as to indicate the sounds which they represent. Thus *qāmāç* (ā); *pathach* (a); *çērē* (ē); but *segōl* (e); *shûrûq* (û); but *qibbuç* (s°phātháim) which means "gathering together of the lips" (u); *chîrîq* (î); *chîriq* (i); *chōlem* (ō); *qŏmŏç* (o). Some of these words are barbarous in form, but the system has the virtue of being practical.

[2] The beginner may need to be reminded that ע and ח are *never quiescent*, but always strong gutturals. The only verbs which ought to be called verbs ל״ה are those which end in ה, in which this *h* is a strong consonant retained (but, of course, without the *mappiq*) when followed by another letter, thus from נָגַהּ "shone" (Is. ix. 1), we have נָגְהָם *nogḥām* "their light" (Joel ii. 10). Verbs which end in *quiescent* ה like גָּלָה, should be termed (as they are by Jewish grammarians) ל״ה נָחִי "with *quiescent* hē as the 3rd root-letter." It must be remembered, too, that ַי ָי *ay āy* at the end of a word is always a closed syllable (but see Excurs. III. 1, p. 149).

7. (α) If a *B*ᵉ*GaDC*ᵉ*PhaTh* letter have a dagesh *lene*, then it is certain that this letter begins a syllable, as מַלְכִּי *mal-cī* "my king."

Except (1) in the 2nd pers. sing. fem. Perf. of verbs with three strong consonants, such as פָּקַד, which gives פָּקַדְתְּ *pā-qádt*, this is but a shortened form of פָּקַדְתִּי *pā-qád-ti*. (2) In the apoc. Imperf. of certain verbs *quiescent* ל״ה, of which the second root-letter is a *B*ᵉ*GaDC*ᵉ*PhaTh*, as וַיֵּבְךְּ *vayyḗbhc* "and he wept," וַיַּחַדְּ *rayyíchad* "and he rejoiced." The full forms of these Imperfects would be יִבְכֶּה and יֶחְדֶּה with the second root-letter *hard*, consequently in the apoc. form the hard pronunciation of the letter is retained.

(β) But the converse is not true (viz. that if a *B*ᵉ*GaDC*ᵉ*PhaTh* letter have no *dagesh* it cannot begin a syllable). For, if the syllable preceding it, either in the same word, or sometimes in the preceding word (see Excurs. III. A. 2), be *open* (see rule 6), then even an *un*-dagesh-ed *B*ᵉ*GaDC*ᵉ*PhaTh* letter may begin a new syllable. E.g. נֹאבְדָה *nō-bhᵉdhāh* (Jon. i. 14), וַאדֹנָי *va-dhōnāy* (Zech. ix. 14), כָּהֹה תִכְהֶה *Cāhōh thic-heh* (xi. 17).

(γ) But a *B*ᵉ*GaDC*ᵉ*PhaTh* letter cannot be without Dagesh *lene* when preceded by a *quiescent* shᵉva.

Except (1) in the names of the two Towns יָקְתְאֵל *Yoq-thᵉēl* (Judg. xv. 38), יָקְדְעָם *Yoq-dhᵉām* (ver. 56). (2) In some anomalous formations such as יַרְכָתוֹ *yar-cāthō* (Gen. xlix. 13), יִקְבְךָ *yiq-bhᵉcā* "thy winepress" (Deut. xv. 14, xvi. 13), see Excurs. III. B. 3, N.B. To these it is possible that we ought to add Infinitives Qal with suffixes beginning with a vowel, such as פָּקְדִי (Amos iii. 14) "my visiting," which may be pronounced *poq-dhī*; but it is possible that the *shᵉva* is *moving*, and that the word should be pronounced *poqᵉdhī* (see rule 9). There are but three instances of such an Infin. with *dagesh* in the 3rd root letter, viz. הָפְכִּי *hophci* (Gen. xix. 21), נָפְפוּ *noqpū* (Ex. xii. 27), עָצְבִּי *'oçbi* (1 Chron. iv. 10), see *Fragment of T. B. Psachim* p. 95, note 36.

8. A *long* vowel in a closed syllable (see rule 6) must have the tone accent, or *metheg* (see Excurs. II. 5), as קָטַנְתִּי *qāṭóntī*, אָנָּא *ānnā́* "O I pray." Therefore, if the tone be moved from a long vowel it must be (α) shortened as יָכֹלְתִּי *yācóltī*, יָכָלְתִּיו *y-col-tīv*, יֵלֶךְ *yēlec*, וַיֵּלֶךְ *rayyḗlec*; or (β) it must take Fixed *metheg*, as בֵּית־אָבִיךָ *bēth-ābhíc* (Gen. xxiv. 23), מְבָרֵךְ *mᵉbhárēc* (Is. lxvi. 3), see Excurs. II. A. 4. (3). (γ).

9. A *short* vowel may stand in a *closed* syllable, either accentuated or unaccentuated.

A *short* vowel may also stand in an *open* syllable: (a) with accent, as q'ṭalānī "he killed me," ná-chal "a valley" (for the older Semitic form *nachl*), bá-yith (for *bayt*), הרף héreph (for *harph*), יִגֵל yi-gel (for *yagl*), שִׁמְעַת shāmā-'at (for the older shāmā́-ti); (β) in the case of *Light* vowels whether without *metheg* as מַלְכִּי ma-l'cḗ, or with *metheg* as אֲשֵׁרֵי a-sh'rḗ, חֶשְׁכַּת chè-sh'cath (Ps. xviii. 12), אֲמָרוֹת ĭ-m'rōth (xii. 9), שָׁמְרֵנִי sho-m'rēnī (xvi. 1); (γ) when the said short vowel is attached to the consonant immediately preceding the consonant bearing the moving *sh'ra* which always precedes the suff. *cém* and *cén* as *d'bha-r'cém*, *tŏ-ra-th'cém*; (δ) in the case of the def. art., or *he* interrog., prefixed to a monosyllable beginning with a guttural as הַהוּא ha-hū́, הָעֵת ha-'ḗth, הֶחָפֵץ ha-chḗpheç; (ε) with *metheg* in the 3rd syllable from the tone (Excurs. II. A. 1) as קָדָשִׁים qŏ-dāshím and (Excurs. II. B. 1) לַמְנַצֵּחַ la-m'naçḗ'ch; (ζ) anomalously when *metheg* is on the syllable next before the tone, see Excurs. II. A. 4 NOTE; and C. 4.

EXCURSUS II.

ON METHEG[1].

A small vertical line placed under a letter, in order to show that the voice should dwell slightly on that letter in pronunciation, is called מֶתֶג *métheg*, מַאֲרִיךְ *ma"rīc*, or גַּעְיָא *ga'yā*.

There are three kinds of Metheg: A, *Light Metheg* (מֶתֶג קַל): B, *Heavy Metheg* (מֶתֶג כָּבֵד): C, *Orthophonic Metheg* (מֶתֶג לְתִקּוּן הַקְּרִיאָה).

A.

Light Metheg is of two kinds: I. *Ordinary* (פָּשׁוּט *pāshūṭ*), and II. *Fixed* (תָּמוּךְ *tāmūc*).

A. I. ORDINARY METHEG.

1. Ordinary *metheg* must (unless the intervention of some other rule prevent it) be placed (a) under a consonant bearing a *long* vowel

---

[1] In writing this Excursus we have made use of Baer's Article in *Merx's Archiv*. But as we do not adopt the principles of syllable-dividing therein expressed, we have been compelled to rewrite most of the rules.

third from the *tone*-syllable (both inclusive); or (β) any such *short* vowel, provided it be not followed by a consonant bearing *sh'va* or *dagesh forte*. E.g. (a) *chărāshím*, *hărīshōním*, *Pōṭīphár*, *hărḥāṭím*, *vā'ōmár*; (β) *hăchillám*, *mǐsabbṓth* (Ex. xxviii. 11), *ŭmǐhartḗm*, *yăharg̱ún* (Zech. xi. 4).

NOTE. Rule A. II. 9 forms an exception to this rule, thus we have הָאֹכְלִים *hā'ōc'lím* (not *hă'ōc'lím*).

The conjunction וּ does not take this *metheg*, thus we have וּמֵאָלָה Gen. v. 4 (comp. xii. 1, iii. 10, xi. 4).

Words joined by *maqqeph* are, of course, treated as one word, thus we have כֹּה־אָמַר (Zech. i. 16), לֹא־נָשָׂא (ii. 4), כַּמָּה־רְחָבָהּ (ii. 1).

2. (a) If the *third* syllable from the tone be disqualified from taking this *metheg*, but the *fourth* be not disqualified, then this fourth syllable takes the *ordinary metheg*, as מַעֲלֵיכֶם (Zech. i. 4), תֹּאכַל־עָלָיו (Deut. xvi. 3).

(β) If the *fourth* be also disqualified, then the *fifth* may take it, as מֵהַתַּחְתֹּנוֹת (Ezk. xlii. 5), פָּרַס־וּמָדַי (Est. i. 18).

(γ) If both the *third* and *fifth* be qualified, they will both take it, as הָאֲשֻׁרִיאֵלִי (Numb. xxvi. 31).

(δ) The *fourth* and *fifth* may also both take ordinary *metheg*, as לֹא־יַעַבְרוּ־בָהּ.

(ε) If both the *third* and *fourth* be qualified, only the *third* takes it, as לִירוּשָׁלַיִם (Zech. i. 14, 16).

3. If a word ending in accentuated י ֵ, יָ ֵ, וּ, or הָ ‍, be joined by *maqqeph* to a word beginning with a consonant with *sh'va* and accentuated on the *first* syllable, the consonant bearing the said *ī*, or *ō*, will take *metheg*: as כִּי־לְבָדְךָ (2 Kings xii. 8), מִי־לְךָ (Gen. xix. 12), וּמְרִיא־וְצֹאן (1 Kings i. 19), אוֹ־בְבוֹר (Numb. xviii. 17), שְׁלֹמֹה־בְנִי (1 Chron. xxviii. 9).

A. II. Fixed Metheg.

Fixed metheg is so called, because nothing short of a change in the form of the word can move it from its place. Thus in rule 9 it will be seen, that *Fixed* metheg interferes with *Ordinary* metheg, but that the reverse is not the case.

4. Fixed *metheg* is used,

(α) To distinguish a *long* vowel from a short one (in cases where the orthographic sign renders the case doubtful) before a consonant bearing a *sh'va* in the syllable next before the tone, and to ensure that the said *sh'va* be read *moving*.

(1) To distinguish *qāmāç* from *qomoç*, as אָֽכְלָה *āc'lāh* "she ate," but אִכְלָה *oc'lāh* "eat thou" (Gen. xxvii. 29), or "to eat" (1 Sam. i. 9). (Comp. also, *with* metheg Lam. i. 7, Zech. ix. 22, Deut. xv. 9, and *without* metheg 2 Chron. vi. 42, Ps. lxix. 19, Ex. xxxvi. 2.) הִמָּלְטִי *himmāl'ṭî* (Zech. ii. 11), בָּשְׂמַת *Bās'māth* not *Bosmath* (Gen. xxxvi. 3), יָדְעָ *yād'ʿā*, הָרְכָשׁ *hār'cāsh* (xiv. 21).

(2) *Chīrīq* written *defectivè* from short *chīriq*, as יִֽרְאוּ *yīr'û* "they fear" (2 Kings xvii. 28) = יִֽרְאוּ (Ps. xxxiii. 8), distinguished from יִרְאוּ *yir-û* (Ex. xvi. 32) "they see" (without *metheg*); so too יִֽשְׁנוּ *yīsh'nû* "they sleep" (Prov. iv. 16), but יִשְׁנוּ *yishnû* "they will change"; and again צִֽקְלַג (Josh. xv. 31) = צִֽיקְלַג (1 Chron. xii. 1. 20), and יִֽשְׂמְךָ *y'sīm'cā* (Gen. xlviii. 20).

(3) *Qibbuç* written *defectivè* for *shūrūq* as גֻּנַּבְתִּי (Gen. xxxi. 19), גֻּבְלָךְ (Deut. xii. 20), נְאֻם־יְהוָה (Zech. i. 4).

(β) To ensure a *sh'va* being read moving after an evidently long vowel, as in בֵּֽיתְךָ *bêth'cā*, מֵֽתְךָ *mêth'cā*, יִֽרְאוּ (*supra*), תֵּֽצְאוּ *têç'û*, נֵֽרְדָּה *nêr'dhāh*, רֹֽאשְׁךָ *rôsh'cā*, אֹֽרְחַת *ôr'chāth*, וַיֹּֽאמְרוּ *vayyôm'rû*, גֵּֽרְשֹׁם *Gêr'shôm*, יֹֽדְעִים *yôd'ʿîm*.

(γ) When a word ends in a syllable with *çērē* and the accent is drawn back to the preceding syllable, but it is still wished to retain the ç*ērē* in the last syllable, a Fixed Metheg (called in this case הָעֲמָדָה *Ha‘amādāh*, i.e. Conservative Metheg) is used, as וַיָּבֶן (Hos. xiv. 10), וַיֵּצֵא (Gen. iv. 16).

NOTE. Had the use of this *metheg* been confined to such cases it would have been of inestimable value. But unfortunately it is sometimes used with pretonic *short qomoç*. Thus we have עָמְדָךְ *‘ŏmdk‘ca* (Obad. ver. 11), where the grammatical consideration that the word comes from *‘ŏmōd*, taken with the fact that the Cod. Petrop. reads *o*, proves that ָ is here certainly *qomoç* not *qāmāç*. So שָׁמְרֵנִי *shom‘rēnī* (Ps. xvi. 1) compared with שָׁמְרֵנִי (xxv. 20) and שָׁפְטֵנִי (xxvi. 1), and so too הַקָּרְבָּן *haqqŏr‘bhân* (Ezek. xl. 43), Cod. Petrop. *haqqorban*.

Again, *Ordinary* metheg (in the place third from the tone, Rule 1) is as compatible with *qomoç*, as with *qāmāç*, thus קָדְשַׁי (Ezek. xliv. 13) is *qŏdāshây* (not *qādāshây*), as may be seen from the pointing of קָדָשִׁים in the same verse, and the vocalization of Cod. Petrop., which is *qodāshây*. While on the other hand שָׁרָשָׁיו (which is from *shóresh*, as *qŏdāshây* is from *qódesh*) is given by Cod. Petrop. (Jer. xvii. 8, Hos. xiv. 6) as *shărāshăv*, and אָהֳלֵיהֶם (Jer. xlix. 29) as *ăhŏlēhăm*, and even אָהֳלֵי (Zech. xii. 7) as *ăhŏlē*, and פָּעָלְךָ (Hab. iii. 2) as *pā‘ŏl‘că*. With these variations of pronunciation we may compare רֹאשׁ *rósh* plur. רָאשִׁים *rāshím*; the Ashkenazic pronunciation of *qāmāç* as *aw* or *o*, and the Sephardic as *ā*; the pronunciation of עַמָּא by Western Syrians as *‘amō*, and by Easterns as *‘ammā*. Taking these phenomena in conjunction with the fact that both systems of vocalization use the *qāmāç*-sign *with sh‘va* to represent *qomoç*, we come to the conclusion that, at the time (or times) of the stereotyping of a traditional pronunciation by the *writing* of vowel-signs, *qāmāç* and *qomoç* were much alike in sound. Thus *qāmāç* would appear to have had the sound, not of the *a* in *father*, nor of that in *call*, nor yet of the *oa* in *coal*, but rather an intermediate sound such as of tho *o* in the Fr. *mode*, or in the Romaïc γεγονότων *yeghonóton*. The ϙomoς would represent the same sound, only *short*[1].

5. Fixed *metheg* is also used to enable a long vowel to remain in a closed syllable, when it has not the tone, as בְּלִטְשַׁאצַר, עִין־דַּגֵּן, לְעֵת־עֶרֶב. To this place belongs that much-disputed word בָּתִּים, בָּתֵּיכֶם. The use of *metheg* in this case would of itself not be sufficient to guarantee the pronunciation of the ָ as *â* (see NOTE on the preceding page). But, the fact that the ָ must have arisen from י ־ as in אָן for אַיִן, and הֹתַיִן (Gen. xxxvii. 17) and דֹתָן (2 Kings vi. 13), would predispose one to conclude that the ָ means *â*. While the fact that *Cod. Petrop.* distinctly reads it as *qâmâç* is decisive (see in Is. iii. 14, v. 9). Three important facts are to be learnt from the *Cod. Petrop.* punctuation of the word, (1) the ָ is *qâmâç*, (2) the ת is hard, (3) the ת is not doubled (in other words the *dagesh* in it is *lene*), thus the word is not *báttîm* or *bottîm*, but *bâtîm* (comp. the Syr. *bâtē*). This case of an unaccentuated *qâmâç* before a B^rG^aDC^eF^aTh letter with *dagesh lene* is, I believe, unique. Another case of the use of this *metheg* is in אָנָּא *ânnâ* "O I pray," the *Cod. Petrop.* however does not double the *nūn* but reads *ânâ* (Is. xxxviii. 3). [According to *Codex Petropolitanus* the word is *mil‘el* in Jon. iv. 2 *ânâh*.]

6. Fixed *metheg* is always placed with the vowel preceding the consonant which bears a *compound sh‘va*, whether the vowel agree with that in the compound *sh‘va* as יַעֲמֹד; or not, as שָׁמְעָה (Ps.

---

[1] If the student think it strange that there should be a difference of opinion about the pronunciation of a vowel in Hebrew, he is reminded that we have similar difficulties in English: thus "cough" is by some pronounced *kawf*, and by others *käff*; "coffee," *kawfy* and *käffy*; "laugh," *lâf* and *läff*. With regard to the vowel *â* we will here give a few facts (kindly communicated to us by Mr Eiríkr Magnússon). Swedish *â* is sounded like English *aw* but *deeply guttural*. The etymol. equivalent in Danish is *aa*, which has the same sound as the Swedish *â* *without the guttural element*, and so is more like the English *ô*. The Icelandic equivalent is *á*, pronounced almost like *ow* in *now*. Let us take a few examples showing how these sounds tend at times to *â*, and at others to *ô*. Thus Germ. *mahl* (mâl), Ice. *mál* (mowl), Dan. *maal* (môl), Swed. *mâl* (mawl).—Ice. *ár* (owr), Dan. *aare* (ore), Swed. *âr* (awr), Engl. *oar*.—Germ. *Thor* (tôr), Dan. *daare* (dôre), Swed. *dâre* (dawre), Ice. *dári* (dowry).—Germ. *Lohn* (lôn), Dan. *laan* (lôn), Swed. *lân* (lawn), Ice. *lán* (lown).

xxxix. 19), וְטֹהַר־יָדַיִם (Job xvii. 9), comp. Gen. xxi. 6, ii. 12, xxvii. 25.

NOTE. Sometimes we have a syllable which, according to Rule 1, would take Ordinary *metheg*, and, according to Rule 6, would take Fixed *metheg*; in such a case the Metheg is *Fixed* metheg, e.g. הָעֲשִׂירִי (Gen. viii. 5), אֵרֲדָה־נָּא (xviii. 21).

In Zech. xiii. 4 we have the anomalous formation בְּהִנָּבְאֹתוֹ in which the *Ordinary* metheg is used in accordance with Rule 1; but the regular form בְּהִנָּבְאוֹ (ver. 3) has *Fixed* metheg, in accordance with Rule 4. (1).

In such a form as צֹעֲקִים the Fixed *metheg* is placed in accordance with both 4. β. and 6.

When such a form as יַעֲמֹד becomes יַעַמְדוּ the *metheg* becomes the *Ordinary* metheg (Rule 1), or when מַעֲלָל becomes מַעַלְלֵיכֶם the *Ordinary* metheg is placed in accordance with Rule 2.

7. All forms of the verbs *hāyāh* "he was," and *chāyāh* "he lived," which have הּ or חּ, take Fixed *metheg* with the preceding letter: thus וֶחֱיֵה, לִהְיוֹת "and live thou" (Gen. xx. 7), so *yih'yeh* (Gen. i. 29), *nih'yethā* (Deut. xxvii. 9), *vehʻyēh* "and be thou" (Gen. xii. 12), *vich'yū* "and live ye" (xlii. 18).

8. (a) Two Fixed *methegs* may be placed on a word without any intervening vowel, as וַאֲבָרֲכָה (Gen. xii. 3), וְלִהְיֹתְךָ (Deut. xxvi. 19).

(β) A *Fixed* metheg may be placed immediately before an *Ordinary* metheg, as וַהֲקִמֹתִי, לַאֲדֹנֵיהֶם.

9. (a) An *Ordinary* metheg may precede a *Fixed* metheg, if at least one syllable intervene, thus וְאֶשְׁתַּחֲוֶה.

(β) If no syllable intervene the Ordinary *metheg* is omitted, thus הָאֹכְלִים (not *hā'oc'līm*), יֵאָמְנוּ *yē'ām'nū* (not *yē'ām'nū*). Similarly לֹא־עֻבְּדָה (Nah. iii. 19), הָאָחֹוֶה (Zech. xi. 14), הָאַחֲרוֹן (xiv. 8),

לֹא־יִהְיֶה (ver. 6) with no *Ordinary* metheg with the first syllable, because the next syllable has *Fixed* metheg.

N.B. *Light* metheg (*Ordinary*, or *Fixed*) may sometimes become a *conjunctive* accent. Hence the syllable which bears a *light* metheg may be called the *semi*-tone-syllable. This change may take place if the word bearing the *metheg* has a *dis*junctive accent, and be immediately preceded by a word with a *dis*junctive accent. E.g. וְהָאָדָם (Gen. iv. 1), comp. Zech. i. 1, 6, 7; vii. 6, 14, xii. 6, 10, xiv. 2, 21, Hos. xi. 6, Joel i. 17, ii. 2, Obad. 20, Jon. i. 4, &c.

Some of the effects to this *semi-tonic* value of *Light* metheg will be seen by a reference to B. 2. (β) and 3ª, and III. B. 5.

B.

HEAVY METHEG.

1. *Heavy* metheg stands with the Article הַ (or the prefixes בַּ, כַּ, לַ), when it stands before a consonant with sh^eva from which the *dagesh forte* has been omitted: e.g. הַמְיַלֶּדֶת (Gen. xxxviii. 28): and that even before a *Fixed* metheg, as הַמִּתְעַבִּים (Mic. iii. 9), הַמְשָׁרְתִים (1 Chr. xxvii. 1).

EXCEPTIONS. (α) When the said initial consonant of the word is י, then *metheg* does *not* stand with the הַ of the deft. art., as הַיְאֹרִים (Ex. viii. 1).

(β) Nor on the syllable immediately before the tone, as הַמְעַט (Numb. xxxv. 8).

(γ) Immediately after *ordinary* metheg, *heavy* metheg cannot stand, e.g. בְּא־הַמְשֻׁגָּע (2 Kings ix. 11 in correct copies), where ה has no *heavy* metheg because it is immediately preceded by the *ordinary* metheg, which stands in accordance with A. 1. 2. (α).

2. *Heavy* metheg is placed, as a rule, with ה interrogative (when pointed with full *pathach*). It is (in the prose books) usually to the right, instead of the left of the vowel (chiefly for the purpose of distinguishing the interrogative *he* from the definite article). Thus הַֽמִכְסֶה (Gen. xviii. 17), הַאֵלֵךְ (Ex. ii. 7).

EXCEPTIONS. This *metheg* is not placed (a) when the letter after the הַ is י, e.g. הַיְֽדַעְתֶּם (Gen. xxix. 5).

(β) Nor on the syllable immediately preceding the *tone*, or the *semi*-tone (see A. II. 9, N.B.), e.g. הַאַף (Gen. xviii. 24), הַֽלְעוֹלָמִים (Ps. lxxvii. 8).

N.B. In הַאֱמֶת (Gen. xlii. 16) the *metheg* is of course *Fixed* metheg (A. 6).

(γ) Nor if a *dagesh* be put in the letter which follows הַ, as הַֽבְּצַעֲקָתָהּ (Gen. xviii. 21), הַיֵּטַב (Lev. x. 19); comp. Numb. xiii. 19, 20, Is. xxvii. 7, Job xxiii. 5; or, as it is sometimes, even in ר, as הֲרִאִיתֶם (1 Sam. x. 24, 2 Kings vi. 32).

3—4. CASES DEPENDENT ON THE PRESENCE OF A DISJUNCTIVE ACCENT.

3. If a word have a *disjunctive* accent, and the tone-syllable begin with a consonant bearing *moving* sh'va, and the *third* syllable from the tone contain *ă, ĕ, ĭ, ŭ* or ו "and" followed by a consonant with sh'va, expressed or understood (see Excurs. I. 1 and 4. β), then this vowel third from the tone will take *Heavy* metheg: e.g. וַיִּשְׁמְעוּ (Gen. iii. 8), עַל־מַֽחֲבַת (Lev. vi. 14).

EXCEPTION. If the pre-tonic syllable have a long vowel with Fixed *metheg* (according to A. 4. *a* (1), or β (1)), and is *not* followed by a consonant with a *compound* sh'va, then the said short third vowel from the tone does not take *metheg*; e.g. מִשְׁבְּךָ (Ex. vii. 28), וַיֹּאמְרוּ (Gen. xi. 3), לִרְצוֹנְכֶם (Lev. xix. 5).

If this long vowel be *ō*, then even when it *is* followed by a consonant with *compound* sh'va, the said third vowel from the tone does not take *metheg*, as הַשֹּׁאֲבֹת (Gen. xxiv. 11), עַד־בֹּאֲךָ (xix. 22).

But if, in this last case, the compound sh'va be under the first of *two like consonants*, then the original rule holds good, as וַיִּתְפֹּצְצוּ (Hab. iii. 6).

3ª. Since the *Light* metheg has a certain accent value (see A. 9, N.B.), if the word have a *disjunctive* accent, and the third syllable from the one bearing *light* metheg conform with all the above conditions, it will take *Heavy* metheg, e.g. מִמַּחְשְׁבוֹתֵיכֶם׃ (Is. lv. 9). Comp. Ps. xviii. 45, 2 Kings v. 18.

N.B. Of course *all* the conditions must be fulfilled or the *metheg* will not be placed in the case of 3 and 3ª. Thus, if the word have a *conjunctive* accent, or if the tone (or semi-tone) syllable do *not* begin with a *moving* sh°va, or if the third syllable therefrom do *not* contain ă, ĕ, ĭ, ŭ, or u "and," the *Heavy* metheg is not placed.

4. If a word with a *disjunctive* accent, have in the pre-tonic syllable ā or ē, and the third syllable before the tone-syllable have ĕ, ĭ, ŭ, or וּ "and" followed by sh°va expressed or understood, this last mentioned syllable will take *Heavy* metheg: e.g. הַמִּתְהַפֶּכֶת (Gen. iii. 24), מִשְׁנֶה־כֶּסֶף (Gen. xliii. 15), וְנִשְׁמַת־מִי (Job xxvi. 4), קַדְמַת־עֵדֶן׃ (iv. 16), אֲשֶׁר־כְּנַעֲנִים (Obad. ver. 20), וְסֹחַר־כּוּשׁ (Is. xlv. 14). See further under C. 3.

N.B. As in 3 and 3ª, all three conditions must be simultaneously observed or the Heavy *metheg* will not be placed.

EXCEPTION. Although *miqrā'-qōdesh* has ā, not ă, in the pretonic syllable, it always takes *Heavy* metheg, when accentuated with *Pashtā*, e.g. מִקְרָא־קֹדֶשׁ (Lev. xxiii. 21, 27).

4ª. If, in words which would otherwise come under rules 3 or 4, the syllable fourth from the tone-syllable take *Ordinary Light* metheg (in accordance with A. 2. a) then the *Heavy* metheg is dropped from the following syllable, e.g. וַיִּשְׁתַּחוּ (Gen. xxiv. 48), וָאֶתְאַבְּלָה (Neh. i. 4), וָאֶתְחַנַּן (Deut. iii. 23).

5. With a *disjunctive* accent the words זַרְעֲכֶם זַרְעֲךָ take *heavy* metheg under the ז, e.g. זַרְעֲךָ (Gen. iii. 15), זַרְעֲכֶם (Lev. xxvi. 16).— But not with a *conjunctive* accent, e.g. וְזַרְעֲךָ (Gen. xvii. 9). Or if the word have such a prefix as will take *Heavy* metheg (according to rule 3) then the ז takes none, e.g. אֶת־זַרְעֲךָ (xxvi. 4).

6. The word וַיְהִי if accentuated with *Pashṭā*, or if joined to the next word by *maqqeph*, or וַיְהִי if joined to the next word by *maqqeph*, takes *Heavy* metheg under the ו, thus וַיְהִי (Gen. iv. 8), וַיְהִי־לוֹ (xii. 15), וַיְהִי־שֵׁת (v. 6).

7. (α) If the Imperf. singl. Qal of a regular verb be joined to the next word by *maqqeph*, and the ō of the last syllable be changed into o, then the first syllable of the Imperf. takes *Heavy* metheg, as יִקְטָל־עָנִי (Job xxiv. 14); comp. Is. xlii. 1, Ps. cxxi. 8, Prov. iv. 4, Job iii. 5, Zech. ix. 2, 3. But the rule is not always observed, e.g. Gen. iii. 16, iv. 7, xli. 12 (ed. Baer).

(β) The rule holds good also with the Infin., with prefix לְ, as לִשְׁבָּר־אֹכֶל (Gen. xliii. 22); but neither is it consistently observed in this case, comp. Joel ii. 17.

(γ) When the long ō is retained, it takes, of course, *Fixed* metheg (A. 5) and there is no *Heavy* metheg, as תָּרְדְּךָ־זִית (Mic. vi. 15). [N.B. The *metheg* of : תִּשְׁתֶּה־יָּיִן of that verse is in accordance with B. 4.]

NOTE. A few words take an anomalous *metheg*, e.g. *ul'yishmā'ēl* (Gen. xvii. 20), *min-haṣṣādēh* (xxx. 16), *'al-hammizbē'ch* (Ex. xxix. 21), *ēth-yiśrā'ēl* (Numb. xxi. 23), *ēth-ha'ay* (Josh. x. 1), *ēl-haṣṣādēh* (2 Kings iv. 39), *miccol-hamm'qōmōth* (Ezr. i. 4), *umigdālīm* (2 Chron. xiv. 6), all accentuated with *Zarqā*; comp. *min-haggōyīm* (Ps. cvi. 47) with *'ōlěh v'yōrēd* (Baer).

HEAVY METHEG WITH SH'VA.

8. If a word begin with a consonant bearing *simple sh'va*, and be accentuated with *Gershayim* ("), or *Pazer* (҆), without a conjunctive accent immediately preceding, and there be at least two vowels between the ו and the tone-syllable, then, if the first syllable have not already

Ordinary light *metheg* the וְ will take *Heavy* metheg, e.g. וְאֶת־פִּתְרֹ֛סִים
(Gen. x. 14), בְּכָל־הַדְּבָרִ֔ים (Deut. ix. 10).

But in Jer. xxxv. 1 the וְ of *v'col-chēlō* does not take Heavy *metheg*, because the preceding word is accentuated with *munach*, comp. Ezek. xx. 40.

And the וְ of *v'āmartā* (Ezek. xvi. 3) does not take Heavy *metheg*, because the 'ā has already *ordinary* metheg.

9. This *sh'va-ga'yā*[1] also stands on words beginning with a consonant with *simple sh'va*, (α) when accentuated with *Dargā* (֧) as a duplicate conjunctive before *R'bīă* (֗) as שְׁלֵמִ֣ים הֵ֣ם אִתָּ֑נוּ (Gen. xxxiv. 21); (β) with *Qadmā* (֨) as duplicate conjunctive before *Pashtā* (֙) or *T'bīr* (֛) as וְחִלַּ֨ת מַצָּ֤ה אַחַ֨ת (Numb. vi. 19), וְחִלַּ֥ת לֶ֣חֶם שֶׁ֗מֶן (Ex. xxix. 23); (γ) with *Mūnāch* (֣) as triplicate conjunctive before *T'līshā g'dōlāh* (֠ on the *first* letter), or *T'līshā q'ṭannāh* (֩ on the *last* letter) e.g. בְּהָנִ֣יחַ יְיָ אֱלֹהֶ֣יךָ לְךָ֗ (Deut. xxv. 19), וְקָרָ֣אתָ בַמְּגִלָּ֗ה אֲשֶׁר־כָּתַ֣בְתָּ מִפִּ֔י (Jer. xxxvi. 6).

N.B. In all these cases given in 9 there must be at least *one* vowel between the *sh'va* and the tone-syllable: also the syllable beginning with the consonant with *sh'va* must not carry the *Ordinary* Light-metheg, or the *sh'va-ga'yā* will fall away, e.g. Deut. xxiv. 9; but the *Fixed* Light-metheg does not prevent the presence of *sh'va-ga'yā*, e.g. Numb. iv. 14.

C.

Orthophonic Metheg.

1. (α) If a word, accentuated with a *conjunctive* accent, end in *pathach 'Ayin* and be *mil''el*, or end in *'Ayin* with *furtive-pathach* and be *mil''ra*, and the following syllable be accentuated, then the final ע takes *orthophonic* metheg, to prevent its being slurred over in pronunciation: as יֵ֥לַע קֹ֖דֶשׁ (Prov. xx. 25), לִשְׁמֹ֥עַ לִ֖י (Lev. xxvi. 21).

(β) Or, if a word ending in *pathach 'Ayin* be joined by *maqqeph* to a word beginning with *'Ayin*, as תֵּ֥שַׁע־עֶשְׂרֵ֖ה (Gen. xi. 25).

---

[1] There are several additional rules for placing *sh'va-ga'yā* in the books of Job, Proverbs and Psalms (in which the system of accentuation is different); but they need not be mentioned here.

2. If a word, accentuated with a *conjunctive* accent, end in (α) *pathach* and a *guttural*, or (β) *pathach* and *rēsh*, or (γ) in *āk*, and be *mil‛el*; or (δ) end in a guttural with *furtive pathach* and be *mil‛ra*; then, if the second word begins with a *similar* (not necessarily a *like*) letter, the final letter of the first word will take *orthophonic metheg*: as (α) זֶבַח הַשְּׁלָמִים (Lev. iv. 26), (β) צָרַר רוּחַ (Hos. iv. 19), (γ) פַּדֶּנָה אֲרָם (Gen. xxviii. 2), (δ) גְּבִיעַ הַכֶּסֶף (xliv. 2).

3. If a word ending in a *guttural* preceded by *pathach* be joined by *maqqeph* to the next word in such a way as to come under Rule B. 4, then in addition to the *Heavy* metheg, the guttural will take *orthophonic metheg*: as נִקְחָ־לָנוּ (Gen. xxxiv. 16), נִשָּׁבְעָ־לִי (xxiv. 7).

4. *Orthophonic* metheg is sometimes used with a *pre-tonic short vowel*, to ensure the *sh‛va*, which follows, being read *moving* either (α) regularly, or (β) irregularly, or (γ) in a pronunciation altogether anomalous; e.g. (α) אַשְׁרֵי (in some Codd. even אַשְׁרֵי) *ashrē̂*, סַבְכֵי *sibhkē̂* (Is. x. 34), עַרְבֹת *‛arbhôth* (Numb. xxxi. 12), חָרְבוֹת *chŏrbhôth* (Josh. v. 2), מָשְׁכוּ *mŏshkû* (Ex. xii. 21), חַסְדֵי *chasdhê̂*, דַּרְכֵי *darkhê̂* (Is. lxiii. 7, Jer. xii. 16), אָרְבְּאֵל *‛orbhê'l* (Hos. x. 14), וַיִּתְיַלְדוּ *vayyithyaldhû* (Numb. i. 18), רָדְפוּ *rŏdhkphû* (Ps. lxxi. 11).—(β) עָלָן *‛alvān* (Gen. xxxvi. 23), עָלָוָה *‛alvāh* (ver. 40), הִשְׁחִיתוּ *hishchîthû*, הִתְעִיבוּ *hith‛îbhû* (Ps. xiv. 1), הַרְחִיק *hirchîq* (ciii. 2), אֶבְחַר *ébchar* (Job xxix. 25, cp. Ps. lxv. 5, lxviii. 24, Prov. xxx. 17, Job xxxix. 18), תַּדְשֵׁא *tadhshê'* (Gen. i. 11) [שִׂבְמָה *Sibhmāh*, Numb. xxxii. 38, Is. xvi. 8, 9 : this word ought, perhaps, rather to come under the rule A. 4, a. 2], לִשְׁבֹת *lishbôth*.—(γ) שָׁרְשׁוֹת *shŏrshôth* (Ex. xxviii. 22) for שַׁרְשְׁרֹת (ver. 14), סַלְכָה *Sálkāh* (Deut. iii. 10), כַּדְכֹּד *cadhkôdh* (Is. liv. 12).

NOTE.—In the instances given under (β) the *metheg* seems to perform the duty of the so-called *dagesh dirimens*, as in הַצְּפִינוֹ *haççphînô*, or *haççphînō* (Ex. ii. 3), מִקְּדָשׁ *miqqdāsh*, or *miqdāsh* (xv. 17). It would be perhaps better to call it *heterophonic* metheg.

EXCURSUS III.

Dagesh in the First Letter of a Word.

A.

B⁽ᵉ⁾GaDC⁽ᵉ⁾PhaTh Letters.

1. If a word beginning with a B⁽ᵉ⁾GaDC⁽ᵉ⁾PhaTh letter be preceded by a word ending in a non-quiescent consonant, the B⁽ᵉ⁾GaDC⁽ᵉ⁾PhaTh letter takes *dagesh lene*, as עֵין פְּרִי.

EXCEPTIONS. To this rule there are only *three* exceptions, viz.

אֲדֹנָי בָּם (Ps. lxviii. 18), where, perhaps, the word is exceptionally pronounced *Adonái*, instead of *Adonáy;* קַו־תֹּהוּ (Is. xxxiv. 11) where the word is, perhaps, pronounced *qau* (cow), not *qav;* and שָׁלֵו בָּהּ (Ezek. xxiii. 42) where the word is, perhaps, pronounced *shāleu* not *shālév*.

2. But if a word beginning with a B⁽ᵉ⁾GaDC⁽ᵉ⁾PhaTh letter be preceded by a word ending in a long vowel, or quiescent letter, and bearing a conjunctive accent, the B⁽ᵉ⁾GaDC⁽ᵉ⁾PhaTh letter is *r⁽ᵉ⁾phūyáh* (without *dagesh*), thus (Hos. ii. 5) וְשִׂמְתִּיהָ כַמִּדְבָּר, (iv. 4) כִּמְרִיבֵי כֹהֵן.

EXCEPTIONS. If the second word begin with בְּפ, בְּכ, בְּמ, בְּב, or כַּב, the בְּ or כְּ takes *dagesh lene*, as (Jud. i. 14) וַיְהִי בְּבוֹאָהּ, comp. Gen. xlvi. 27, Is. lix. 21, Josh. viii. 24.

But if the first of these letters have a full vowel, rule 2 still holds good, thus כֹּהֲנֵי בָמוֹת (1 Kings xiii. 33).

N.B. Rule A. 2 gives way before B. 4 (α), except in the cases of the *prefixes* בְּ and כְּ; it also yields to B. 4 (β), and B. 4 (γ) EXCEPTIONS.

3. (α) Also if such a word be preceded by a word ending in a long vowel, or quiescent letter, and bearing a *dis*junctive accent, the initial

BeGaDCePhaTh letter still takes *dayesh lene*, as וְאַתָּה תְּשׁוּפֶנּוּ (Gen. iii. 15).

(β) Or if the accent be *conjunctive*, but *P'siq* be placed between the two words, as גַּת ׀ וְרַדוּ (Amos vi. 2, cf. viii. 9, &c.).

B.

Dayesh Conjunctionis.

1. If a word ending in הֶ ‎ be joined by *maqqeph* to a word accentuated on the first syllable, the first letter of the latter word takes *dayesh conjunctionis*, as (Hos. vi. 4) אֶעֱשֶׂה־לָּךְ, (viii. 7) יַעֲשֶׂה־קָּמַח, מַעֲנֵה־רַךְ (Prov. xv. 1), יִבְנֶה־בַּיִת (2 Sam. vii. 13).

2. When זֶה or מָה is prefixed to a word by *maqqeph*, the first letter of the word takes *dayesh conjunctionis*, wherever the accent may fall, as מַה־זֹּאת (Gen. xii. 18), מַה־נּוֹרָא (xxviii. 16), וְזֶה־מִּזְבֵּחַ (1 Chr. xxii. 1).

3. If a word end in ה ָ, *and its last syllable begin with a consonant bearing moving sh'va* and it be joined by *maqqeph* to a word accentuated on the first syllable, the first letter of the second word takes *dayesh conjunctionis*, as אוֹבְחָה־לָּךְ (Jon. ii. 10), סְאָה־סֹּלֶת (2 Kings vii. 1), שְׁלָחָה־לּוֹ (Ezek. xvii. 6).

N.B. But if the last syllable do not begin with a consonant bearing *moving sh'va*, there is no *dayesh conjunctionis*, e.g. וּפְנֵה־דֶרֶךְ (Mal. iii. 1), נֶגְדָה־נָא (Ps. cxvi. 18). Neither is there after an Infin. or Imperat. Qal with final *he*, e.g. וּלְדָבְקָה־בוֹ (Deut. xi. 22), שִׁמְעָה־לִי (Job xxxii. 10).

4. The first letter of a word accentuated on the first syllable takes *dayesh conjunctionis* under the following conditions:

(a) If it be preceded by a word ending in ָ, הָ‎ or הֶ‎, accentuated with a *conjunctive* accent on the *penultimate*, provided the penultimate be the *proper tone-syllable* of the word, as עָשִׂיתָ זֹּאת

(Gen. iii. 14), בְּאֵרָה שֶׁבַע (xlvi. 1), לְמַעְלָה רֹאשׁ (Ezr. ix. 6), אֵלֶּה לָּךְ (Gen. xxxiii. 5), וְשַׂמְתָּ שְׁמוֹ (Neh. ix. 7).

EXCEPTIONS. The prefixes בו״כל *with simple sh'va* do not take this *dagesh*, e.g. יְדַעְתִּיךָ בְשֵׁם (Ex. xxxiii. 12), נִהְיֵיתָ לְעָם (Deut. xxvii. 9).

But לָךְ always takes this *dagesh*, thus חֲלִילָה לְּךָ (Gen. xviii. 25): and after the analogy of *l'ca* we have in Ps. xix. 3 וְלַיְלָה לְּלַיְלָה.

(β) If the accent of the former word be *drawn* back to the penultimate, which would otherwise have had *Fixed* metheg (in accordance with Excurs. II. A. 4), as יַלְדָה בֵּן (Gen. xix. 38), נִירְשָׁה־לָּנוּ (Ps. lxxxiii. 13).

(γ) But if the accent thus drawn back be on a syllable which could not take *metheg*, no *dagesh conjunctionis* is used, as שָׂדֶה טוֹב (Ezek. xvii. 8), חָרָה לָךְ (Gen. iv. 6).

EXCEPTIONS. Imperfects and Participles of verbs quiescent ל״ה are an exception to (γ), thus וּמוֹרֶה שֶׁקֶר (Hab. ii. 18), עֹשֶׂה פְּרִי (Gen. i. 11), יַנְקֵה רָע (Prov. xi. 21).

(δ) If it be joined by *maqqeph* to a preceding word ending in ה־ָ or ה־ֶ with *metheg* on the preceding syllable (in accordance with Excurs. II. A. 1, NOTE) as יַלְדָה־לּוֹ (Gen. xxi. 3), קָבָה־לִּי (Numb. xx. 11), בֹּנֶה־בַּיִת (2 Chron. ii. 3), עֹשֶׂה־פְּרִי (Gen. i. 12).

5. Rule 4 (a) holds good when the second word has not the *tone*, but merely the *semi-tone* (see Excurs. II. A. 9, N.B.) on the first syllable, as אֵלֶּה־יַּעֲקֹב (Gen. xxix. 31), וְעָשִׂיתָ סִרְתָיו (Ex. xxvii. 3), שָׁמָּה קְבָרוּ (Is. xliv. 21).

EXCEPTION. But a *B'GaDC'PhaTh* letter does not take *dagesh* in these circumstances, thus אֵלֶּה תּוֹלְדוֹת (Gen. ii. 4), לָמָּה

תַּעֲמֹד (xxiv. 31), פָּעַלְתָּ בִימֵיהֶם (Ps. xliv. 2). [Except two, וִישִׂימֵהוּ תֵל־עוֹלָם (Job viii. 29), כְּמֹכָה בָּאֵלִם (Ex. xv. 11).]

N.B. From the foregoing rules it will be understood that if the latter of two words have neither the tone nor semi-tone on the first syllable, or if the former end in any open syllable except $ā$, $āh$, or eh, then the *dagesh conjunctionis* is not used, e.g. בֵּרַכְתָּ בָרֵךְ (Numb. xxiii. 11), שִׁירוּ לוֹ (ver. 21), עָשָׂה פֶלֶא (Ezek. xv. 11), עָשִׂיתִי כֵן (Neh. v. 15).

6. But, if the first word be *mil'el* and end in $ū$, and the next word begin with a *sibilant* or *liquid*, and an *accentuated syllable*, *dagesh conjunctionis* is used, as קוּמוּ צְּאוּ (Gen. xix. 14), וַיַּחְדְּלוּ מְּעָט (Hos. viii. 10). Also לוֹ and לֹא take *dagesh* after וַיֹּאמְרוּ in Gen. xix. 2, Judg. xviii. 19, 1 Sam. viii. 19, Esth. vi. 13.

Delitzsch[1] gives 17 exceptions to the above rules, confirmed by the *Massôreth*, viz. Ex. xv. 1, 21, xv. 11, 13, 16, Deut. xxxii. 6, 15, Is. liv. 12, Jer. xx. 9, Ps. lxxvii. 16, xciv. 12, cxviii. 5, 18, Job v. 27, Dan. iii. 2, 3, v. 11.

C.

Orthophonic Dagesh.

1. When a word ending with a liquid, is joined by *maqqeph* or a conjunctive accent to a word beginning with the same liquid, the initial liquid of the latter word should take *orthophonic dagesh*, as אִם־מָּחוּט (Gen. xiv. 23), עַל־לֵּב (xxxiv. 3), בֶּן־נּוּן (Ex. xxxiii. 11), וְנֶעְלַם מִּמֶּנּוּ (Lev. v. 2), וְהֵיבֵל לְּבָבֶל (Ezr. vi. 5).

2. (α) When לֹא לוֹ come together (as Gen. xxxviii. 9, Hab. i. 6, ii. 6, Prov. xxv. 17), or לוֹ לֹא (as Deut. xxxii. 5), לֹּא takes *dagesh*.

(β) Whenever לֵאמֹר is preceded by the word מֹשֶׁה with a conjunctive accent, the לּ takes *dagesh* (e.g. Ex. vi. 10, 29, xiii. 1, xiv. 1).

---

[1] This Excursus is (with a few modifications) merely an epitome of Delitzsch *De primarum vocabulorum literarum dagessatione*, in his Preface to Baer's edition of the Text of Proverbs.

EXCURSUS IV.

Some of the uses of Siman Rapheh.

Siman rapheh (a small horizontal line placed over a letter to show that it has no *dagesh*) is abundantly used in some MSS. and Edd., and in others hardly at all. In none is it used uniformly.

1. It is used to indicate the intentional omission of a grammatical DAGESH FORTE, (α) after the *def. art.* as הַיְקוּם (Gen. vii. 4)—but Baer omits it in ver. 23—to show that the *yūd* is not dageshed as it is in הָיְעוּצָה (Is. xiv. 26): so too frequently with מְ, as הַמְעֻשָׁקָה (Is. xxiii. 12), לָמְנִי (lxv. 11).—(β) After *he* interrog. as הַזֹּבְחִים (Amos v. 25).—(γ) After *min* as מִקְצֵה (Gen. xlvii. 21), comp. vi. 16, xxv. 23. —(δ) In the middle of Pi'elistic (or dageshed) forms, as וַיְקַנְאוּ (Gen. xxvi. 14), עֹרִים (Is. xlii. 16), so בִּקְשֻׁהוּ (Hos. vii. 10), but וּבִקְשׁוּ (v. 15), הַמַּקְלוֹת from *maqqēl*, but on the contrary מִפַּסְאוֹ (Jon. iii. 6), comp. Is. xiv. 10, &c., from *cissē'*.—(ε) With other dageshed forms such as וָאֶקְחָה (Gen. xviii. 5), וַיְחַקּוּ (Job xix. 24), תִּתְצוּ (Is. xxii. 10); תְּאָמַנָה for *tē'āmán-nāh* (Is. lx. 4), וּמַשְׂאֵת (Amos v. 11), and וַיִּשָּׂאוּ (Jon. i. 15).—(ζ) To avoid the doubling of a letter before an anomalous *dagesh lene* as מִשְׁתִּים־ (Jon. iv. 11), comp. Zech. iv. 12.— (η) To show, in cases where a quiescent *yūd* or *aleph* is omitted after *segōl*, that the following letter is not to be doubled, as תִּכְלֶנָה (Job xvii. 5), comp. Mic. iii. 12, Zech. i. 17, v. 9.—(θ) To mark the omission of the *dagesh forte* in the objective suffix *ēcā*, as יָדְךָ (Is. xxxviii. 19), comp. lviii. 8, Job v. 19, Obad. ver. 3, Prov. iii. 3, xxix. 17.

2. *Siman Rapheh* is also used: (a) to mark the *anomalous* omission of DAGESH LENE after a *quiescent* sh°va, as יִפְגָּשְׁךָ (Gen. xxxii. 18), יָרְכָתוֹ (xlviii. 13), יִקְּבְךָ *yiq-bhécā* (Deut. xv. 4), but xvi. 13 without the *siman rapheh*, and so too בִּגְדוֹ *big-dhó* (Hag. ii. 12, Prov. xx. 16), but נֶגְדָּה־נָּא *ney-dhāh-nā* (Ps. cxvi. 18), where the omission of *dagesh conjunct.* in the *nūn* shows that in such cases the sh°va is *quiescent* (see III. B. 3, N.B.), מַרְבַדִּים *mar-bhaddím* (Prov. vii. 16, xxxi. 22).—(β) Or after a *moving* sh°va as סָרְגוֹן, see also examples in II. C. 4.—(γ) To emphasize the correct omission of a *dagesh lene*, as חַסְדֵי (Is. lv. 3), as contrasted with the anomalous חַסְדֵי (which in our present texts is found in Lam. iii. 22, 2 Chron. vi. 42), comp. Gen. xix. 33, Ps. xviii. 13, xlv. 9, lxxvi. 4, יְלִדְתְךָ (ex. 3), בִּנְפֹל (Job iv. 13), קַשְׁתוֹתָיו (Is. v. 28), *qash'thōthāv* (see close of Excurs. II.), not *qashtōthāv*, תְּשַׁגְּשֵׁנִי (xvii. 11).

3. *Siman Rapheh* is often used (a) to show that the letter after *shūrūq* written *defective* (`) is not to be doubled, as אֵלָי (Gen. xxiv. 39), בְּעָלֹת (xx. 3), עֲנוֹת (xviii. 16), מָצֹק (Job xi. 15); comp. Is. xv. 4, xlix. 20, Mic. iv. 3, Zech. i. 13, Gen. xxxi. 26, &c.; מְרֹשָׁתִי (Is. xxi. 10), הַשִּׂים (Gen. xlvi. 22), and so often to distinguish between roots of the form of קוֹם and סבב; such is the case also in שָׁסוּ (Ps. xliv. 11), מָטָה (lx. 4). Or, to prevent the doubling of a letter after *chīrīq* written *defective*, as סְעָפִיהָ (Is. xvii. 6), הַחֲמִשִׁי (Zech. vii. 3). (β) To distinguish between conjugations, as וַיִּמַח (Gen. vii. 23) to show that it is Qal, not Niphal, קִבְצוּ (Joel ii. 16), שִׁלְחוּ (Gen. xlii. 16), חִזְקוּ (Is. xxxv. 4) as being Impert. Qal, not Perf. Pi°el. (γ) To distinguish between like words, e.g. אָנָה "whither" (Zech. xvi. 8) and even אָנָה (Ps. cxxxix. 7) as differ-

ing from אָנָּא, "I pray"; between לָמָּה mil'ra, and לָמָה mil'el "why"; to distinguish בְּחָנֵנִי (Ps. xxvi. 2) as being from Rt. *bāchăn*, and not the infin. of *chānăn*; the subst. אָמְצָה *āmçāh* (Zech. xii. 5) from the Imperative Pi'el; מִנָּלָם (Job xv. 29) to show that מ is not the *prep.* מִן; יִתְּנוּ (Hos. viii. 10) to show that the root is not *nāthăn*. (δ) To prevent the involuntary doubling of a consonant after an *accentuated short* vowel, as חִתַּתָּנִי (Job vii. 14); Zech. xiii. 5, Ps. xxx. 4, xxxi. 9, cxxxix. 1, Job ix. 19, xli. 3; יִגְּשׁוּ (ver. 8), עֹשֶׂךָ (Is. li. 13), קָרְבֻּנָה (Gen. xli. 21); תּוֹרֶךָ "thy dove" (Ps. lxxiv. 19) as distinguished from תּוֹרְךָ "she will teach thee"; or even after a *long* vowel as וָאֶתְּנָה (xxvi. 6).—In Gen. i. 6 לָמַּיִם to show that the *qāmaç* is merely euphonic.

4. *Siman Rapheh* is also used with *final he*, (α) to show that though soft it is equivalent to הּ as עֹונָה בָהּ (Numb. xv. 31); (β) to show that the *he* is really quiescent (and not equivalent to הּ) Zech. iv. 7, or to show that it is equivalent to א, Zech. ix. 8. Comp. Is. xviii. 5, xxi. 3, xxii. 17, 18, xxx. 32, lxv. 18, Job xxxi. 22, xxxix. 13, Hos. ii. 13, ix. 10, Amos i. 11, Hab. iii. 11, Zeph. ii. 14, Prov. xii. 28, xxi. 22, &c.

5. To indicate that the *initial* letter of a word is purposely without *dagesh*, and that the rules given in Excurs. III. have not been overlooked.

From the foregoing examples it will be seen that (as in the case of *metheg*, and the sign for *qāmaç*) the utility of *Siman rapheh* is much impaired by its being used for diametrically opposite purposes.

www.ingramcontent.com/pod-product-compliance
Lightning Source LLC
Chambersburg PA
CBHW022112160426
43197CB00009B/997